ROYAL HISTORICAL SOCIETY
STUDIES IN HISTORY
New Series

TRADE AND TRUST IN THE
EIGHTEENTH-CENTURY ATLANTIC WORLD
SPANISH MERCHANTS AND THEIR
OVERSEAS NETWORKS

Studies in History New Series
Editorial Board

Professor John Morrill (*Convenor*)
Professor Barry Doyle (*Economic History Society*)
Professor Nigel Goose (*Economic History Society*)
Dr Emma Griffin (*Literary Director*)
Dr Rachel Hammersley
Professor Michael Hughes (*Honorary Treasurer*)
Professor Colin Kidd
Professor Daniel Power
Dr Bernhard Rieger
Professor Alec Ryrie
Dr Selina Todd (*Past and Present Society*)

This series is supported by annual subventions from the
Economic History Society and from the Past and Present Society

TRADE AND TRUST IN THE EIGHTEENTH-CENTURY ATLANTIC WORLD

SPANISH MERCHANTS AND THEIR OVERSEAS NETWORKS

Xabier Lamikiz

THE ROYAL HISTORICAL SOCIETY
THE BOYDELL PRESS

© Xabier Lamikiz 2010

All Rights Reserved. Except as permitted under current legislation no part of this work may be photocopied, stored in a retrieval system, published, performed in public, adapted, broadcast, transmitted, recorded or reproduced in any form or by any means, without the prior permission of the copyright owner

The right of Xabier Lamikiz to be identified as the author of this work has been asserted in accordance with sections 77 and 78 of the Copyright, Designs and Patents Act 1988

First published 2010
The Royal Historical Society, London
in association with
The Boydell Press, Woodbridge
Paperback edition 2013
The Boydell Press, Woodbridge

ISBN 978 0 86193 306 8 hardback
ISBN 978 1 84383 844 9 paperback

Transferred to digital printing

The Boydell Press is an imprint of Boydell & Brewer Ltd
PO Box 9, Woodbridge, Suffolk IP12 3DF, UK
and of Boydell & Brewer Inc,
668 Mt Hope Avenue, Rochester, NY 14620–2731, USA
website: www.boydellandbrewer.com

A CIP catalogue record for this book is available
from the British Library

The publisher has no responsibility for the continued existence or accuracy of URLs for external or third-party internet websites referred to in this book, and does not guarantee that any content on such websites is, or will remain, accurate or appropriate.

This publication is printed on acid-free paper

FOR OLATZ

Contents

List of maps and tables	viii
Acknowledgements	ix
Abbreviations	xi
Introduction	1

PART I: INTERNATIONAL TRADERS: BILBAO AND 'THE NORTH'

1 Bilbao merchants	27
2 Basque ship captains and seamen	51

PART II: COLONIAL TRADERS: CÁDIZ AND PERU

3 Trading with Peru	73
4 Long distance communications	95
5 Merchants and networks	116

PART III: TRUST AND DISTRUST

6 Confidentiality	141
7 Risk and competition	162
Conclusion	182
Bibliography	187
Index	201

Maps and Tables

Maps

1. Cities and ports in western Europe in the eighteenth century	28
2. Coastline of the Basque Country in the eighteenth century	64
3. Major trading routes between Spain and America before 1739	76

Tables

1. *Galeones* and isthmian fairs, 1550–1739	79
2. *La Perla*'s mail destinations	102
3. Juan de Eguino's addressees, May 1779	158

Acknowledgements

This book developed out of my interest in eighteenth-century Atlantic trade. The research was undertaken thanks to the very generous financial support of the Department of Education, Universities and Research of the Basque Government, whose postdoctoral scholarship facilitated my study in the United Kingdom. I owe a particular debt to Penelope J. Corfield for her constant encouragement, enthusiasm and intellectual stimulus without which I would never have completed this book. Special thanks go to Julian Hoppit, my mentor at University College London, who read part of the book and gave me useful comments and suggestions. I am also grateful to María Rosario Porres of the University of the Basque Country for her encouragement and support. For their invaluable comments and suggestions I am further indebted to Jeremy Black at the University of Exeter; Uriel Heyd at Royal Holloway; Hannah Barker of Manchester University; Christine Linehan at the Royal Historical Society; the anonymous readers of the manuscript; and the participants in the 'British History in the Long Eighteenth Century' seminar (at the Institute of Historical Research, London), which I have attended since 2001. I would also like to express my gratitude to the Departments of History at Royal Holloway and University College London. Michael Marsden afforded professional support to help me to polish my English. My lifetime friend Lander Gurtubai made the maps for the book. Whatever shortcomings may remain are due to me.

Others who have contributed advice or assistance include several friends and scholars in the Basque Country, Britain, Spain and Peru: Jaione Agirre, Oier Alonso, Ada Arrieta, James Dixon, Eñaut Etxebarri, Jonathan Garabette, Amanda Goodrich, Regina Grafe, Margarita Guerra, James Guppy, Jeanette Hansen, Takashi Ito, Joseph Kruk, Toby Lincoln, Cristina Mazzeo, Carlos Sánchez, Marc Stevenson, Rafael Torres, Susan Whyman, Aingeru Zabala, Iñaki Zurutuza, and, of course, my brother Unai and our mother Irene.

I am grateful to the various archives and libraries that have allowed me to use materials in their possession. In particular, I wish to thank the National Archives (London), the British Library (London), the Institute of Historical Research (London), the Instituto Riva-Agüero (Lima), the Archivo General de la Nación (Lima), the Archivo General de Indias (Seville) and the Archivo Foral de Bizkaia (Bilbao). I am indebted further to many people who shared my interest in the eighteenth-century Atlantic trade and discussed the subject at seminars and conferences. To participate in those discussions has been a privilege, and a fascinating entry into the world of historical research. Eskerrik asko guztioi.

Parts of this book appeared in the *Revista de Historia Económica*, the

International Journal of Maritime History and the *Hispanic American Historical Review*. I would like to thank their editors and anonymous readers for their invaluable comments and suggestions.

That my family and friends have put up with me during years of intensive and all-absorbing work seems a miracle to me. Without their encouragement and patience the present book would have been impossible. Finally, I wish to express my sincere thanks to my partner Olatz Ormazabal, who has always motivated and supported me. This book is dedicated to her.

Xabier Lamikiz
September 2009

Abbreviations

AFB	Archivo Foral de Bizkaia (Bilbao)
AGI	Archivo General de Indias (Seville)
AGN	Archivo General de la Nación (Lima)
AGS	Archivo General de Simancas (Simancas, Valladolid)
AHN	Archivo Histórico Nacional (Madrid)
ARA	Archivo Ramírez de Arellano (Lima)
ATHA	Archivo del Territorio Histórico de Álava (Vitoria-Gasteiz)
BL	British Library (London)
C	Chancery
FHL	Friends House Library (London)
FP	Fondo Prestamero
HCA	High Court of Admiralty
IRA	Instituto Riva-Agüero (Lima)
LGL	London Guildhall Library
NRO	Norfolk Record Office (Norwich)
PC	Privy Council
SP	State Papers
TC	*Tribunal del Consulado*
TNA	The National Archives (London), formerly Public Record Office
AEA	*Anuario de Estudios Americanos*
AHR	*American Historical Review*
EcHR	*Economic History Review*
HAHR	*Hispanic American Historical Review*
IJMH	*International Journal of Maritime History*
JbLa	*Jahrbuch für Geschichte von Staat, Wirtschaft und Gesellschaft Latinamerikas*
JEcH	*Journal of Economic History*
JLAS	*Journal of Latin American Studies*
RHA	*Revista de Historia de América*
RI	*Revista de Indias*
WMQ	*William and Mary Quarterly*
Add.	Additional
doc.	*documento*
exp.	*expediente*
H	Hacienda
leg.	*legajo*
MS	manuscript

Introduction

'How could a merchant of this kingdom send his goods to a strange kingdom if he did not trust his correspondent? How is he to buy manufactures if there is an absence of good faith to make the purchase on credit, or of trust to make a remittance of money in advance?' Such were the questions posed by the Spaniard Simón Codes in 1803 in his award-winning essay on how to eradicate dishonest bankruptcies.[1] Those were, of course, rhetorical questions for which there was only one answer: no merchant would ever risk leaving his goods or money in the hands of a correspondent whom he did not trust. What Codes was trying to do, however, was to draw attention to the economic implications of the situation, namely that overseas trade could not be carried out unless merchants learned to trust each other. It is precisely this learning process that this book sets out to explore. For all its economic ramifications, being able to trust another human being for trade purposes has always entailed factors other than the purely economic. Indeed, the process of building trust in the context of trade, as in any other social activity, is permeated with beliefs, customs, experiences and perceptions; it is inextricably linked with the culture of economic life. This book is therefore a cultural exploration of overseas trade. Its setting is the eighteenth-century Atlantic, and its protagonists are primarily Spanish merchants.

Iberian merchants and the eighteenth-century Atlantic trade

Spanish merchants may appear an odd choice because for most of the seventeenth and eighteenth centuries Spaniards in general do not seem to have been particularly attracted to mercantile activities. Writing in the 1690s, the Bristol merchant and economist John Cary contended that 'Spaniards are stately People, not much given to Trade or Manufactures themselves ... other trading Nations, such as the English, French, Dutch and Genoese, take Advantage of them.'[2] This was a view shared by the great majority of his contemporaries. Even eighteenth-century Spanish policy-makers held similar opinions. For instance, the minister José del Campillo y Cossío, in his 1743 *Nuevo sistema de gobierno económico para América* (not published until 1789), acknowledged that, as well as being 'greedier' and 'more industrious',

---

[1] Simón Codes, *Memoria sobre qué providencias convendrían tomarse para precaver las quiebras o bancarrotas fraudulentas*, Madrid 1803, 31–2.
[2] John Cary, *Discourse on trade and other matters relative to it* (1690s), 1st edn, London 1745, 65.

foreigners had 'a different application and conduct from ours'.³ The situation was particularly damaging in international trade, where Spanish merchants played a marginal role. This relative inactivity may have been explained by a lower level of industriousness and by Spaniards' general liking for values associated with landowning and rent-seeking, but for those merchants who were willing to trade with other European countries there was an additional problem, as the Navarrese mercantile thinker Gerónimo de Uztáriz explained in 1724.

In the last two chapters of his influential *Theórica y práctica de comercio y marina*, a competent analysis of Spain's economic decline that included numerous ideas and *proyectos* designed for recovery, Uztáriz contended that it should be Spaniards' priority to engage more actively in international trade: '[i]t is one of the indispensable conditions, to render commerce an advantage to any kingdom or state whatsoever, that the trade carried on by the natives be active, at least in a great measure, and not passive, as we find it in Spain, to our great prejudice'.⁴ It was painful to see that Spanish merchants could only buy the goods that they needed at very high prices from foreign merchants established on the Iberian peninsula. For Uztáriz, the problem facing his compatriots was the lack of reliable correspondents abroad: '[w]e are at as great a loss for factors and other persons to be confided in and of our own nation, whom we may charge with the purchase and shipping of [goods] to Spain'.⁵ True, there were foreigners who lived in their own countries while maintaining correspondence with Spanish merchants, sending and receiving commissions, but in Uztáriz's opinion they were very few. In an attempt to encourage his compatriots to trade with European countries such as Britain and France, Uztáriz stated that it was first necessary to provide trustworthy correspondents for the Spaniards. And how could this be done? Simply by having a Spanish factor, accompanied by a bookkeeper, in eighteen European sea-ports. Appointing factors, with salaries, to places such as London, Amsterdam and Hamburg would be the first step in encouraging Spanish merchants to settle with their families abroad, which would in turn enable their compatriots at home to participate in international trade. In this way Spaniards could form:

> a mutual correspondence ... for buying, selling, depositing goods, remittances, and other transactions, as is done by the generality of other nations,

---

³ José del Campillo y Cossío, *Nuevo sistema de gobierno económico para América* [1743] (1st edn, Madrid 1789), Oviedo 1993, 301.
⁴ Gerónimo de Uztáriz, *The theory and practice of commerce and maritime affairs*, London 1751, ii. 378. Due to its censorious and controversial nature, Uztáriz's book was initially published in 1724 in a limited edition, and it was not until 1742 that it was printed for a wider audience. It was subsequently translated into English (1751) and French (1753), and is generally regarded as the most important Spanish economic work of the eighteenth century.
⁵ Ibid. 393.

particularly in Spain, where we find many French, English, Dutch, Germans, Swedes, Italians and others, trading, and making this kingdom, as it were, their place of abode.[6]

It is an overstatement to say that a lack of compatriots resident abroad was responsible for preventing Spanish merchants from trading with foreign countries, and yet the modern reader should not dismiss its significance altogether. Uztáriz did not go as far as to explain why Spaniards were unwilling to settle abroad, but his understanding of how trading networks were constituted and, more important, of what merchants considered a trustworthy correspondent, is none the less very telling. Although his plan was never put into practice and has received very little attention from historians, nobody disputed Uztáriz's assessment of the national and ethnic character of overseas trading networks. In fact, his British contemporaries held a similar view: in its entry entitled 'factors', Malachy Postlethwayt's updated edition of the *Universal dictionary of trade and commerce*, published in London in 1751, included a full transcription of the last chapter of *Theórica y práctica*, and, rather revealingly, Uztáriz's plan was regarded as 'the natural way of first establishing commerce with distant countries'.[7] It seems that merchants' perception of trustworthiness was intimately associated with their correspondents' nationality or ethnicity.

By focusing on the merchants involved in Spain's trade with both northern Europe and America, this study examines the role played by merchant communities in providing the members of the extended national, ethnic or religious group with a community that supplied a solid foundation for trust, even though in practice trust sometimes broke down. From a cultural and historical point of view the question is not whether the merchant who belonged to a particular group was more reliable than an outsider, but whether he was perceived to be more reliable, and if so, why. This is an important question because the perception of trustworthiness appears to have been a crucial factor in determining who participated in the trade (or who exerted control over it) and who did not.

Apart from focusing upon the local and overseas interaction between different merchant communities, this book also regards the Atlantic as a crucial arena of historical inquiry. In the last two decades or so historians have become interested in what has been termed Atlantic history, a field that adopts the ocean as a unit of analysis, as a common sphere of economic and cultural exchange between Europe, the Americas and Africa.[8] According to John Elliott, the 'new' Atlantic history may be defined as 'the

---

[6] Ibid. 394.
[7] Malachy Postlethwayt, *The universal dictionary of trade and commerce, translated from the French of the celebrated monsieur Savary*, London 1751, i. 761.
[8] For a comprehensive introduction to the idea of Atlantic history see Bernard Bailyn, *Atlantic history: concepts and contours*, Cambridge, MA 2005, 3–56.

history, in the broadest sense, of the creation, destruction and re-creation of communities as a result of the movement, across and around the Atlantic basin, of people, commodities, cultural practices, and ideas'.[9] The Atlantic was at once unifying and divisive, connecting and fragmenting communities through space and time, and compelling those communities to adapt themselves to changing political and economic conditions. Furthermore, '[f]or Atlantic history the relevant distinction is between a history of places around the Atlantic versus a history of the Atlantic'.[10] There is, however, a tendency to see Atlantic history, including the slave trade, in Anglophone terms. This book aims to make its own distinct contribution to Atlantic history by looking at goods, people, information and ideas that circulated around and across the ocean mostly in Spanish.

The phenomenon of merchants settling in foreign countries and forming communities is well-documented from the Middle Ages up to the eighteenth century and beyond. As the French historian Frédéric Mauro stresses, throughout the centuries the social base of the trader universe was represented by merchant communities organised on the basis of common national, ethnic or religious identity.[11] The members of the Hanseatic League, the foreign merchant communities of Antwerp in the sixteenth century, or the Huguenot, Jewish and Armenian diasporas, had as great an influence on trade as did geography, politics and commercial institutions, mechanisms and techniques. An important organisational strategy for foreign merchant communities was the establishment of factories. The so-called 'factory system' ('the semi-public establishment of separate premises for foreign merchants or factors', in the words of Philip Curtin) had first evolved in medieval Flanders but began to disappear in Europe in the sixteenth century, just as the use of local commission agents became increasingly common.[12] In early modern times the factory system became the common way of dealing with European trade with Asia and Africa. What has not been sufficiently emphasised, however, is that northern European countries used the factory system (understood as a body of privileges and special jurisdictions granted to foreign merchant communities rather than the establishment of separate premises for them) in the trade with both Spain and Portugal until the beginning of the nineteenth century.

Things had been substantially different in the fifteenth and sixteenth centuries when Iberian merchants had played an important role in interna-

---

[9] John H. Elliott, 'Atlantic history: a circumnavigation', in D. Armitage and M. J. Braddick (eds), *The British Atlantic world, 1500–1800*, New York 2002, 239.
[10] Alison Games, 'Atlantic history: definitions, challenges, and opportunities', *AHR* cxi (2006), 745.
[11] Frédéric Mauro, 'Merchant communities, 1350–1750', in James D. Tracy (ed.), *The rise of merchant empires: long-distance trade in the early modern world, 1350–1750*, Cambridge 1990, 255. See also Sanjay Subrahmanyam (ed.), *Merchant networks in the early modern world*, Aldershot 1996.
[12] Philip D. Curtin, *Cross-cultural trade in world history*, Cambridge 1984, 4.

tional trade. Spaniards had participated actively in the trade with northern Europe and their success derived to a large extent from their factories (Castilians and Basques each had their own factory) in Bruges and Antwerp, where, along with Italian, German, English, Flemish, Portuguese and French merchants, they had carried on an extensive trade in wool and cloth, metals, cereals, wine, spices and other staples. For that period, therefore, it is clear that traditional ideas concerning the inferiority of the Spanish merchant must be discarded.[13]

The problems facing Spaniards started in the last quarter of the sixteenth century with the outbreak of the Flemish war and the gradual weakening of Spain as a European power. Spanish traders disappeared from northern Europe. Furthermore, several disadvantageous and unbalanced treaties signed by Spain throughout the seventeenth century, most notably those of Westphalia (1648), the Pyrenees (1659) and Madrid (1667), granted privileges (special jurisdiction, religious protection, tax reductions and so on) to Dutch, French and English merchants residing in Spain. As a result:

> Foreign merchant enclaves structured like family enterprises formed culturally and economically hermetic undertakings, maintaining security by relying upon speaking and keeping business records in their native tongue, recruiting among their ethnic group, and buying primarily from producers at home.[14]

Like Uztáriz a few decades later, seventeenth-century Spanish economic thinkers (the so-called *arbitristas*) such as Juan de Castro (writing in the 1660s) and Miguel Álvarez Osorio y Redín (1686) complained bitterly that foreigners had taken over Spain's international trade, and exhorted Spaniards to make purchases directly from European producers rather than from foreign intermediaries.[15]

At least in theory, colonial trade should have been more favourable to Spaniards since foreigners were officially excluded from trading with and settling in the American colonies. Nevertheless the Spanish monopoly appears to have been thoroughly penetrated both by foreign goods and foreign merchants established in Lower Andalusia. In 1675, in his highly popular *Le Parfait Negociant*, the Frenchman Jacques Savary described the widespread method of using Spanish merchants as a front for business actually conducted by foreigners.[16] Similarly, in his 1764 book on the origins of

---

[13] See Carla R. Phillips, 'Spanish merchants and the wool trade in the sixteenth century', *Sixteenth Century Journal* xiv (1983), 259–82; Constance J. Mathers, 'Family partnership and international trade in early modern Europe: merchants from Burgos in England and France, 1470–1570', *Business History Review* lxii (1988), 367–97; Jean-Philippe Priotti, *Génesis de un crecimiento: Bilbao y sus mercaderes, h. 1520–h. 1620*, Bilbao 2004.
[14] Stanley J. Stein and Barbara H. Stein, *Silver, trade and war: Spain and America in the making of early modern Europe*, Baltimore 2000, 72.
[15] Ibid. 94–7.
[16] Jacques Savary, *Le Parfait Negociant, ou instruction générale pour ce qui regarde le commerce des marchandises de France & des pays etrangers*, Paris 1675, 76–80.

commerce, the Englishman Adam Anderson described the Andalusian city of Cádiz as 'the proper Center of the whole Spanish American Commerce', adding that '[h]ither other European Nations send their Merchandize, to be shipped off in Spanish Bottoms for America, sheltered (or, as our old English Phrase has it, coloured) under the Names of Spanish Factors'.[17] The supposed Spanish monopoly of colonial trade thus existed in name only, due to Spaniards who were willing to act as front men (*prestanombres*) for foreigners in exchange for a commission. Furthermore, due to their lack of capital, those Spaniards who were involved in the colonial trade had no option but to resort to foreign lenders and traders.[18]

The history of early modern Portuguese merchants is also one of decline, starting in the middle of the seventeenth century, just when the crisis of Spanish imperial dominion in the Atlantic became apparent. In the fifteenth and sixteenth centuries the Portuguese had been even more successful than the Spaniards, opening commercial routes and creating networks that encompassed the Atlantic and Indian Oceans.[19] The disarticulation of their transatlantic networks came as a result of religious persecution in the 1630s (the most prominent Portuguese merchants in Iberia and America were accused of secretly professing the Jewish faith) and the rupture of Luso-Spanish relations in 1640. By the eighteenth century little remained of their illustrious commercial past. Portugal had seen the arrival of numerous foreign merchants in the second half of the seventeenth century, most notably the English. The Methuen Treaty of 1703 between Portugal and England greatly strengthened the English traders' position in Lisbon and Porto. Thanks to this Portugal retained a political position strong enough as to preserve the territorial integrity of Brazil, but in compensation it renounced further manufacturing development, implicitly transferring to England the dynamic impulse created by the Brazilian gold mines discovered in the 1690s. English merchants in Portugal were granted several privileges and fiscal exemptions, protection from the inquisition, and a special jurisdiction which, combined with their larger capital and extended networks, gave them overt control of Portugal's international trade.[20] Rather surprisingly, by the mid-eighteenth century there were only three Portuguese merchant houses in Lisbon which

---

[17] Adam Anderson, *An historical and chronological deduction of the origin of commerce from the earliest accounts to the present time*, London 1764, ii, appendix 97.

[18] Antonio García-Baquero, *Cádiz y el Atlántico, 1717–1778: el comercio colonial español bajo el monopolio gaditano*, Seville 1976, i. 479–97; Antonio-Miguel Bernal, *La financiación de la Carrera de Indias: dinero y crédito en el comercio colonial español con América*, Seville 1992, 353–62; Manuel Bustos Rodríguez, *Cádiz en el sistema atlántico: la ciudad, sus comerciantes y la actividad mercantil, 1650–1830*, Madrid 2005, 158–65.

[19] See Charles R. Boxer, *The Portuguese seaborne empire, 1415–1825*, London 1969, and Daviken Studnicki-Gizbert, *A nation upon the ocean sea: Portugal's Atlantic diaspora and the crisis of the Spanish empire, 1492–1640*, Oxford 2007.

[20] L. M. E. Shaw, *The Anglo-Portuguese alliance and the English merchants in Portugal, 1654–1810*, Aldershot 1998.

had the experience and general commercial expertise to engage in business with foreign markets, and even these houses had some foreign partners.[21] Furthermore, by 1703 the English were also allowed to participate in the trade with Brazil. Portuguese merchants, just like their Spanish neighbours, played a subsidiary role in their country's overseas commerce.

British contemporaries saw religion as one of the reasons why the Iberian countries had a poor mercantile record. In 1764 Adam Anderson contended that Protestant countries had 'undoubtedly considerable Advantages beyond those of the Popish Persuasion, both in their Commerce and Manufactures'. He offered four reasons for this: 'none of their useful Hands are shut up in Convents'; 'they are not obliged to Celibacy'; 'Neither are they interrupted from following their lawful and commendable Employments, by superstitious and nonsensical Holidays and Processions'; and finally 'By the latter's persecuting all of a different religious Persuasion from their own, whereby Multitudes of useful People are prevented from settling in Popish Countries!'[22]

Religion does indeed seem to have played a major part in Portugal's decline, but not for the reasons given by Anderson. In the first half of the seventeenth century most Portuguese merchants had been 'new Christians' or *cristãos novos* (known as *conversos* in the Spanish empire), with Jewish ancestors, and were therefore suspected of being crypto-Jews. The correlation, widely spread in both Portugal and Europe, between new Christians, Judaism and the merchant profession seems to have been an important factor in diminishing the interest of the Portuguese in the mercantile arts. The fact that throughout the seventeenth and eighteenth centuries the word 'Portuguese' was synonymous with 'Jew' in foreign countries was a source of national embarrassment.[23]

However, the famous Weberian explanation for Protestantism as the lynchpin of 'the spirit of capitalism', which has given rise to much controversy regarding the impact of religious belief on economic life, would appear to be of little use here.[24] In fact, other historians have shown that Catholics also participated rather successfully in the British and French colonial trades.[25] Michel Zylberberg, for example, attributes French traders' successful dealings in Cádiz primarily to 'a Catholic capitalism'.[26] It would appear

---

[21] Kenneth R. Maxwell, *Conflicts and conspiracies: Brazil and Portugal, 1750–1808*, Cambridge 1973, 25.
[22] Anderson, *Historical and chronological deduction*, i, p. viii.
[23] Boxer, *Portuguese seaborne empire*, 271–2.
[24] See Max Weber, *The Protestant ethic and the spirit of capitalism*, London 1930. For an insightful critique of Weber's views see Kurt Samuelsson, *Religion and economic action*, trans. Geoffrey French, London 1961.
[25] Thomas M. Doerflinger, *A vigorous spirit of enterprise: merchants and economic development in revolutionary Philadelphia*, Chapel Hill 1986, 163; John F. Bosher, *The Canada merchants, 1713–1763*, Oxford 1987, 47–67.
[26] Michel Zylberberg, *Une si Douce Domination: les milieux d'affaires français et l'Espagne vers 1780–1808*, Paris 1993, 122.

that the geographical spread of national, ethnic and religious groups had a much bigger impact on determining who participated in commerce than the cultural and spiritual imprint of religion itself. John Bosher argues that in the late seventeenth century Huguenot merchants 'had an advantage over French Catholic merchants in that they belonged to the great and growing Protestant Atlantic world' and therefore could use Dutch and English facilities such as ships, ports, merchandise, loans, bills of exchange, insurance and so on.[27] The advantage held by the members of the 'Protestant International', and by the French Catholics over their Iberian co-religionists, was that they were allowed to settle in Iberia under very favourable conditions, whereas Iberian Catholics (and all Iberians were Catholics by the end of the eighteenth century) were not welcome in either England or Holland, and had no immunities in France similar to those enjoyed by the French in Spain. Finally, Iberians' reduced participation in international trade can also be explained by the massive and rich American colonies upon which they could focus their attention.

In the eighteenth century both Spain and Portugal made great efforts to modernise their empires and to tighten their control over their American colonies by copying many of the mercantilist policies implemented by the British. Although the reforms encompassed a wide range of areas, from colonial administration and taxation to defence and national manufacturing, particular attention was paid to commerce. In Spain successive ministers pursued a British-style empire of commerce, as in Portugal did Sebastião José de Carvalho e Melo (future marquès de Pombal, 1750–77), who designed his nationalistic policies 'to remove the necessity for the residence of foreign factors in Portugal'.[28]

An explanation based upon the role of 'trade diasporas' would appear to solve the problem of why the Spanish and Portuguese did not participate actively in international trade.[29] However, if attention is paid to the Iberian colonial trades, then the same explanation does not seem to apply to the foreigners established in Cádiz, Lisbon and Porto: they were not allowed to travel to either Spanish America or Brazil but nevertheless seem to have obtained enormous benefits from the Iberian colonial trades. To what extent did they have to rely on Portuguese *commissários volantes* (itinerant traders travelling to Brazil) and Spanish *encomenderos* (agents travelling to Spanish America)? This form of division of labour, where Iberians were the intermediaries and the foreigners the principals (or owners of the merchandise), generated problems of distrust in the eighteenth century.

---

[27] John F. Bosher, 'Huguenot merchants and the Protestant International in the seventeenth century', WMQ lii (1995), 98.
[28] Maxwell, *Conflicts*, 32.
[29] The term 'trade diaspora' refers to networks of proactive merchants set up to buy and sell their goods along established trade routes: Robin Cohen, *Global diasporas: an introduction*, Seattle 1997, 83.

INTRODUCTION

Trading networks and the concept of trust

The sociologist Niklas Luhmann, who has paid careful attention to the role of trust in facilitating economic and social exchange, notes that 'if you choose one action to others, in spite of the possibility of being disappointed by the action of others, you define the situation as one of trust'.[30] In other words, trust is an act of faith, based upon personal judgement, but there is no deity involved – only human beings. When the uncertainties arising from long distances and slow and often unpredictable communications are added to this equation, it becomes very clear that interpersonal trust was crucial to early modern overseas trade. The agents in many diverse markets had information that the principal merchants and traders did not (i.e. asymmetric information), and monitoring their honesty and performance was anything but easy. The risk was twofold: on the one hand the agent could be tempted to cheat his principal, and on the other the principal, not having direct access to information, could easily grow suspicious of his agent. This potential source of distrust is essentially what economists and economic historians call 'the principal-agent problem'.[31]

In the early modern period the concept of trust was intimately linked with two others: credit and reputation. Referring to early modern England, Craig Muldrew asserts that 'more than anything credit was a public means of social communication and circulating judgement about the value of other members of communities'.[32] To have credit in a community meant that an individual could be trusted to pay back his or her debts. According to Muldrew, the early modern economy was a system of cultural and material exchange in which the central mediating factor was credit or trust.[33] That credit, reputation and trust were tightly interwoven is also shown by Natasha Glaisyer, who states that the term credit had three interconnected meanings: payments to be made later, one's capacity to pay later and one's reputation: 'It is important not to separate these meanings because an individual's reputation, to a large extent, determined whether others were prepared to trust him, or her, to pay later.'[34] In recent years historians have also emphasised

---

[30] Niklas Luhmann, 'Familiarity, confidence, trust: problems and alternatives', in Diego Gambetta (ed.), *Trust: making and breaking cooperative relations*, Oxford 1988, 97.
[31] See, for example, Ann M. Carlos and Stephen Nicholas, 'Agency problems in the early chartered companies: the case of the Hudson's Bay Company', *JEcH* l (1990), 853–75; Avner Greif, 'Reputation and coalitions in medieval trade: evidence on the Maghribi traders', *JEcH* xlix (1989), 857–82; David Hancock, '"A world of business to do": William Freeman and the foundations of England's commercial empire, 1645–1707', *WMQ* lvii (2000), 3–34.
[32] Craig Muldrew, *The economy of obligation: the culture of credit and social relations in early modern England*, Basingstoke 1998, 2. See also Laurence Fontaine, 'Antonio and Shylock: credit and trust in France, *c.* 1680–*c.* 1780', *EcHR* 2nd ser. liv (2001), 39–57.
[33] Muldrew, *Economy of obligation*, 7.
[34] Natasha Glaisyer, *The culture of commerce in England, 1660–1720*, London 2006, 38.

the importance of these concepts in the characteristically risky environment of early modern overseas trade.³⁵ In the words of Nuala Zahedieh, '[c]redit in the sense of belief, confidence, faith, trust, the estimate in which a character is held, reputation, was the elusive but fundamental key to success in early modern commerce'.³⁶

Trust was also imperative because merchants were very reluctant to disclose the state of their businesses even to their contacts and correspondents. Rather paradoxically, merchants regarded confidentiality both as absolutely necessary for commerce and as a potential source of distrust. A good reputation, built on past behaviour, was often the only reliable antidote to the effects of distrust. This explains the numerous references to the sincerity of intentions, or good faith, in the economic literature of the time. 'Good faith, which is the mother of trust and credit', stated Simón Codes in 1803, 'is needed for everything, and much more for trade; because without it all men are in a continuous hostility unable to rely on anyone but on themselves'.³⁷

How did merchants cope with the uncertainties arising from the agency problem? Resorting to one's family was the first obvious strategy, and indeed the importance conferred by historians on the role of the family in creating partnerships and trading networks is grounded in solid arguments.³⁸ Apart from the emotional link that naturally gave relatives an aura of dependability, merchants had access to more practical information about the conduct and capabilities of their relatives than about those of anybody else. However, it was frequently the case that merchants did not have relatives residing in the places with which they traded, and therefore were compelled to find other people to act as their agents. In practice, merchants sought additional grounds upon which to base trust, as the examples of national, ethnic and religious merchant communities clearly show. Within the Spanish colonial empire terms designating geographical provenance and ethnicity – such as

---

³⁵ See, for example, Luuc Kooijmans, 'Risk and reputation: on the mentality of merchants in the early modern period', in C. Lesger and L. Noordegraaf (eds), *Entrepreneurs and entrepreneurship in early modern times: merchants and industrialists within the orbit of the Dutch staple market*, The Hague 1995, 25–34; Nuala Zahedieh, 'Credit, risk, and reputation in the seventeenth-century colonial trade', in Olaf U. Janzen (ed.), *Merchant organization and maritime trade in the north Atlantic, 1660–1815*, St John's 1998, 53–74; Peter Mathias, 'Risk, credit and kinship in early modern enterprise', in John McCusker and Kenneth Morgan (eds), *The early modern Atlantic economy*, Cambridge 2001, 15–35; and Xabier Lamikiz, 'Un "cuento ruidoso": confidencialidad, reputación y confianza en el comercio del siglo XVIII', *Obradoiro de Historia Moderna* xvi (2007), 113–42.
³⁶ Zahedieh, 'Credit', 53.
³⁷ Codes, *Memoria*, 31–2.
³⁸ See, for example, Susan M. Socolow, *The merchants of Buenos Aires, 1778–1810: family and commerce*, Cambridge 1978; Paloma Fernández Pérez, *El rostro familiar de la metrópoli: redes de parentesco y lazos mercantiles en Cádiz, 1700–1812*, Madrid 1997; and Richard Grassby, *Kinship and capitalism: marriage, family and business in the English-speaking world, 1580–1740*, Cambridge 2001.

montañés (from modern Cantabria), *vizcaíno* (a term used to refer to Basques in general), *catalán, gallego, criollo* and so on – were more meaningful than the more general *español* (Spaniard). The sense of common identity based on ethnic and regional origin was known in Spanish as *paisanaje*. In eighteenth-century Buenos Aires, for example, in order to lessen the risks inherent in commerce, merchants preferred overwhelmingly to trust family members in commercial transactions: 'if there were no family members to turn to, fictive kin, or merchants from the same regional origin were next in order of preference'.[39] Likewise for the merchants of Mexico City, according to John Kicza, such ties were 'the best guarantee of loyalty and trustworthiness available' in the eighteenth century.[40] These views are in tune with anthropologists' theoretical approach to the problem of how merchants built their own reputations and monitored the trustworthiness of their agents and partners across cultural and geographical divides. Merchant networks are thus seen in practice as synonymous with the internal organisation of trading diasporas.[41] However, this theoretical assumption, which concentrates on intra-group relations, fails to explain commercial cooperation between the members of different communities.

The second main theoretical approach to explaining how commercial networks were formed comes from economic historians' use of 'new institutional economics'. They have explored the relationship between institutional change and economic activity, showing that evolving economic institutions (both formal and informal) facilitated commercial exchange between merchants who, under more uncertain conditions, would have been more reluctant to trust one another.[42] The theoretical approach of the scholars inspired by these views lies in the assumption that merchant coalitions were the product of self-interested individuals who cooperated only as long as it was economically advantageous to do so. However, this strictly rational understanding of commercial cooperation pays little attention to the role of culture and social relations. The notion of culture is indeed particularly problematic for this approach because it refers to inherited ethical and

---

[39] Socolow, *Merchants*, 170–1.
[40] John E. Kicza, *Colonial entrepreneurs, families and business in Bourbon Mexico City*, Albuquerque 1983, 52.
[41] Curtin, *Cross-cultural trade*, 1–14; Abner Cohen, 'Cultural strategies in the organization of trading diasporas', in C. Meillassoux (ed.), *The development of indigenous trade and markets in West Africa*, London 1971, 266–84.
[42] See, for example, Douglass C. North, 'Institutions, transaction costs and the rise of merchant empires', in James D. Tracy (ed.), *The political economy of merchant empires*, Cambridge 1991, 22–40; Paul E. Lovejoy and David Richardson, 'Trust, pawnship, and Atlantic history: the institutional foundations of the Old Calabar slave trade', AHR civ (1999), 333–55; and Avner Greif, *Institutions and the path to the modern economy: lessons from medieval trade*, Cambridge 2006. See also Janet T. Landa, *Trust, ethnicity, and identity: beyond the new institutional economics of ethnic trading networks, contract law, and gift-exchange*, Ann Arbor 1994.

normative habits that vary over time and between different communities, and is therefore not the exclusive product of rationality.[43] The impact of culture on economic life is none the less unquestionable, and as important a factor for explaining economic progress as population, capital, technology and market characteristics. Hence, to work on the basis of certain universal assumptions about human nature (as economists often do – primarily in their basic model of human beings as 'rational utility maximisers') may restrict the historical understanding of the distinctiveness of particular societies.[44] This is clearly exemplified by the process of developing trust in somebody: it involves making decisions based on information and experience, and is therefore a rational choice – but only up to a certain point. As long as choices influenced by culture arise out of habit and are embedded in social and cultural norms, trust is not entirely the result of rational calculation. It also expresses hope, faith and expectation, all of which may eventually prove to have been misplaced.

Other historians have criticised the traditional anthropological and economic approaches, proposing alternative ways of looking at early modern trading networks. Working on the (religiously-speaking) 'hybrid and heterogeneous' networks of the Portuguese 'nation' in the sixteenth and seventeenth centuries, Daviken Studnicki-Gizbert criticises traditional explanations based exclusively either on ties of religion, kinship and provenance, or on rational self-interest. Instead he proposes the concept of interdependence, which describes the cultivation of mutual understanding and collective obligation normatively, cognitively and in day-to-day social practice.[45] Francesca Trivellato, who has adopted a network approach to studying cross-cultural trade, states that the question is not whether merchants of different nationalities and religions traded with each other (given the expansion of trade in the seventeenth century that question is rhetorical) but rather 'why and how such diverse traders kept their promises'.[46] The network analysis approach (understood in micro-analytical rather than mathematical terms) allows her to look at inter-group commercial relations and to examine the workings of specific informal networks (based on mechanisms of reciprocity and reputa-

---

[43] Clifford Geertz defines culture as 'an historically transmitted pattern of meanings embodied in symbols, a system of inherited conceptions expressed in symbolic forms by means of which men communicate, perpetuate, and develop their knowledge about and attitudes toward life': *The interpretation of cultures*, New York 1973, 89.

[44] Francis Fukuyama, *Trust: the social virtues and the creation of prosperity*, London 1995, 33–5.

[45] Daviken Studnicki-Gizbert, 'Interdependence and the collective pursuit of profits: Portuguese commercial networks in the early modern Atlantic', in Diogo Ramada Curto and Anthony Molho (eds), *Commercial networks in the early modern world*, Florence 2002, 100–17.

[46] Francesca Trivellato, 'Jews of Leghorn, Italians of Lisbon, and Hindus of Goa: merchant networks and cross-cultural trade in the early modern period', ibid. 61.

tion control) that traversed commonly defined geographical, political and cultural areas. The typicality of her intercontinental Jewish-Italian-Hindu networks, however, is highly questionable.

The existence of inter-group and cross-cultural trade in the early modern period is undeniable, but it was not free of problems, particularly in the context of long-distance exchanges. As the British merchants residing in Lisbon put it in 1716, 'we have often experienced great inconveniences by trusting our own and our friends' effects in the hands of Portuguese Factors in the Brazils, who by reason of the distance of the place (which hinders sueing them by law) render accounts of our effects when and how they please'.[47] The British considered it necessary that their countrymen be allowed to reside in Brazil, a concession that the Portuguese government, despite the Methuen Treaty, was always reluctant to make. Both the French and the British merchants established in Cádiz made similar complaints in the 1760s. They were growing very dissatisfied with their Spanish frontmen who 'increasingly were being found dishonest and unreliable'.[48] These examples say a great deal about perceptions of trust and distrust – but to what extent were such perceptions the by-product of actual experience and how much the result of merchants' natural fear of being cheated? Moreover, was it not enough for merchants to make friends with colleagues belonging to other groups, or simply to marry their daughters, in order to foster collaboration? Rather than adopting or proposing a theoretical approach to answering those questions, this study explores the formation of trading networks by looking at merchants' daily experience of trust and distrust, and how that experience, seen from different angles, affected their participation in trade. In so doing, the book hopes to go some way towards filling the gap in historians' understanding of how cultural factors impinged upon economic life.

To identify the economic and social consequences of trust and distrust it is necessary to place merchants' activities in an evolving historical context. Cultural norms were moulded by practice and experience, while the latter was subject to numerous historical variables. In early modern commerce, people's ability to trust was affected by three major factors: first, the efficiency of the legal system in enforcing contracts; second, the availability of information, which was closely but not exclusively linked to the frequency and quality of communications; and, lastly, the risks associated with the system and pattern of trade, including the distance and difficulty of navigation, the opportunities for the marketing of goods, the level of competition and the use of credit. It is by paying attention to those variables, and how merchants experienced them, that the rationale behind both Uztáriz's plan

---

[47] Charles R. Boxer, 'Brazilian gold and British traders in the first half of the eighteenth century', *HAHR* xlix (1969), 462–3.
[48] Allan Christelow, 'Great Britain and the trades from Cádiz and Lisbon to Spanish America and Brazil, 1759–1783', *HAHR* xxvii (1947), 18.

to settle Spanish factors in Europe and the complaints made by the foreign merchants involved in the trade with Brazil and Spanish America may be explained.

Spanish merchants and the Bourbon reforms

At the turn of the eighteenth century, with the arrival of the new Bourbon dynasty, Spain and its policy-makers adopted the Colbertian model of mercantilism,[49] but as the century progressed the British 'empire of commerce' became the example to admire and to follow. In the first half of the century important efforts towards reform were made by ministers such as José Patiño, José del Campillo and the marqués de la Ensenada, but it was the ascension to power of Charles III in 1759 that really gave added vigour to the ongoing attempts to modernise the Spanish empire. The reign of Charles III has unsurprisingly received much attention from historians, who have concentrated either on the political and economic impact of his reforms (in particular the 'free trade' regulations of 1765 and 1778) or on the correlation between the pressure put on the colonies by the royal measures and the foundations of Spanish American emancipation.[50]

How did the reforms affect Spanish participation in Spain's international and colonial trade? It is a question that the existing literature leaves unanswered. After three decades in which they labelled eighteenth-century merchants as *burguesía mercantil* (mercantile bourgeoisie), historians are now less inclined to tackle the question of whether or not the members of the merchant elite regarded themselves as a distinctive, well-defined social group.[51] Some argue that the very use of the term *burguesía* has had an isolating effect, and that for a comprehensive understanding of merchants' activities it is essential to analyse their ties with the rest of society.[52] However, for all the interesting work that has been done in recent years, merchants' ties with other colleagues living overseas remain virtually unexplored. The numerous studies dealing with the communities on either side of the Atlantic make

---

[49] This was a set of policies implemented by the French minister of finance Jean-Baptiste Colbert (1619–83). They included support for national manufactures by creating state-owned factories, abolition of barriers to internal trade and discrimination against foreign trade.

[50] For recent examples see Patricia H. Marks, *Deconstructing legitimacy: viceroys, merchants, and the military in late colonial Peru*, University Park, PA 2007, and Josep María Delgado Ribas, *Dinámicas imperiales (1650–1796): España, América y Europa en el cambio institucional del sistema colonial español*, Barcelona 2007.

[51] See, for example, Pere Molas Ribalta, *La burguesía mercantil en la España del antiguo régimen*, Madrid 1985; Antonio García-Baquero (ed.), *La burguesía de negocios en la Andalucía de la Ilustración*, Cádiz 1991; and Luis Miguel Enciso Recio (coor.), *La burguesía española en la edad moderna*, Valladolid 1996.

[52] Fernández Pérez, *Rostro familiar*, 5.

few references to transatlantic connections.[53] Similarly, the several works on individual traders and families do not pay much attention to the genesis and functioning of such networks.[54] Moreover, once a few interconnected merchant names have been detected, the assumption seems to be that there are no further questions worth asking. This A-traded-with-B approach is usually followed only by brief and straightforward remarks on the importance of family in providing trustworthy contacts:[55] the details of how such networks functioned, or failed to function, has not been addressed.

The effects of the Bourbon reforms on the traders in the major Spanish and American commercial centres have been studied primarily in connection with their respective *consulados* or merchant gilds. That is partly the reason why in the historiography merchants' individual attitudes, views and business practices appear greatly overshadowed by studies of institutional activities and discourses. The institution of the *consulado* emerged from the medieval economy of Mediterranean towns, first appearing in Sicily in the twelfth century then reaching Spain in the mid-thirteenth century, where it became established in Valencia and Barcelona. From a simple maritime court it evolved into a permanent tribunal with both original and appellate jurisdiction in mercantile disputes. In addition to judicial tasks it was in charge of promoting commerce, collecting taxes, enforcing trade regulations and implementing infrastructure improvements in roads and ports. The *consulado*'s governing body, along with several representatives, also represented the gild membership before the crown and before other institutions such as local councils and regional assemblies. The gild membership or *matrícula* included resident merchants, the eligibility of whom depended on their age, property and occupation. The governing body, made up of a *prior* (headman) and two *consules*, was elected by the members themselves every one,

---

[53] See, for example, Manuel Bustos Rodríguez, *Los comerciantes de la Carrera de Indias en el Cádiz del siglo XVIII, 1713–1775*, Cádiz 1995; María Jesús Arazola, *Hombres, barcos y comercio de la ruta Cádiz-Buenos Aires, 1737–1757*, Seville 1998; David A. Brading, *Miners and merchants in Bourbon Mexico, 1763–1810*, Cambridge 1971; Kicza, *Colonial entrepreneurs*; C. R. Borchart de Moreno, *Los mercaderes y el capitalismo en la ciudad de México, 1759–1778*, Mexico City 1984; Jackie R. Booker, *Veracruz merchants, 1770–1829: a merchant elite in late Bourbon and early independent Mexico*, Boulder 1993; Socolow, *Merchants*; Cristina A. Mazzeo (ed.), *Los comerciantes limeños a finales del siglo XVIII: capacidad y cohesión de una élite, 1750–1825*, Lima 2000; and Jesús Turiso Sebastián, *Comerciantes españoles en la Lima borbónica: anatomía de una élite de poder, 1701–1761*, Valladolid 2002.

[54] See, for example, María C. Torales Pacheco (coor.), *La compañía de comercio de Francisco Ignacio de Yraeta, 1767–1797*, Mexico City 1982; José Garmendia Arruebarrena, *Tomás Ruiz de Apodaca: un comerciante alavés con Indias, 1709–1767*, Vitoria 1990; Richmond F. Brown, *Juan Fermín de Aycinena: central American colonial entrepreneur, 1729–1796*, Norman, OK 1997; Cristina A. Mazzeo, *El comercio libre en el Perú: las estrategias de un comerciante peruano, José Antonio de Lavalle y Cortés, 1777–1815*, Lima 1994.

[55] See, for example, Victoria E. Martínez del Cerro, *Una comunidad de comerciantes: navarros y vascos en Cádiz (segunda mitad del siglo XVIII)*, Seville 2007, 208–54.

two or three years. These leaders were judges in the *consulado* court, and also members of an executive council or *junta*.[56]

From the end of the thirteenth century to the early nineteenth century the Spanish crown granted *consulados* to over thirty cities and towns in Spain and the colonies, and the institution was introduced in ports involved primarily in the Atlantic trade at the end of the fifteenth century. In 1497 the merchants of Burgos were granted a *consulado*, and so were their competitors in Bilbao in 1511. Similarly, in 1543, the rapidly growing merchant community of Seville (the monopoly port of colonial trade until 1717, when it was moved to Cádiz) was granted another *consulado*. Half a century later the two Spanish American viceroyal capitals would get theirs, Mexico City in 1592 and Lima in 1613.[57] The merchants of other American commercial centres such as Caracas, Guatemala, Havana, Buenos Aires, Veracruz and Cartagena would not be granted *consulados* until the mid-1790s.[58]

The *consulados* were important sources of income for the crown, whether in the form of loans or donations. Naturally they also became powerful lobbyists for their own (usually monopolistic) cause, sending numerous petitions and supplications to Madrid, and initiating frequent disputes both among themselves (particularly in the colonial trade) and with the crown. In the eighteenth century these clashes were exacerbated by various Bourbon reforms.[59] As a result, historians are generally happy to imply that commercial networks in the colonial trade were moulded according to the merchants' gild affiliations. However, such assumptions are greatly misleading, for what merchants cared about most was the trustworthiness of their correspondents, regardless of *consulado* affiliations.

---

[56] Robert S. Smith, *The Spanish guild merchant: a history of the consulado, 1250–1700*, Durham 1940.

[57] See Manuel Basas Fernández, *El consulado de Burgos en el siglo* XVI, Madrid 1963; Teófilo Guiard Larrauri, *Historia del Consulado y Casa de Contratación de Bilbao y del comercio de la villa*, Bilbao 1913–14; Antonia Heredia Herrera, 'Apuntes para la historia del Consulado de Cargadores a Indias, en Sevilla y en Cádiz', AEA xxvii (1970), 219–79; Clarence N. Guice, 'The *consulado* of New Spain, 1594–1795', unpubl. PhD diss. Berkeley 1952; and María E. Rodríguez Vicente, *El Tribunal del consulado de Lima en la primera mitad del siglo* XVII, Madrid 1960.

[58] See Bernd Hausberger and Antonio Ibarra (eds), *Comercio y poder en América colonial: los consulados de comerciantes, siglos* XVII–XVIII, Madrid 2003.

[59] See, for example, Guillermo Céspedes del Castillo, 'Lima y Buenos Aires: repercusiones económicas y políticas de la creación del Virreinato del Plata', AEA iii (1946), 669–874; Brian R. Hamnett, 'Mercantile rivalry and peninsular division: the *consulados* of New Spain and the impact of the Bourbon reforms, 1789–1824', *Ibero-Amerikanisches Archiv* ii (1976), 273–305; Geoffrey J. Walker, *Spanish politics and imperial trade, 1700–1789*, London 1979; Pedro Pérez Herrero, 'Actitudes del *consulado* de México ante las reformas comerciales borbónicas (1718–1765)', RI xliii (1983), 97–182; and Patricia H. Marks, 'Confronting a mercantile elite: Bourbon reforms and the merchants of Lima, 1765–1796', *The Americas* lx (2004), 519–58.

INTRODUCTION

By the 1790s there were clear signs that Spaniards had become more active in their country's trade. Foreigners were still predominant, but the Spanish merchant houses were gradually taking on a greater role. In the second half of the century the foreigners of Cádiz themselves would acknowledge that the Spanish increasingly began to trade on their own account instead of being mere intermediaries.[60] In 1796 the Frenchman Jean François de Bourgoing, having recently visited Spain, stated that his compatriots in the peninsula were facing 'the competition of indigenous merchants who everyday learn more about their real interests and finally want to do by themselves what they have seen foreigners doing successfully for too long'.[61] The story of how Spaniards overcame their previous limitations is still to be told.

Bilbao, Cádiz and Atlantic history

This study looks at Spanish merchants involved in two different and contrasting trades: Bilbao's trade across and around the North Atlantic, and Cádiz's colonial trade with the viceroyalty of Peru. Although the economic details of these trades will be explored at length in chapters 1 and 3 respectively, it is useful here to briefly mention their main characteristics. The port of Bilbao, in northern Spain, was a major redistribution node within the Castilian economy. It traded in a wide range of products (meat, wax, wood, onions and chestnuts, to mention a few), but its main exports were Castilian wool and Basque iron, while its main imports were ironmongery and textiles from England, France and Holland, as well as dried codfish from Newfoundland and North America. The southern port of Cádiz, on the other hand, was the monopoly port of the Spanish colonial trade for most of the eighteenth century. The trade with the viceroyalty of Peru (on the Pacific coast) was one of the richest with Spanish America. From Cádiz large quantities of textiles, wax, paper and other commodities were sent to Peru in exchange for American silver and gold. A major problem was the enormous distances: in the eighteenth century the journey from Cádiz to the Peruvian capital of Lima entailed five to six months of hazardous navigation.

There seem to have been important differences between the merchants of Bilbao and Cádiz. Crucially, the indigenous merchants of Bilbao are regarded as having participated in international trade more actively than any other Spanish merchants in the eighteenth century, whereas the Spaniards of Cádiz concentrated on the monopoly trade with the vast American dominions, leaving the trade with Europe almost entirely in the hands of foreigners.[62]

[60] Bernal, *Financiación*, 366–7; Bustos, *Cádiz*, 172–84.
[61] Jean-François Bourgoing, *Tableau de l'Espagne moderne*, Paris 1797, iii. 130.
[62] See, for example, Ana Crespo Solana, *El comercio marítimo entre Amsterdam y Cádiz, 1713–1778*, Madrid 2000, 145–50, and Arnaud Bartolomei, 'La Bourse et la vie: destin collectif et trajectories individuelles des marchands français de Cadix, de l'instauration

The commercial arrangement with the colonies, based on a rigid system of fleets in which, at least officially, only Spaniards could participate, had been created in the mid-sixteenth century following the model established a few decades earlier by the merchant gild of the Castilian town of Burgos and its wool exports to northern Europe. Burgos's fleets to Flanders did not survive beyond the sixteenth century, whereas the fleets of the colonial trade continued well into the eighteenth. Bilbao played an important part in providing shipping for Burgos's wool exports to the north in the sixteenth century, but none the less its merchant community remained in a secondary position. It was only in the middle decades of the seventeenth century that Bilbao gradually became the most important commercial centre in northern Spain. But its newly acquired pre-eminence owed nothing to the monopoly of wool and the system of fleets to the north that had encumbered Burgos a century before. Rather, Bilbao's success was explained by its incorporation into the multilateral trade of the north Atlantic system, a trade controlled mostly by a large community of English and Dutch merchants residing in the town. It was not until the 1680s that the Bilbao merchants' relationship with those foreigners became one of fierce competition for the trade with 'the North' (north-west Europe and the north Atlantic). In Cádiz, however, there was no such competition between Spaniards and foreigners. As a result of their dissimilar experiences, the merchants of Cádiz and Bilbao are taken in the historiography to epitomise two contrasting mentalities in the eighteenth century. Antonio Domínguez states that the *bilbaínos* (the indigenous merchants of Bilbao) formed a 'more authentic bourgeoisie' than the *gaditanos* (the Spaniards resident in Cádiz).[63] Similarly, María Jesús Arazola notes that by the 1730s the intellectual evolution of the merchants of Bilbao was closer to that in France and Britain rather than to the rest of Spain, and as a result they had 'a more open-minded mentality' than that fostered by the monopolistic commercial arrangement with Spanish America.[64] This book attempts to explore and evaluate those contrasting mentalities by focusing on the strategies employed by *bilbaínos* and *gaditanos* as they participated in their respective Atlantic trades.

Within the Atlantic there were systems of cohesion such as the triangular or multilateral trade, the plantation complex or the *Carrera de Indias* (the system of Spanish colonial trade). There were also inter-imperial links, which have received little attention from historians.[65] Although the supra-

du *comercio libre* à la disparition de l'empire espagnol (1778–1824)', unpubl. PhD diss. Marseille 2007, 163–8.

[63] Antonio Domínguez Ortiz, *Sociedad y estado en el siglo* XVIII *español*, Barcelona 1976, 397–8.

[64] Arazola, *Hombres*, 41.

[65] For an example of inter-imperial trade see David Hancock, '"A revolution in the trade": wine distribution and the development of the infrastructure of the Atlantic market economy, 1703–1807', in McCusker and Morgan, *Early modern Atlantic economy*, 105–53.

national conception of Atlantic history entails dealing with more than country or empire, in the Spanish case, for two important reasons, this can also be done within the empire itself. First, because Spain's international and colonial trades were greatly affected by other developments occurring in the Atlantic basin – for instance the activities of the indigenous merchants of Bilbao were transformed as a result of the rise of the English and Dutch multilateral Atlantic trades in the seventeenth century. Similarly, in the late seventeenth and first half of the eighteenth centuries the Spanish colonial trade suffered a profound crisis due to foreign contraband shipped through the Caribbean, which eventually compelled the Spanish government to reform the system of transatlantic trade. The second reason why the Spanish imperial trade can be considered supranational is the important participation of foreign merchants established firstly in Seville and then in Cádiz. If the level of foreign participation in the Spanish empire is taken into account, it can safely be said that there was hardly any Atlantic trade that could be considered purely Spanish. The American silver that arrived in southern Spain, and was then funnelled all over Europe, was one of the engines of the Atlantic system.[66] And through the Spanish official channels foreign goods and ideas were shipped to Spanish America. Even though the apparatus of the *Carrera de Indias* was officially Spanish, its character was hardly uniquely Spanish, despite the views of some historians.[67]

Despite the important differences in the structure of the European colonial trades, all merchants involved in the Atlantic invariably had to cope with the problems involved in trusting other people. The British case offers the most obvious comparison. As John Elliott has put it, for the British '[t]he variety of routes, leading to a variety of settlements yielding a very diverse range of produce, made it difficult to think in terms of a Spanish-style system of fixed annual sailings in convoy'.[68] And yet, despite these differences, there was a shared predicament when it came to building trust. Historians who have studied the British colonial trade naturally emphasise the importance of having dependable correspondents overseas, but they have hardly begun to investigate the role of trust in the genesis and evolution of those trading networks.[69] For instance, when explaining the growing involvement of the tobacco planters in the consignment trade across the Atlantic, Jacob Price

---

[66] Stein and Stein, *Silver*, 19.
[67] For instance Carlos Martínez Shaw and José María Oliva Melgar argue that there was 'an Atlantic system specifically Spanish (or Hispanic)': 'Presentación', in C. Martínez Shaw and J. M. Oliva Melgar (eds), *El sistema atlántico español (siglos XVII–XIX)*, Madrid 2005, 12.
[68] John H. Elliott, *Empires of the Atlantic world: Britain and Spain in America, 1492–1830*, New Haven 2006, 112.
[69] For two exceptions see Nuala Zahedieh, 'Making mercantilism work: London merchants and Atlantic trade in the seventeenth century', *Transactions of the Royal Historical Society* ix (1999), 143–58, and Sheryllynne Haggerty, *The British-Atlantic trading community, 1760–1810: men, women, and the distribution of goods*, Leiden 2006, 109–41.

and Paul Clemens state that such developments 'presupposed the existence in London and other English ports of commission merchants who could not only obtain the necessary cargo space but could also command the confidence of these larger Chesapeake planters'.[70] But how was that confidence created, maintained or destroyed, and what problems did it entail? Similarly, in his book on the integration of the British Atlantic community during the middle decades of the eighteenth century, David Hancock devotes barely three pages to the importance of having overseas correspondents, predictably concluding that '[c]ommercial linkages to men with established, tested skills were culled and cultivated from a collection of blood, ethnic and neighbourhood connections'.[71]

Scholars inspired by the world-systems approach and global history criticise the idea of Atlantic history, depicting it as a myth.[72] Other historians, most notably the French, do not seem to be particularly interested in Atlantic history.[73] Nevertheless the utility of the ocean as a unit of analysis has been repeatedly demonstrated.[74] Rather than economic exchange it seems it was the spread of cultural values that created a common arena of social, political and economic interaction throughout the Atlantic world.[75] David Armitage has identified three types of Atlantic history: 'cis-Atlantic history', which looks at a particular place or region within an Atlantic context; 'trans-Atlantic history', which emphasises a comparative approach between places on either side of the Atlantic; and 'circum-Atlantic history', which takes the Atlantic basin as a whole.[76] Naturally the latter poses the biggest challenge for historians because it requires research in various languages and continents. This book attempts to combine the three types of transatlantic history by paying attention both to merchant communities in their places of residence and to their relationships with their overseas correspondents. The inclusion of Peru as part of the Atlantic world makes sense if its colonial

---

[70] Jacob M. Price and Paul G. E. Clemens, 'A revolution of scale in overseas trade: British firms in the Chesapeake trade, 1675–1775', JEcH xlvii (1987), 16.
[71] David Hancock, *Citizens of the world: London merchants and the integration of the British Atlantic community, 1735–1785*, Cambridge 1995, 139–41 at p. 140. For an exception see Lovejoy and Richardson, 'Trust, pawnship, and Atlantic history'.
[72] For a defence of Atlantic history see Nicholas Canny, 'Atlantic history and global history', in R. Pieper and P. Schmidt (eds), *Latin America and the Atlantic world, 1500–1850: essays in honor of Horst Pietschmann*, Cologne 2003, 25–34.
[73] Cécile Vidal, 'The reluctance of French historians to address Atlantic history', *Southern Quarterly* xliii/4 (2006), 153–89.
[74] The most remarkable contributions come from historians working on the transatlantic slave trade. See, for instance, Philip D. Curtin, *The rise and fall of the plantation complex: essays in Atlantic history*, Cambridge 1990, and David Eltis, *The rise of African slavery in the Americas*, Cambridge 2000.
[75] David Eltis, 'Atlantic history in global perspective', *Itinerario* xxiii/2 (1999), 143–4.
[76] David Armitage, 'Three concepts of Atlantic history', in Armitage and Braddick, *British Atlantic world*, 11–27.

history is considered: the viceroyalty of Peru, one of the richest Spanish American territories, was moulded and radically transformed by the rise of the Atlantic economy.

Sources

The canniness of early modern merchants led them to keep their records as secret as possible. As a result very few of their account and letter-books have survived, either in Spain or elsewhere. However, the archive of the British High Court of Admiralty in the National Archives, London, contains remarkable, previously undiscovered, material which qualifies this situation. During the eighteenth-century wars the British navy captured hundreds of Spanish merchant ships, privateers and men-of-war. During the double war of Jenkins' Ear and Austrian Succession (1739–48), for instance, at least 131 ships were captured, ninety-two during the three years of Spanish participation in the Seven Years' War (1761–3), and 140 during the four years of participation in the American War of Independence (1779–83). Along with the ships and their cargoes, the British also managed to intercept thousands of letters and documents of all kinds. This material is poorly catalogued, which is why no one has used the correspondence taken from Spanish prizes previously. The documents are of variable quality. When they were about to be captured, Spanish captains commonly got rid of the ship's papers – by the simple method of throwing them overboard – in order to conceal political, military and commercial information that could be useful to the enemy. Usually they kept only the bills of lading, so that the owners could demand their cargo during the subsequent trial at the High Court of Admiralty (a trial that determined whether the capture had been made lawfully). Fortunately, however, there were several instances when the British were also able to seize many other papers and documents.

There are three outstanding sources that provide invaluable information about key moments in the eighteenth-century colonial trade. The first is two mail boxes aboard one of the ships in the Spanish fleet that was intercepted by the English while returning from Veracruz in December 1702. The second is a box containing 293 envelopes taken from several Spanish ships returning from the Spanish Caribbean between 1743 and 1746. The third, and most remarkable, is the contents of the ship *San Francisco Xavier*, alias *La Perla*, which set sail from Callao (Lima's seaport) for Cádiz on 12 May 1779. From *La Perla* the British took several bags containing nearly 2,000 envelopes of personal correspondence. Along with these there were other, smaller ships that were captured while sailing off the peninsular coast. From these the British took papers and personal correspondence belonging to several Basque captains involved in the trade of Bilbao and San Sebastián, and these provide a vivid picture of the pattern of trade in which the merchants of Bilbao were involved.

This study relies on further research in several archives in Spain, Britain and Peru, where material more familiar to historians was consulted. In the Archivo General de Indias in Seville documents dealing with the local *consulado* and the Lima *consulado* were particularly useful, as were the private records of the Cádiz merchant Juan Vicente Marticorena (1782–7). In the Archivo Foral de Bizkaia in Bilbao documents from the Bilbao *consulado* were examined, especially the correspondence that the heads of the *consulado* conducted with representatives in Madrid, and several mercantile litigations. In the Archivo General de la Nación, Lima, several judicial records of great interest were used, as well as a few private records, most significantly the 1758–9 letter-book of the merchant Juan Cranisbro, as was the private correspondence of the merchants Andrés and Domingo Ramírez de Arellano held in the Instituto Riva-Agüero. The Lima *consulado*'s only surviving letter-book, from the years 1778–82, is particularly valuable as a means of contrasting the merchants' actual practices with the institutional discourse of their gild. In Britain, as well as diverse documentation in The National Archives (London), several other archives and libraries hold valuable material: manuscripts dealing with Spanish trade held in the British Library, the London Guildhall Library, the London Friends House Library and the Norfolk Record Office (Norwich) have been used to shed light on issues ranging from reforms in the colonial trade to the activities of British manufacturers trading with Cádiz and Bilbao.

Such material is linked with printed primary sources (handbooks to trade, economic writings and so forth) and situated within the already developed debates among historians, particularly in relation to the Bilbao and Cádiz merchants and their overseas networks. By combining the literature on the Spanish Atlantic trade and the synchronic primary sources, this book attempts to give both a long-term account of trends and a detailed cross-hatching of the state of the trade. This is in accordance with Penelope Corfield's emphasis on the need for historians to be more aware of the diachronic/synchronic nature of the past, including not only the historians' capacity to reconstruct past societies synchronically on their own terms but also to provide a retrospective analysis of the long-term patterns and diachronic developments that mesh the past to the present.[77] Where applicable, comparisons are made with Britain, France and Portugal, based mainly on the rich secondary literature. Quotations from sources in Spanish, Basque and French have all been translated into English, taking care to preserve the style of the correspondence as far as possible.

The book is structured into three parts. First, chapters 1 and 2 deal with merchants and ship captains involved in Bilbao's trade with northern

---

[77] For the concept of 'diachromesh' see Penelope J. Corfield, *Time and the shape of history*, New Haven 2007, passim, esp. p. xv.

Europe and the north Atlantic, paying special attention to the relationship between local and foreign merchants residing in Bilbao. In the second part, chapters 3, 4 and 5 explore the experience of the merchants (both Spanish and foreign) involved in the trade between Cádiz and Lima. The focus here is on the transformations that took place in both the trading route and the system of communications throughout the eighteenth century, and how those changes moulded the networks linking Spain and Peru. Finally, chapters 6 and 7 discuss several topics (such as confidentiality, enforceability of contracts, use of credit, decision-making and competition) which affected all the merchants who featured in the previous chapters.

PART I

INTERNATIONAL TRADERS: BILBAO AND 'THE NORTH'

1

Bilbao Merchants

In September 1763, after the Spanish monarchy had granted a 4 per cent tax reduction to Castilian wool exported through the non-Basque port of Santander, the Bilbao *consulado* complained bitterly on behalf of the *bilbaíno* merchants. In a petition to the king, the *consulado* pointed out that for the previous eighty years the indigenous merchants of Bilbao had played an essential role in recovering the Castilian wool trade from foreign hands. Spain's international trade had been dominated by foreigners for most of the seventeenth century, and the *consulado* acknowledged that Bilbao 'could not avoid getting infected but was one of the gaps through which foreign industry entered the kingdom'.[1] The locals had been at the mercy of English and Dutch merchants who had bought Spanish commodities cheaply and sold their manufactures to the Spaniards at exorbitant prices. Fortunately, however, out of all the Spanish merchants the *bilbaínos* had been:

> the first who started to shake off such an unfair yoke from our shoulders ... by working hard in all branches of trade, the members of the *consulado* not only equalled but surpassed foreigners, first by taking possession of the wool trade ... and then of the entire cloth trade by going to the factories and buying there at reasonable prices, having built ships and employed in them a large number of local mariners.[2]

Though that is a somewhat exaggerated account of the commercial awakening of the indigenous merchants of Bilbao, the process was indeed the first sign of a more active Spanish participation in the trade with northern Europe – something that Spanish historians are eager to stress. For instance, in his monumental *Historia de la economía española*, Jaime Carrera Pujal states that 'the bilbaínos must be given credit for establishing national control over wool exports, while in Seville and Cádiz the Spaniards allowed foreigners to seize the trade with America'.[3] According to the traditional historiography, it was the united efforts of the town hall of Bilbao, the provincial government

---

[1] Bilbao *consulado*'s petition to the king, Bilbao, 28 Sept. 1763, AFB, Consulado 549, fo. 30r.
[2] Ibid. fo. 30r–v.
[3] Jaime Carrera Pujal, *Historia de la economía española*, Barcelona 1944, ii. 148. See also Luis María Bilbao, 'Crisis y reconstrucción de la economía vascongada en el siglo XVII', *Saioak* i (1977), 157–80, and Juan José Laborda Martín, 'El arranque de un largo protagonismo: la recuperación comercial de Vizcaya a comienzos del siglo XVIII', *Saioak* ii (1978), 136–81.

Map 1. Cities and ports in western Europe in the eighteenth century
(by Lander Gurtubai)

of Vizcaya and the *consulado* itself that gave the locals the opportunity to end foreign dominance. However, stressing the confrontation between locals and foreigners only explains part of the story. The infrastructural networks that supported the Bilbao trade and allowed it to grow also made an important contribution to the Bilbao merchants' new-found confidence.

This chapter explores the origin and nature of those networks by paying attention to several institutional arrangements that enhanced relationships of trust between locals and foreigners. Crucially, some of those arrangements were not part of any economic strategy, but rather were based on 'custom' and were meant to preserve the cultural and religious identity of the inhabitants of Vizcaya, the Basque province in which Bilbao was located. The discussion also casts light on the tensions between locals and foreigners, showing that the *bilbaínos* did not increase their participation in international trade by expelling foreign merchants, but rather by making the Bilbao *consulado* and its members more creditable.

The *fueros* of Vizcaya and Bilbao's trade

In the eighteenth century, Bilbao boasted a merchant community of about 250 members, and nearly 300 ships entered and left its sheltered harbour each year, all of which spoke to its role as a hub of international trade. Strategically situated on the banks of the Nervión River in the *Señorío* (lordship) of Vizcaya, Bilbao was Castile's chief means of access to the northern seas. But this alone does not explain its prominence. More important for Bilbao than its accessibility from Castile was Vizcaya's peculiar set of home rules, the so-called *fueros*, a series of laws formulated by the Basque territories and first codified in 1371. The Basque Country (*Euskal Herria* in Basque) is the region in which the Basque language (*euskera*) is spoken.[4] It is located on the Atlantic side of the Pyrenees and includes the northern Spanish provinces of Vizcaya, Guipúzcoa, Álava and the kingdom of Navarra, and three provinces located in south-western France (Labourd, Basse-Navarre and Soule).[5] Each of the Spanish Basque provinces had its own *fueros*, which were regarded as equivalent to a constitution.[6] Apart from serving as a legal system, the *fueros* also guided the relationship of the Basque territories with

---

[4] Basque is the only one of western Europe's ancient languages to have survived until the present day. Due to its highly unusual structure – indeed, there seem to be no other languages to which it is related – it has long been an object of curiosity and speculation: Robert L. Trask, *The history of Basque*, London 1997.
[5] In their Basque form the seven provinces are known as Bizkaia, Gipuzkoa, Araba, Nafarroa, Lapurdi, Nafarroa Behera and Zuberoa. In this book the Spanish form, the form appearing in the primary sources, will be used.
[6] The Spanish government did not abolish the *fueros* until 1873–4. The current statutes of autonomy of the País Vasco (1979) and of Navarra (1982) were inspired by the *fueros*.

the successive kings of Castile (and later of Spain). While spending a few days in Bilbao in January 1780, John Adams, the future American president, wrote that:

> It may seem surprising, to hear of free Provinces in Spain: But such is the Fact, that the High and independent spirit of the People, so essentially different from the other Provinces, that a Traveller perceives it even in their Countenances, their Dress, their air, and ordinary manner of Speech, has induced the Spanish Nation and their Kings to respect the Ancient Liberties of these People, so far that each Monarch, at his Accession to the Throne, has taken an Oath, to observe the Laws of Biscay.[7]

The *fueros* arose from a series of customs and habitual practices that were themselves a reflection of a specific way of thinking and feeling. They were maintained by democratically elected assemblies (*juntas*) to which every town and village sent representatives. There were a great many laws, some of which were essential in defining the Basque identity.[8] Notably, the Basque territories had the right of self-defence against anyone, including the king (who was not regarded as king but as lord of Vizcaya, and whose troops could not enter the country); residents were exempted from military service and enjoyed the rank of *hidalgos* (that is all who could prove Basque parentage for two generations belonged to the nobility, although this meant little more than exemption from servitude and taxation); they were exempted from the most important Castilian taxes on consumption (the so-called *alcabala*, *cientos* and *millones*); and, decisively, residents of Vizcaya, Guipúzcoa, Álava and Navarra enjoyed complete commercial freedom both internally and externally, since no customs dues were payable on the coast though they were inland, on the route to Castile. Commercial freedom and tax exemption were a function of the combined effect of the region's agricultural deficiencies (the terrain was mountanous and heavily forested) and relatively high population density. Vizcaya's population was never very large, although it grew steadily from 70,000 in 1704 to 111,000 in 1797; the other coastal province, Guipúzcoa, had similar numbers.[9] As for Bilbao itself, the population rose from 6,000 in 1700 to 11,000 in 1800, with the most rapid growth occurring between 1746 and 1768.[10]

---

[7] John Adams, *Diary and autobiography of John Adams*, ed. Lydon H. Butterfield, Cambridge, MA 1961, iv. 234.
[8] Anon., *Fueros, franquezas, libertades, buenos usos, y costumbres, del muy noble, y muy leal señorío de Vizcaya*, Bilbao 1704.
[9] Emiliano Fernández de Pinedo, *Crecimiento económico y transformaciones sociales del País Vasco, 1100–1850*, Madrid 1974, 87.
[10] Mercedes Mauleón Isla, *La población de Bilbao en el siglo XVIII*, Valladolid 1961, 49–80. As Jan de Vries shows, in the eighteenth century urban centres with 5,000–9,900 people were far more numerous than cities with populations of 10,000 and above. In 1750 there were 668 such cities in Europe: *European urbanization, 1500–1800*, Cambridge, MA 1984, 66–9.

In the early eighteenth century, English merchants estimated that customs duties averaged only 1 per cent of cargo value in Vizcaya and Guipúzcoa, in comparison with 7 per cent in Valencia and Aragón, 7 to 10 per cent in Catalonia, 10 per cent in Andalusia and 20 per cent in Alicante.[11] This shows that the economic implications of the Basque *fueros* were far-reaching. As John Adams himself put it in 1780, '[i]t is not at all surprizing that a Constitution, in its nature so favourable to commerce, should have succeeded'.[12] It is clear that Bilbao's role as a commercial centre can only be understood in the context of the *fueros*, whose influence was as much economic as political and cultural.

As a free port, Bilbao received imports and served as a major redistribution node within the Castilian economy. Its main export was Castilian wool from León, Segovia and Soria. In the first half of the eighteenth century, Spain exported an average of around 3,500 tons of wool a year. Between them, the northern ports of Spain and the French port of Bayonne handled around 73 per cent of total wool exports, with Bilbao accounting for around 56 per cent of that amount.[13] The main destinations were England and Holland, particularly London and Amsterdam. London's share rose significantly as the eighteenth century progressed (from 30.5 per cent between 1765 and 1779 to 51.5 per cent between 1790 and 1805), while the share to Amsterdam and the troubled Dutch economy declined (from 34 to 18.4 per cent in the same period). The share exported to the Austrian Netherlands via Ostend also rose initially but then declined steeply (from 10 to 25 per cent in the 1780s, and then to only 1.4 per cent between 1790 and 1805), while the share going to northern Germany via Hamburg increased (from 1 to 12 per cent).[14] In an attempt to gain an increased fiscal benefit from the lucrative and expanding wool trade, the Spanish government decided in 1763 to grant a 4 per cent discount to the wool exported through Santander, but even then Bilbao remained the principal wool exporter.[15]

Bilbao exported a range of other goods including meat, wax, wood, onions and chesnuts, and it imported a variety of textiles and ironmongery from France, England and Holland. Unfortunately, the true dimensions of the import trade cannot be established with precision because Bilbao's port books (*libros de avería*) are not entirely reliable. Nevertheless, the available data, used with caution, suggest that despite declining English exports to

---

[11] Jean O. McLachlan, *Trade and peace with old Spain, 1667–1750: a study of the influence of commerce on Anglo-Spanish diplomacy in the first half of the eighteenth century*, Cambridge 1940, 183.
[12] *Diary of John Adams*, iv. 235.
[13] Carla R. Phillips and William D. Phillips, *Spain's golden fleece: wool production and the wool trade from the Middle Ages to the nineteenth century*, Baltimore 1997, 265–6; Aingeru Zabala, *Mundo urbano y actividad mercantil: Bilbao, 1700–1810*, Bilbao 1994, 266.
[14] Zabala, *Mundo urbano*, 389.
[15] Román Basurto Larrañaga, *Comercio y burguesía mercantil de Bilbao en la segunda mitad del siglo* XVIII, Bilbao 1983, 162–4.

Spain after the 1760s, Bilbao managed to maintain a stable export trade in textiles and ironmongery to England until the mid-1790s.[16]

In addition to European trade, Bilbao also imported large quantities of dried, salted codfish from Newfoundland and the British American colonies, accounting for nine million pounds (26 per cent) of total Spanish imports of English cod during the 1770s. Although Cádiz, with its greater population (70,000), imported more (eleven million pounds or 31.7 per cent), supplies from both ports were conveyed inland to meet consumer demand in places such as Madrid, Seville and Toledo. Other major Spanish ports such as Barcelona (16.4 per cent), Alicante (14.4) or Valencia (2.9) were way behind Bilbao and Cádiz in the volume of their cod imports.[17]

The iron and shipbuilding industries were very influential in Vizcaya. High-quality iron ore was easily extracted from the mines of Somorrostro (ten miles west of Bilbao), and charcoal was obtained from ample supplies of oak and beech. Numerous small ironworks were scattered across Vizcaya and Guipúzcoa, in places where Basque was virtually the only language spoken. This turned out to be an advantage for the *bilbaíno* merchants over their foreign competitors because they could communicate more easily with iron producers. If any foreign merchant wanted to trade in Basque iron, he often had no option but to do so through a *bilbaíno*. Crucially, the production and trade in iron was a source of capital for the indigenous merchants. This was true even in the seventeenth century, when the Basque iron industry was in a state of crisis. From 1720 to 1775, the industry staged a prolonged recovery thanks to rising Castilian, international (mainly Dutch, French, France, English and Portuguese) and colonial demand (through Cádiz).[18] After 1775, however, competition from Swedish iron and the loss of colonial market brought new challenges.

With its densely wooded and mountainous terrain, the region around Bilbao was not easily cultivated for agricultural purposes, which largely explains why local communities had long traditions of emigration to the American colonies and of fishing and seafaring to acquire the resources necessary for survival. This, in turn, fostered numerous small shipyards along the indented coast. As with the iron industry, shipbuilding experienced uneven fortunes, suffering greatly during the seventeenth century, flourishing after the War of the Spanish Succession and entering a new period of crisis toward the end of the eighteenth century.[19]

---

[16] Rafael Uriarte Ayo, 'Anglo-Spanish trade through the port of Bilbao during the second half of the eighteenth century: some preliminary findings', *IJMH* iv/2 (1992), 211.

[17] James G. Lydon, 'Fish for gold: the Massachusetts fish trade with Iberia, 1700–1773', *New England Quarterly* liv (1981), 542.

[18] See Rafael Uriarte Ayo, *Estructura, desarrollo y crisis de la siderurgia tradicional vizcaína, 1700–1840*, Bilbao 1988.

[19] See Lourdes Odriozola Oyarbide, *Construcción naval en el País Vasco, siglos XVI–XIX: evolución y análisis comparativo*, San Sebastián 2002.

Along with the legal imports and exports, the *fueros* also paved the way for a flourishing trade in contraband. The War of the Spanish Succession, for instance, gave rise to a substantial contraband trade in tobacco from the Caribbean and the British colonies. To stop this tobacco entering Castile illegally, the Spanish crown decided to move against the *fueros*, and in August 1717 ordered that the inland customs be moved to the coast. A year later, when the royal order was effectively implemented, a major riot broke out in the Basque provinces, the so-called *matxinada*. In Vizcaya, around 5,000 country people entered Bilbao on 4 September 1718 to defend the *fueros*. The crowd lynched and killed the *diputado general*, who was the head of the government of Vizcaya, while the *corregidor*, the king's highest official in Vizcaya, and several other members of the provincial elite, who were accused of supporting the king, had to run for their lives. The riot was stopped by 3,000 royal troops sent from Madrid. That same year, the crown reconsidered its position and decided to return the customs to their former position.[20]

In effect, the rioters had won. But there was a paradoxical defeat alongside their victory. Throughout the eighteenth century, the Bilbao *consulado* repeatedly tried to get permission to trade with the Spanish American colonies, but for the crown the *fueros* and the colonial trade were totally incompatible. Bilbao was to be excluded from colonial trade even in 1765 and 1778, when the trade to Spanish America was gradually opened to all the major Spanish ports, on the grounds that Bilbao already had its own separate economic rights.[21]

Competition with foreign merchants

The relationship between the *bilbaínos* and the foreign merchants in the eighteenth century can only be understood if the seventeenth-century background is taken into account. Between the 1620s and 1650s at least ninety English merchants stayed in Bilbao for six or seven years on average. At certain times, as in 1644, there had been almost as many English merchants active in Bilbao as locals.[22] The number of foreigners decreased slightly in the second half of the century: in 1687 there were fourteen English firms, fourteen Dutch and Flemish, and seven French.[23] Nevertheless Bilbao's trade with northern Europe was almost entirely in their hands. During the Franco-Spanish war of 1684, the Spanish consul in Amsterdam was told to record all

---

[20] Xabier Lamikiz, 'Bizkaitar eta gipuzkoar nekazariak 1718ko matxinadan', *Uztaro* xxxiii (2000), 21–41.
[21] Carmen Torija Herrera, *El libre comercio vasco con América*, Vitoria 1985, 128–9.
[22] Regina Grafe, *Entre el mundo ibérico y el Atlántico: comercio y especialización regional, 1550–1650*, Bilbao 2005, 196–9.
[23] AFB, Corregimiento 2927/022, fo. 25.

commodities transported to Spain.²⁴ His notes showed that all the shippers in Amsterdam and the great majority of the consignees in Bilbao were either Dutch or Flemish merchants.

The foreigners' presence in Bilbao followed the rise in the seventeenth century of the Atlantic economy. The English, for example, created a new pattern of trade that differed substantially from the traditional two-way exchange with northern Europe. This was a triangular trade that linked England, the emerging North American mainland colonies and northern Spain. Castilian wool and Basque iron were sent from northern Spain to England; manufactured goods went from England to the North American mainland colonies; and dried, salted codfish from North America was then transported to northern Spain.²⁵ This expanding trade remained in foreign hands simply because the Spaniards had no contacts either in England or in North America. As Bernard Bailyn has shown, the New England merchants trading with Spain 'almost invariably dealt with Englishmen resident in the port towns'.²⁶ In fact, foreign merchants established throughout the peninsula were to predominate within the trade of Spain and Portugal with northern Europe and the North Atlantic for most of the seventeenth and eighteenth centuries. But in Bilbao their situation had developed in a very special way.

In the mid-seventeenth century, foreign merchants were welcomed in Bilbao because their presence allowed the local economy to benefit from their trade. Nevertheless, the English and the Dutch residing in Bilbao did not forge family links with the indigenous merchants,²⁷ although in that respect their behaviour did not differ much from that of their compatriots in the rest of Spain and Portugal. What was different, however, was the fact that foreign merchants were not allowed to have their own gild institutions within Bilbao, and, more important, they could neither own properties anywhere in Vizcaya nor live on their own. In the first decades of the eighteenth century, the English and the French petitioned to the Spanish crown several times to revoke those restrictions, but the king could do nothing, for the restrictions arose from the *fueros*.²⁸ Law no. 13 of the *fueros*, established in the fifteenth century, forbade any descendant of Muslims, Jews and converted Christians to reside in Vizcaya. 'Since such people can come from

---

²⁴ Juan A. Sánchez Belén, 'Bilbao y el comercio de importación anglo-holandés durante la Guerra de Reuniones de 1684', in M. Rodríguez Cancho (coor.), *Historia y perspectivas de investigación: estudios en memoria del profesor Angel Rodríguez Sánchez*, Badajoz 2002, 269–78.
²⁵ Grafe, *Entre el mundo ibérico y el Atlántico*, 135–59.
²⁶ Bernard Bailyn, *The New England merchants in the seventeenth century*, New York 1964, 90.
²⁷ Grafe, *Entre el mundo ibérico y el Atlántico*, 201–2.
²⁸ Between 1704 and 1713 the French tried several times to appoint Juan Capdeville as their consul in Bilbao, but to no avail: AHN, Consejos, leg. 51439/exp. SN. The British were equally unsuccessful in trying to appoint William Frankland in 1714–16: TNA, SP 94/213, fo. 19.

remote Kingdoms', reads the law, 'and since they are unknown, and so are their lineage and genealogy, ... anyone that wants to reside or to settle in Vizcaya ... must provide information of his or her lineage and genealogy.'[29] Furthermore, those who wanted to acquire citizenship (*avecindamiento*) and could prove their 'purity of blood' (which was a tremendously time-consuming and difficult bureaucratic process) and *hidalguía* (lowest nobility) had to be Catholics.[30] Without citizenship, foreigners could not own property in Vizcaya. In practice they were left in legal limbo by the *fueros*, and it was up to each town to regulate the foreigners' situation. In Bilbao, since at least the sixteenth century, foreigners were obliged to lodge in the house of some local in the premises of a *huésped* (host). As the head of the Bilbao *consulado* stressed in 1717, the major reason for compelling foreigners to lodge with local families was to avoid any introduction of 'diabolic rites' by Protestant ministers. It was further noted that several foreigners had even converted to Catholicism, thanks to that measure.[31]

In Bilbao, most English and Dutch merchants seem to have been Protestants, and therefore had no access to citizenship. That status was usually achieved only by Irish and French merchants who had lived for many years in Bilbao and were married to local women.[32] But even so they could not be elected to institutional positions such as offices in the town hall, the provincial *Juntas* and the consulado. Citizenship exempted them only from the payment of the *prevostada*, a 2.5 per cent tax on food, drink and fuel imports that only foreigners had to pay. Nevertheless, religious differences were not a barrier to social interaction. In 1685, for instance, the English merchant community had no problem in celebrating along with the town of Bilbao 'the glorious coronation in England of the very Catholic James Stuart'.[33] The fiesta took four days and included events such as bullfighting and a procession led by four representatives of the town of Bilbao and four English merchants. The best musicians of the Basque Country were hired for the occasion, and a poem (a *romance endecasílavo*) was composed especially for the occasion.

Apart from protecting the town against 'diabolic rites', the *huésped* institution also allowed locals to get a portion of the foreigners' business. The host

---

[29] Anon., *Fueros*, 20–1.
[30] For example, in 1797 the English merchant William Hopkinson and his wife Elizabeth acquired citizenship only after adopting the Catholic faith: AHN, Consejos, leg. 2656/exp. 36. See also Mauleón, *Población*, 30–3.
[31] Juan Martín Landecho to Joseph Lauro, Bilbao, 10 May 1717, AFB, Consulado 536.
[32] For example, in 1721, after a process lasting several years, the Irish merchants Edmund Shee, John Power and Arthur Lynch, all of whom were married to Basque women, were granted citizenship: AHN, Consejos, leg. 30/exp. 2.
[33] Anon., *Relación de las fiestas que celebró en esta muy noble villa de Bilbao, de el señorío de Vizcaya, la ... muy leal nación inglesa en la gloriosa ocasión de averse coronado en Inglaterra el muy Cathólico Jacobo Estuardo*, Bilbao 1685.

was entitled to a rent and to a 1 per cent share of the merchant's profits.[34] But having a foreigner at home also entailed a great responsibility. Since foreigners had no property in Bilbao, there was always the danger for any local merchant that a foreign debtor could simply disappear, leaving behind his unpaid debts. To minimise that risk, hosts were required to provide surety for their foreign guests' dealings.[35] No doubt the binding of the foreigner to a local offered some assurance that dealings with foreigners were not too risky. A crucial side effect of the *huésped* institution, however, was that it contributed to forging a close friendship between some locals and their foreign guests. Indeed, the host often helped the newly-arrived foreigner both to market his products and to establish contacts with wool and iron suppliers. It is no wonder, then, that the most important merchants of Bilbao were interested in hosting successful foreign merchants.

Yet a good understanding between locals and foreigners also had a potentially dark side. After 1680, the *bilbaínos* themselves gradually began to participate in exporting wool, leading to fierce competition with the foreigners. Historians explain the increasing participation of the indigenous merchants by resorting to one economic factor: *bilbaínos* entered the wool trade because the Basque iron industry was in crisis. It is true that after 1650 people with Basque surnames began to appear in the major wool producing areas of Segovia as flock owners and wool buyers, and that significant improvements were made in the port of Bilbao and in the road network to Castile, enhancing Bilbao's options of attracting the export trade.[36] However, historians have paid no attention to what was initially the *bilbaínos'* main problem: the lack of trustworthy correspondents in northern Europe. In 1673, for example, one of the first attempts made by a Bilbao merchant to ship wool to northern Europe ended with the merchant bitterly complaining that 'if any local shipped them on his own account, the wool for sale in the north arrived, with such impost and the wool sold at such low price that they [the foreign merchants] obliged him not to repeat the experience'.[37] In other words, if the merchants of Bilbao managed to trade with England and Holland after 1680 it was only because they managed to find trustworthy correspondents. With that, they could take good advantage of changing economic circumstances. In 1687 the Dutch merchants in Bilbao attempted to move their trade to Santander, but the impossibility of securing tax advantages there left them no option but to remain in Bilbao. The attempt to transfer to Santander was a sign of growing competition in Bilbao, which provoked a series of battles in the early eighteenth century. On 12 September 1700, eight English

---

[34] Carrera, *Historia*, ii. 181.
[35] Grafe, *Entre el mundo ibérico y el Atlántico*, 205–7.
[36] Angel García Sanz, *Desarrollo y crisis del antiguo régimen en Castilla la Vieja: economía y sociedad en tierras de Segovia, 1500–1814*, Madrid 1977, 241–2; Bilbao, 'Crisis', 179.
[37] Aingeru Zabala Uriarte, 'The consolidation of Bilbao as a trade centre in the second half of the seventeenth century', in Janzen, *Merchant organization*, 171.

merchants agreed with the town of Santander to move their trade from Bilbao in exchange for several privileges.[38] This agreement had followed the publication of Bilbao's new municipal ordinances in December 1699. Although article no. 64 of the ordinances (which was also included in the municipal ordinances of 1622), banned foreigners from trading in Bilbao, the truth is that it was never enforced.[39] Therefore, it seems more likely that the English used article no. 64 as an excuse to seek tax exemptions in Santander, where they would face no local competition.

With the 1700 agreement, Santander intended to enhance its economy by allowing the English to stay, just as Bilbao had done throughout the seventeenth century. But in Santander it was the English who dictated the conditions. Four of those are key to understanding how different the foreigners' situation was in Bilbao compared to that in other major Iberian ports. First, the English were to have their own legal representative appointed as consul in Santander. Secondly, they were to be allowed to own properties and to live wherever they liked in Santander. Thirdly, the Spanish king was to appoint a special judge (*juez conservador*) for any litigation undertaken by the English nation in Santander, just as was customary in Seville and Cádiz but not in Bilbao. And lastly, Santander was to be exempted, just like Vizcaya, from the three major Castilian taxes on consumption. Both the Santander authorities and the English merchants knew that the Spanish crown would easily grant the first three conditions, but they were doubtful about the fourth one. And indeed the crown did not give Santander the same tax status as Bilbao. The agreement was officially rejected by the king in August 1701.

In 1703, during the War of the Spanish Succession, most English merchants left Bilbao,[40] but some of them returned, probably around 1710, long before the peace was signed. In October 1712 three of them posted two letters to Lord Lexington, the British ambassador in Madrid. The first one went via José de Lauro, the representative of the Bilbao *consulado* in Madrid. In that letter (to which Lauro would have had access) they stressed 'how very considerable a branch of our trade in this place is that of Virginia leaf tobacco, and how necessary it will be to have it admitted here'.[41] The second letter went via an English firm established in Madrid, named Archer and Crean. 'Our trade in this place must be removed', they stressed this time, 'or it will be impossible to carry on our trade by a factory here.'[42] They wanted a permit to import tobacco via Santander so that they could move

---

[38] There is a full transcription of the agreement in Guiard, *Historia del consulado*, ii. 40–7.
[39] Mauleón, *Población*, 98.
[40] Nine of them set out for England via Bayonne in 1703, where they would become prisoners of war: SP 34/36/13. Another four English and two Dutch merchants were forced to stay in Bilbao until they had cleared their debts: José Grimaldo to Francisco Ronquillo, Madrid, 4 Jan. 1707, AHN, Consejos, leg. 12593/exp. SN.
[41] Roger Slingar, Abraham Lordell and John Gosselin to Robert Sutton, 2nd Baron Lexington, Bilbao, 23 Oct. 1712, Lexington papers, BL, MS Add. 46550, fo. 188.
[42] Ibid. fo. 190.

there, stressing that the whole affair 'ought to be kept as private as possible till matters be brought to a head'. Indeed rumours about the removal of the inland customs to the coast would soon start to circulate across Vizcaya, and many *vizcaínos* thought that the English were the instigators of the attack on the *fueros*. In November 1716 the English complained about 'the insults put upon us not only by the people of this Contratation House [the *consulado*], but by all the Biscayners in general of this place'.[43] However, this particular confrontation, as well as foreigners' previous attempts to move their trade to Santander, conceal a contrasting and rather paradoxical situation which historians have ignored. Rather than being constantly at loggerheads, by the 1710s a number of *bilbaíno* merchants were on very good terms with those English and Dutch merchants who had spent several years in Bilbao: so much so that these men became the *bilbaínos*' correspondents in northern Europe.

One of these was the London merchant John Richards (known in Bilbao as Juan Ricardo). Starting in 1716, his account book shows that he traded with Jamaica, Amsterdam, Cádiz, Madrid and, above all, Bilbao. Of the 13,478,118 pounds of wool exported through Bilbao between 1717 and 1721, Richards received 801,325 (5.95 per cent).[44] He operated as a commission agent for fifteen of the most influential members of the Bilbao *consulado*: merchants such as Diego Allende Salazar, José de Arriquibar and Bartolomé de Jussué. Interestingly, Richards received wool only from *bilbaíno* merchants and in Basque ships, and recorded all those dealings in Spanish (his other dealings were written in English).

The importance of having a reliable agent in London can be easily inferred from the tasks Richards fulfilled. For a 2 per cent commission, he sold wool in London (the names of the buyers are also noted in his accounts) and shipped textiles for Bilbao (such as *sempiternas*, *bayetas* and *calamacos*). He also agreed insurance policies in the London coffee houses for both ships and cargoes to and from Bilbao, and, occasionally, he shared the value of a wool cargo with his Bilbao principals on a fifty-fifty basis.[45] The textiles he sent to Bilbao were paid for either with the money from the wool sales or with bills of exchange on London. But who was John Richards? It appears that the Bilbao merchants had not chosen him as their agent by coincidence. The English brothers George and James Richards lived in Bilbao between at least 1674 and 1684, lodging in the house of a certain Aparicio Echevarría for six

---

[43] Stephen Harvey, Samuel Reynolds, Gosselin, Lordell and the company Slingar and Hatchings to Paul Methuen, Bilbao, 20 Nov. 1716, SP 94/213, fo. 68.
[44] For the wool received by Richards see his account book LGL, MS 19017/1. For Bilbao wool exports between 1715 and 1729 see Laborda, 'El arranque', 144.
[45] For example, in July 1719 Diego Allende Salazar and John Richards went fifty-fifty on a cargo of 120 bags of wool (24,803 pounds) that John Richards sold for 3,146 pounds sterling: LGL, MS 19017/1, p. 182.

or more of those years.⁴⁶ Moreover, by 1691 George Richards was established in London and trading with *bilbaínos*.⁴⁷ There is no direct evidence that the three Richards were relatives, but it seems likely that this was the case.

Further evidence from John Richards's account book supports the idea that the indigenous merchants of Bilbao used foreign merchants who had lived in Bilbao as their correspondents in northern Europe. Along with wool commissioned to him, Richards also received wool to be re-exported to Dutch merchants established in Amsterdam. His account book thus shows how the merchant networks branched off into many other relationships: Diego Allende Salazar's correspondent in Amsterdam was Luis Michel; Domingo de Acha sent wool to Juan Benito Mortel; Manuel de Olarte to Josias Tartas; José de Arriquibar and Manuel de Lecanda to Cornelio Van Lintelo and Son; Pedro de Errecarte to the widow and son of Juan Balde; and Miguel Antonio de Jussué and José de Palacio to the widow and son of Pedro Vanveen. Although Richards wrote all those forenames in their Spanish version, the Amsterdam merchants' surnames were neither Basque nor Spanish. It is notable that two of the firms were managed by both the widow and son of late merchants, and a third by a merchant and his son. It is not difficult to guess when and where those connections had been created. In 1667 one Balde, Pedro Balde, lived in Bilbao.⁴⁸ So did one Mortel, Servacio de Mortel and Pedro Vanveen (also Bamben) in 1682–7.⁴⁹ Similarly, Luis Michel lived in Bilbao for several years in the first third of the eighteenth century. Thus it appears that the *bilbaínos'* correspondents in Amsterdam were either Dutch merchants who had lived in Bilbao or members of their families. In Richards's account book, only one Bilbao merchant is noted in relation to a merchant settled in England. Bartolomé de Jussué's correspondent in Bristol was Robert Earle, one of the English merchants who had fled Bilbao in 1703 due to the war. It is clear that while some foreigners were very unhappy at being unable to live on their own in Bilbao, others took their role as lodgers as an opportunity to build relationships of trust with the *bilbaínos*.

English and Dutch merchants virtually disappeared from Bilbao over the course of the eighteenth century, but this was due to the vagaries of trade, not because they were expelled. At any given time during the eighteenth century there were between 200 and 250 merchants in Bilbao,⁵⁰ around 15–20 per cent of whom were foreigners. In 1763, for example, there were forty foreign merchants, eighteen of whom had been granted citizenship:

---

[46] AFB, Corregimiento 0218/005. In 1674 George Richards received dry codfish from Portsmouth, New England: Corregimiento 0260/008.

[47] That year he sent tobacco from London to the *bilbaíno* José de Urquijo in the *San Joseph*, captained by José de Noxa: AFB, Corregimiento 2177/031.

[48] Guiard, *Historia del consulado*, i. 512.

[49] AFB, Corregimiento 2927/022, 0962/042.

[50] A 1787 census listed 240 merchants: Mauleón, *Población*, 148–51.

twenty-four were French (twelve with citizenship and twelve lodging with locals), nine Irish (three with citizenship and six lodging with locals), four Germans (all lodging with locals), one Savoyard (with citizenship), one was English (lodging with a local) and one Dutch (lodging with a local).[51] In 1791 there were forty-five foreign merchants in Bilbao, seventeen of whom were married to Basque women.[52] No doubt, foreigners remained of great interest to the indigenous merchants of Bilbao because they had, as the *consulado* itself put it in 1746, 'greater easiness in connecting and corresponding with the North'.[53] Thanks to the *huésped* institution and the tough process of acquiring citizenship, the foreigners of Bilbao were much closer to the local community than was the case anywhere else in Spain and Portugal. Crucially, this contributed to the creation of trust between the two, giving the locals the opportunity to engage in international trade.

Securing institutional trust and improving merchants' education

The *huésped* institution helped to forge bonds between locals and foreigners, but that alone was not enough to foster reciprocal overseas trade between the two groups. For that, other improvements were required in order to build up trust. From the 1660s up to 1737, the merchants of Bilbao worked hard to improve the expertise of their *consulado* and to cement the efficiency and impartiality of its mercantile court. This institution, in turn, helped to convince their foreign correspondents that it was safe to trade directly with the *bilbaínos*. As a result, the English and Dutch merchant communities of Bilbao gradually became superfluous.

Reliability was a quality to which the mercantile court of the Bilbao *consulado* had always aspired, but in the mid-seventeenth century merchants established in England were not sure that it had been achieved. In the 1640s they solicited the creation of a court in Bilbao formed by an English consul and several resident English merchants and factors, so that

> the said Court shall have power upon an information of the ... dishonest behaviour of any merchant or factor there residing, or at the desire of any merchant, creditor or principal here, or of any other place, using the said trade, or sending goods unto the said port of Bilbao, to demand any books, papers, letters or accounts from the hand of the said merchant or factor.[54]

---

[51] Ibid. 88–92.
[52] Ibid. 284–8. For foreigners in Bilbao in the late eighteenth and early nineteenth centuries see Jon Garay Belategui and Rubén López Pérez, 'Los extranjeros en el Señorío de Vizcaya y en la villa de Bilbao a finales del antiguo régimen: entre la aceptación y el rechazo', *Estudios humanísticos: Historia* v (2006), 185–210.
[53] Mauleón, *Población*, 96.
[54] Anon., *A brief narration of the present estate of the Bilbao trade, with some particulars by agreement, humbly tendred by the marchants trading thither*, London 1640?, 6.

The English merchants resident in Bilbao considered the petition an unnecessary intrusion in their businesses. 'Let every man see what Factor he trusteth, who will best know who to trust', they replied.[55] As for an English consul and an English court, they stressed that 'it is questionable whether these nice and free people would permit them'. From the perspective of the England-based merchants, their petition proves two crucial facts. First, that they did not think that the Bilbao *consulado* and its court could control the dishonest behaviour of their correspondents. And second, the reason why they were concerned about their compatriots' dependability was because it was they with whom they traded at that time, not with the indigenous merchants. For locals to be trusted by foreigners, it was essential that the Bilbao merchants prove to their correspondents in northern Europe that in Bilbao all merchants were under the jurisdiction of a qualified institution. That is precisely what began to happen in the period 1662–76, when the Bilbao *consulado* took important measures designed to make trade safer.[56]

The first defining moment was the publication in 1669 of the *consulado*'s new ordinances, which were aimed primarily at regulating marine insurance and the use of bills of exchange and promissory notes.[57] These improvements allowed indigenous merchants to boost their reputations. The combination of developing institutional improvements and the close relationship between some locals and foreigners greatly contributed to increasing the *bilbaínos*' participation in international trade. In this light, Dutch and English attempts to move their trade to Santander can be seen as a consequence of that growing participation as in Bilbao foreigners were being replaced by indigenous merchants.

That is precisely what the head of the Bilbao *consulado*, Juan Martín de Landecho, pointed out to the *consulado*'s representative in Madrid in January 1717. 'In regard to the English', he stressed, 'I do not think they can complain about anything apart from the fact that the locals are more trusted than they are.'[58] Crucially, he also noted that the English blamed their compatriots for this. For him, merchants based in England who traded with Bilbao had had the opportunity to prove the *bilbaínos*' reliability and punctual correspondence, and no longer sent as many commissions to the now small number of English merchants residing in Bilbao. Hence, it was because of their loss of dominance in Bilbao that those few merchants were now trying to acquire exemptions for Santander. If Castilian wool was exported through Santander, noted Landecho, no one would stop foreigners from regaining total supremacy over the trade.

---

[55] Ibid. 13.
[56] Zabala, 'Consolidation', 159–61.
[57] [Bilbao *consulado*], *Ordenanzas de la Casa de la Contratación de la muy noble y leal villa de Bilbao*, Bilbao 1669.
[58] Landecho to Lauro, Bilbao, 31 Jan. 1717, AFB, Consulado 536.

However unsuccessfully, the foreigners kept trying to move their trade to Santander during the first half of the eighteenth century. The British tried again in 1726–7. In 1742 rumours circulated that the French were about to get exemptions in Santander with the help of their ambassador in Madrid. That incessant pressure was to produce a landmark in the commercial history of Spain. Drawing from their experience in international trade, a group of *bilbaíno* merchants in about 1725 began to work on new ordinances for the *consulado*. Designed 'to provide more security and more advantage to the trade', the Bilbao *consulado*'s updated ordinances were completed and published in 1737. Their prestige was immediately acknowledged throughout Spain and Spanish America. In fact, they soon became the standard code for commercial law in the Spanish empire, and a major step towards the unified commercial code which Spain would adopt in 1829.

The 1737 ordinances were much longer and far more detailed than those of 1669. With over 300 pages divided into twenty-nine chapters and 723 articles, the new ordinances explained in great detail how to deal with crucial aspects of overseas trade under headings such as merchant companies, book-keeping, sales contracts, commissions, bills of exchange, sea-loans, marine insurance, bankruptcies, delayed payments, ships, freights, ship-owners, ship-brokers, ship-captains, crews and so forth.[59] This crucial document was to become the staple mercantile handbook, used by virtually all Spanish merchants throughout the empire. It is safe to say that the Bilbao *consulado*'s 1737 ordinances played a major role in teaching Spaniards the merchant profession.

The reaction of foreign merchants to the ordinances was not very surprising. After all, anything that could make the locals look more knowledgeable and reputable in the eyes of merchants established in northern Europe was potentially damaging to any French, Dutch or English merchant who had taken the trouble to establish himself in Spain. On 8 January 1738, fifteen French, Dutch and English merchants in Bilbao appealed to the Council of Castile for the invalidation of twenty articles from nine chapters of the ordinances. Articles nos 3 and 4 from chapter 9, for example, decreed that every merchant should have four account books, and it further described how they should be arranged and what information they should contain. The foreigners considered such a measure 'unworthy of approval'.[60] Articles nos 4 and 5 from chapter 10 gave detailed instructions for the creation of merchant companies, describing types of companies and the conditions under which they should operate. Companies had to be set up in the presence of a public notary and partners had to provide a great deal of information, for example with regard to each partner's role in the company and the

---

[59] [Bilbao *consulado*], *Ordenanzas de la ilustre Universidad y Casa de Contratación de la m.n. y m.l. villa de Bilbao, (insertos sus reales privilegios) aprobadas y confirmadas por el rey nuestro señor Don Felipe Quinto (que dios guarde) año de 1737*, Madrid 1769.
[60] Ibid. 315.

capital employed. As far as the foreigners were concerned this showed that the ordinances were motivated purely by 'hatred of foreigners'.[61] Similarly, other chapters dealt with risk-reducing measures such as control of commissions, bills of exchange, bankruptcies and marine insurance. Rather revealingly, the foreigners argued that the ordinances had been designed 'for the instruction of beginners'.[62]

The foreigners' complaints are also important because the Bilbao *consulado* chose to publish them. After 1740 numerous editions of the ordinances included a fifty-page appendix containing the foreigners' complaints to Madrid, and also a declaration from the king in which he backed the *consulado*, stating that foreigners had no authority whatsoever with regard to ordinances. By including this long appendix the *bilbaínos* were not simply celebrating victory, as in that case the mere inclusion of the royal decree in their favour would have sufficed. Instead, by publishing every one of the foreigners' complaints, the *bilbaínos* were making their point even more forcefully: foreign merchants in Bilbao were shown as being in fear of the success of the updated ordinances in terms of the ways in which they enhanced the commercial reliability of the *bilbaínos*.

Along with defending its ordinances, the Bilbao *consulado* put a lot of emphasis on preserving its court's jurisdiction over commercial disputes. Indeed, a single commercial court for all merchants would be of crucial importance if the ordinances were to be implemented effectively. The court was formed by the three heads of the *consulado*. The ordinances allowed litigants to appeal twice against their decisions – first to a tribunal formed by two merchants, known as *colegas*, and the *corregidor*, the king's highest official in Vizcaya; and second to a tribunal formed by two different merchants, or *recolegas*, along with the *corregidor*. After that there was no possibility of any further appeal. The *consulado* stressed repeatedly that this judicial system was intended 'to provide more brevity, to expose the truth and to preserve good faith'.[63]

Drastic measures were taken every time a merchant tried to escape the *consulado*'s jurisdiction, as nothing less than 'the public faith of commerce' was at stake.[64] For example, in March 1758 the local merchant Pedro Matías de Loygorri ran away to Madrid after the discovery of several frauds that he had committed. In Madrid he appealed to the Council of Castile. The *consulado* ordered its representative in Madrid, Manuel de Eléxpuru, to arrest Loygorri before he could enjoy the Council's protection. Assisted by four guards, Eléxpuru managed to arrest Loygorri by night in the most extraor-

---

[61] Ibid. 316.
[62] Ibid. 317.
[63] Bilbao *consulado*'s petition to the king, Bilbao, 9 Sept. 1750, AFB, Consulado 539, fo. 273r.
[64] Ventura Francisco Gómez de la Torre to Pedro Mendieta, Bilbao, 27 Mar. 1758, ibid. Consulado 541, fo. 74v.

dinary circumstances, and then immediately send him to jail in Bilbao. Loygorri's dealings with several merchants of Castile and northern Europe (he exported wool) were to be examined before the Bilbao *consulado's* court and nowhere else.[65] Another example from 1758 concerns the case of an Irish ship's captain, Martin Meager, who arranged an insurance policy in Bilbao for a ship that had already been wrecked, thereby cheating both the insurers and several Irish merchants resident in Cork.[66] As soon as the *consulado* began to deal with his case, Meager fled to Madrid where he was assisted by the British ambassador in bringing his case before the Spanish Council of War. Eventually, however, the *consulado* managed to take Meager back to Bilbao for judgement there.

The *consulado* also preserved one crucial foundation of early modern trade: the total confidentiality of merchants' business records. Early in March 1745, the *corregidor* entered the house of the *bilbaíno* merchants Joaquín and Juan Matías de Sarachaga in search of smuggled goods. He found nothing illegal in the house but, to make sure that the Sarachagas were not hiding anything, he seized their account books and papers. This caused such an uproar in the Bilbao merchant community that Domingo del Barco, the head of the *consulado*, wrote immediately to the minister of state, Zenón de Somodevilla y Bengoechea, 1st marqués de la Ensenada. Barco stressed that by violating the merchants' confidentiality it was their correspondents and associates who were being exposed, putting their credit and reputations in jeopardy. The foreigners' situation in Spain was once again brought to the centre of the discussion, since two royal decrees of 1681 and 1714 had assured them that no Spanish official could put his hands on their business records. The *consulado* argued that Spaniards should have that same privilege, because 'if the foreign nations saw that Spaniards had no privilege of confidentiality for their books, they would cease trading with them'.[67]

A royal order was eventually issued on 10 December 1745 granting all Spanish merchants total commercial confidentiality. The several printed copies of the provision that were distributed among the merchants of Bilbao were kept 'as the most important paper in which they assure the faith of their trade, and the inviolable secret that their businesses require'.[68] As soon as the Cádiz *consulado* learned what the *bilbaínos* had achieved, it rushed to get a copy of the provision for its archive. Crucially, the fact that merchants never knew for sure the precise financial situation of their correspondents meant that there was no trade without interpersonal trust. The social and cultural ramifications of trade's inherent confidentiality were far-reaching.

---

[65] Gómez de la Torre to Manuel Eléxpuru, Bilbao, 30 Oct. 1758, ibid. fo. 177v.
[66] Gómez de la Torre to Eléxpuru, Bilbao, 8 July 1758, ibid. fo. 122r.
[67] Bilbao *consulado*'s petition to the king, Bilbao, 2 May 1745, ibid. Consulado 537.
[68] Domingo del Barco to Pedro Mendieta, Bilbao, 27 Dec. 1745, ibid. Consulado 538, fo. 80v.

The Bilbao *consulado* sent copies of the 1737 ordinances to foreign countries in the following years.[69] To date, no foreign testimony specifically acknowledging their importance has been found. However, the fact that Bilbao's trade kept growing is a good indication that the relationship between the *bilbaínos* and their correspondents in northern Europe was certainly good. In 1740, when a new war had just broken out, the British ambassador in Paris was told by his agent in Bayonne that 'the town of Bilbao is so much a friend to the English that they will not fit out a privateer, that they continue to receive English goods, not with standing the king of Spain's prohibition'.[70] The Bilbao *consulado* had done everything in its power to provide suitable conditions for trust to operate. The links with the north had been reinforced, and indeed were visually represented before the eyes of any visitor. On 17 January 1780, after having lunch with the Gardoquis (one of the most important merchant families of Bilbao), the American John Adams was taken to the chamber of 'a curious institution' called the *consulado*. On its walls, along with portraits of the king and queen of Spain, he saw 'Pictures of the royal Exchange London, the Exchange of Amsterdam, of Antwerp &c.'[71]

The merchants of Bilbao had achieved something that their counterparts in Cádiz, Seville, Lisbon and the other Iberian ports would not, namely putting all merchants under one creditable jurisdiction. The situation for foreign merchants in Lower Andalusia and Portugal was very different. Over the course of the eighteenth century the foreign communities of Cádiz would repeatedly stress the importance of being under special jurisdiction. For the British consul in Cádiz, this was absolutely necessary if any British merchant wanted 'to remain in this kingdom with any degree of security'.[72] As for the jurisdiction of the Cádiz *consulado*'s court, neither the British nor any other foreign nation acknowledged its authority. That did not stop trade between foreigners and the Spaniards, but the situation did not contribute to fostering trust and reciprocity between the two. In Bilbao the story was very different.

Spanish merchants in London

The *huésped* institution and improvements in the dependability of the *consulado* enhanced the *bilbaínos*' participation in international trade. However, questions remain about *bilbaíno* merchants' links outside Spain, for if a lack

---

[69] Lorenzo Ignacio Landazuri to Real Junta de Comercio, Bilbao, 1 Apr. 1748, ibid. fo. 256r.
[70] James Waldegrave to Thomas Pelham-Holles, 1st duke of Newcastle, Paris, 24 Sept. 1740, SP 78/224.
[71] *Diary of John Adams*, ii. 432.
[72] Josiah Hardy to Lord Grantham, Cádiz, 23 Aug. 1774, Grantham papers, BL, MS Add. 24168, fo. 249.

of trustworthy correspondents had been an obstacle to trade with northern Europe in the seventeenth century, did the *bilbaínos* try to overcome that problem by appointing their own agents (for example family members, partners or associates) to places such as London or Amsterdam? Existing evidence suggests that Spaniards did not move to northern Europe until the 1750s.

In 1702 Spain had its own consuls in London, Amsterdam, Rotterdam, Middelburg, Lisbon and Marseilles, but these officials fulfilled few, if any, commercial tasks. The situation improved very little in the first half of the eighteenth century, due to Philip V's belligerent foreign policy, the passivity of most Spanish merchants and the weak Spanish mercantile fleet.[73] However, the merchants of Bilbao cannot be accused of being passive. In fact, the Bilbao *consulado* considered that it was important for the *bilbaínos* to move to northern Europe, but problems existed that only Spanish diplomacy could solve, since the *consulado* had powers to sort things out at home, but not abroad. In 1747, when the peace negotiations between Spain and Britain were about to start, the Bilbao merchants complained to the crown that foreigners were much better treated in Spain than Spaniards were treated abroad. This was particularly so in England, where Spaniards had to pay more taxes than the British, and as a result Spanish merchants were disinclined to establish themselves there. In France, the situation was equally bad, due to French inheritance laws that banned foreigners from disposing freely of their properties in their wills. However, in their petition, the merchants of Bilbao significantly said nothing about the situation of foreigners in Vizcaya and the *fueros*.[74]

The treaty eventually signed in Aix-la-Chapelle in October 1748 was as satisfactory as any previous one. As ever, on paper everything seemed ideal. In its second article the treaty confirmed what had been agreed in Utrecht in December 1713: that British merchants resident in Spain and Spanish merchants resident in Britain would not have to pay more taxes than nationals, and would be permitted to own property.[75] The terms agreed with Holland in June 1714 were very similar, and would also be ratified in 1748. The reason why many of the concessions in the treaty of 1714 had remained merely nominal was because political relations between Madrid and London were strained until the middle years of the century. It was the commercial treaty of 8 December 1750 between Spain and Britain that changed the situation, allowing the two countries to improve their diplomatic and

---

[73] Jesús Pradells Nadal, *Diplomacia y comercio: la expansión consular española en el siglo* XVIII, Alicante 1992, 45.
[74] Bilbao *consulado* to José Carvajal, Bilbao, 27 Feb. 1747, AFB, Consulado 538, fos 124–40.
[75] Anon., *Colección de los tratados de paz, alianza, comercio etc. ajustados por la corona de España con las potencias extrangeras desde el reynado del señor don Felipe Quinto hasta el presente*, Madrid 1796, ii. 267–355, 363–97.

commercial relations significantly.[76] However, in August 1751, before the commercial treaty with Britain was implemented, the head of the Bilbao *consulado* was still unhappy with the attitude of the Spanish government. He confided to the *consulado*'s representative in Madrid that '[o]ther nations do not allow foreigners to reside [in their country] when it goes against their interests; but our nation, as though our nationals lacked ability, not only allows foreigners to stay but concerns itself with their convenience'.[77]

In 1753 the *bilbaínos* Pedro Ignacio de Xarabeitia and Pedro de Errecarte were probably the first Spanish merchants to establish themselves in London since the sixteenth century.[78] The Spanish consul in London, Andrés Zedrón, informed Madrid that at long last the Spanish had two compatriots in London who could serve them with more *amor* (love – a notably emphatic noun) than any English correspondent.[79] Following in the footsteps of Xarabeitia and Errecarte, at least another twenty-three Spanish merchants (sixteen of them Basques, of whom nine were from Bilbao) would move to London in the second half of the eighteenth century.[80] Apart from one or two names mentioned in passing, at no point does the historiography even acknowledge their existence.

The merchants' private records have not survived, so not much can be said about their activities, but there appears to have been an affinity between them: virtually every one of them was involved in a partnership with a compatriot. Only three (Juan García from 'Garcias and Lewis', and Juan Miguel Pérez and José de Echalaz from 'Ives, Baseley, Pérez, Echalaz and Co') went into partnership with English merchants. During the three decades that he stayed in London, Pedro de Errecarte was associated first with Xarabeitia, then with Francisco Antonio del Rio, and lastly with Joaquín Uríbarri (his nephew) and Antonio de Aransolo. After 1780, Aransolo would go into partnership with another *bilbaíno*, José Domingo de Larrazábal. The Castilian Antonio Vallejo was a partner of Francisco Antonio del Río and later of the Basque José de Echalaz. Echalaz would be partner of a merchant from Soria (although educated in Bilbao), Juan Miguel Pérez, and of the *bilbaíno* Manuel de Basarrate, before associating with the Norwich manufacturers Ives and

---

[76] McLachlan, *Trade*, 139–45.
[77] José Nicolás Allende to Pedro Mendieta, Bilbao, 23 Aug. 1751, AFB, Consulado 539, fo. 417r.
[78] See Samuel Lee, *A collection of the names of the merchants living in and about the city of London*, London 1677, repr. 1863, and the numerous editions of *Kent's directory* from 1736 onwards.
[79] Andrés Zedrón to Carvajal, London, 11 Apr. 1754, AGS, Estado, leg. 6923.
[80] Their names were Antonio Aransolo, Pedro Atristain, Manuel Basarrate, Manuel Bergareche, Luis Collantes, Andrés Dendaretegui, Fermín Echalaz, José Echalaz, Alfonso Eguino, Francisco Eguino, José Francisco Elorriaga, Matías Gandásegui, Bartolomé Garay, Manuel Garay, Juan García, Lángara, José Domingo Larrazábal, Juan Manuel Martínez, Juan Miguel Pérez, Manuel Antonio del Río, Fermín Tastet, Joaquín Uríbarri and Antonio Vallejo.

Baseley. The *montañeses* (merchants from the Santander area) Collantes and Lángara were both partners. Alfonso de Eguino at first traded alone, and then went into partnership with his nephew Francisco and his fellow Basques, Manuel de Garay and Pedro de Atristain. Similarly, Manuel de Garay, along with his brother Bartolomé, became partners of the *bilbaíno* Manuel de Bergareche. Significantly, every time they needed witnesses for some bureaucratic procedure, they resorted to their compatriots.[81]

Diplomatic back-up was not the only reason for the Spaniards' sudden arrival in London. First, the final defeat of the Jacobite uprising at Culloden in 1746 reduced English anti-Catholicism, at least among the educated political elite, and London became far more willing to relax the laws against Catholics.[82] Second, the rise of London as the dominant capitalist city of Europe attracted numerous foreign merchants in the second half of the eighteenth century. London's trading community became a more heterogeneous mix of nationalities than ever before, with a whole range of competing ethnic and religious cultures as merchants tried to take advantage of the new and wider commercial possibilities that the British capital offered.[83] Those merchants kept close connections with their countries of origin, and, if they succeeded in London, it was because they attracted commissions from their compatriots.

However, this picture needs to be qualified somewhat. In the second half of the eighteenth century, the merchants of Bilbao were not in desperate need of *bilbaíno* merchants in London. The Basque linkages with the north were already developed in the first half of the eighteenth century and would be stronger in the second. In September 1796, when a new war against Britain had just started, the merchants of Bilbao were required to give the names of their correspondents in Britain. The 335 folios of the survey are in a bad condition and some names are illegible. Moreover, many merchants do not seem to have provided the names of all their connections. However, some conclusions can still be drawn.[84] Over 200 merchants had, or had had in recent years, correspondence with Britain. London and Bristol were the main locations, but they also corresponded with merchants in Exeter, Falmouth, Hull, Sheffield, Leeds, Halifax, Norwich, Manchester, Liverpool and Birmingham. The companies and merchants most often mentioned were those established in London and Norwich, particularly the Spanish houses of London and the company of Jeremiah Ives, the leading Norwich

---

[81] See the last wills and testaments of Pedro Atristain (AFB, Corregimiento 1763/013), Alfonso Eguino (TNA, C 12/1401/24), Pedro Errecarte (AFB, Corregimiento 4000/006) and Antonio Vallejo (TNA, C 12/668/1).

[82] Colin Haydon, *Anti-Catholicism in eighteenth-century England, c. 1714–1780: a political and social study*, Manchester 1993, 164–71.

[83] Perry Gauci, *Emporium of the world: the merchants of London, 1660–1800*, London 2007, 123–4.

[84] AFB, Corregimiento 0101/008.

merchant-manufacturer. Other London merchants such as Marc Weyland, the Baring brothers and Dubois and Sons were also repeatedly mentioned. In Bristol, the *bilbaínos*' main correspondents were the English wool merchants Jeremiah Hull and Henry Brooke. In total, the merchants of Bilbao provided about sixty names, although thirty of them appeared far more frequently than others.

In fact, the reason why Spaniards moved to London seems to be more closely connected to Spanish colonial trade than to Anglo-Spanish trade to and from Iberia. The pattern of Spanish colonial trade underwent profound transformation after the 1740s, and Spaniards in London made a major contribution to this process. The main features were similar to those experienced by the international trade in textiles in the second half of the eighteenth century. Fast product innovation encouraged English manufacturers to open up direct channels of distribution for their products. Manufacturers offered up to 500 different cloths to their customers in Spain: woollens, worsteds and mixed goods in a large number of colours, qualities and designs.[85] To market such quantities of cloths more efficiently, manufacturers opted to use commercial travellers. These offered all sorts of textiles to merchants in Spain, but also contributed to extending the range of products by gathering information about consumer taste and fashion, giving an increasing retail orientation to the trade. After the mid-eighteenth century, both competition and the use of credit were greatly encouraged by business networks becoming more closely linked, which in turn contributed to the expansion of trade. The process was extended to the north transatlantic trade, where 'business links between British and American merchants, suppliers and agents in the hinterland of British ports, and manufacturers became more closely intertwined'.[86] Though it is a far less familiar story, that process also took place in Spanish colonial trade, and the Spaniards of London were among the merchants who made it happen.

Xarabeitia and Errecarte, for example, ordered cloths (camblets, florettas, taboretts, sattins, callimancoes and brocades) of specific colours and figures from the Norwich manufacturer Philip Stannard as soon as they established themselves in London.[87] But rather than Bilbao, Cádiz and Spanish America were where they intended to market these fabrics. In 1753, the year that his name first appeared in a London directory, Errecarte and his brother Juan Tomás joined the Cádiz *consulado*, the merchant gild enjoying the monopoly of Spanish colonial trade. On 4 October 1754 Pedro de Errecarte set off

---

[85] John Smail, *Merchants, markets, and manufacture: the English wool textile industry in the eighteenth century*, Basingstoke 1999, 97–8.
[86] Kenneth Morgan, 'Business networks in the British export trade to northern America, 1750–1800', in McCusker and Morgan, *Early modern Atlantic economy*, 40.
[87] For Stannard's letters to Xarabeitia and Errecarte see *The letters of Philip Stannard, Norwich textile manufacturer, 1751–1763*, ed. Ursula Priestley, Norwich 1994, 41, 54, 57, 60, 62, 66, 102.

from Cádiz for the main Spanish American port, Veracruz.[88] He returned to London months later, but his connections with Cádiz and Spanish America remained crucial to his commercial activities. In the 1760s Errecarte brought his nephew, Joaquín de Uríbarri, from Bilbao to work with him in London, while his other nephew, Ramón, joined the Cádiz *consulado* in 1768.[89] Other Spaniards in London followed a similar pattern. For instance, Alfonso de Eguino had a brother in Cádiz, Juan de Eguino, and many connections in Spanish America (most of them Basques like him). In common with Xarabeitia and Errecarte, Eguino had access to a network of trustworthy correspondents who provided him with crucial information about colonial fashion and demand. Trust was to play a crucial part in moulding Spanish colonial trade in the second half of the eighteenth century. Spaniards, being the only merchants legally allowed to travel to the Spanish colonies, found themselves in a privileged position to develop links with their Spanish American counterparts.

However, before analysing transformations in the colonial sphere, there is another crucial aspect of the *bilbaínos*' international trade that deserves careful attention. Along with the institutional arrangements, the local recruitment of ship captains and mariners also played a critical role in establishing reliable and trustworthy commercial conditions for the merchants of Bilbao.

---

[88] AGI, Arribadas 457, fo. 163v.
[89] Ruiz, *Consulado*, 210.

2

Basque Ship Captains and Seamen

Even though no Bilbao merchant established himself in northern Europe until the mid-eighteenth century, Basque ship captains had been travelling regularly to the ports of France, England and the Netherlands since at least the medieval period. The decisive intervention of these captains is another reason for the growing participation of Bilbao merchants in international trade, and, just as the *huésped* institution and the improvements in commercial knowledge contributed to the fostering of interpersonal trust, so local captains played a crucial part in reducing for the merchants of Bilbao the risks arising from the principal-agent problem. It is no accident that in September 1763, while recounting what they had achieved since the 1680s, the *bilbaínos* congratulated themselves on having built a great many ships and having employed on them a large number of Basque mariners.[1]

In fact, the Basque Country had a long tradition of fishing and seafaring and, unlike most parts of Spain, both Vizcaya and Guipúzcoa had an abundant supply of local ship captains and mariners. However, with the exception of those in eighteenth-century Catalonia, ship captains have hardly been studied by historians of Spain.[2] This chapter explores the role played by Basque seamen in connecting *bilbaíno* merchants with merchants overseas, and in making possible an intricate system of collection and distribution, transportation and communication, that linked different commercial areas.

The dearth of private correspondence for Basque ship captains has been partially overcome by using the previously unstudied cache of confiscated personal papers and letters in the British High Court of Admiralty: there were several cases where British naval officials were able to seize the personal papers of ship captains. Moreover, ship captains and crews' depositions at the British High Court of Admiralty provide other unique insights. These rare sources reveal how eighteenth-century ship captains functioned as middlemen for the merchants whom they served, and how they contributed to the creation and maintenance of trading networks.

---

[1] Bilbao *consulado*'s petition to the king, Bilbao, 28 Sept. 1763, AFB, Consulado 549, fo. 30r–v.
[2] See Pierre Vilar, *Catalunya dins l'Espanya moderna: recerques sobre els fonaments econòmics de les estructures nacionals*, Barcelona 1968, iv. 219–424, and Carlos Martínez Shaw, *Cataluña en la Carrera de Indias, 1680–1756*, Barcelona 1981, 19–32.

Basque ship captains as mariners and shipowners

Understanding the ship captain's role requires some basic appreciation of the shipping process. When goods were loaded onto his ship, a captain signed three bills of lading (*conocimientos de carga*) by which he promised to carry and deliver the cargo to a consignee. The bill of lading contained essential information, such as the captain's name and place of residence, the ship's name, ports of loading and unloading, a brief description of the cargo, the shipper and his consignee's names, the freight to be paid and the date. One copy was for the shipper, one for the consignee (which, if possible, was sent to him in advance) and one for the captain. If the cargo was damaged in transit, the captain had to submit a written explanation (a ship's protest, or *protesta de mar*) to a notary public, by means of which he could settle his affairs with the owner of the cargo or the ship. The number of bills of lading on any given ship varied according to the cargo. In October 1710, for example, captain Francisco de la Cuadra was found to be in possession of ninety-seven bills of lading. His vessel's cargo, consisting chiefly of bundles of woollen cloth from Holland, had been shipped by various merchants and was destined for a large number of individual consignees in Bilbao and Cádiz.[3] By contrast, in July 1739, captain Asensio Iguelz left San Sebastián with a bulk cargo of iron for Cádiz; since there was only one shipper and one consignee, the captain carried a single bill of lading.[4] Thus, a bill of lading might represent the entire cargo or only a small part of it.

When a single merchant shipped an entire cargo, the ship could also be chartered, a process that entailed bargaining between the cargo owner (or charterer) and the shipowner to establish a freight rate or price for the proposed voyage. The final terms were incorporated into a legal contract known as a charter party (*carta de fletamento*), which indicated such things as the ship's capacity, the nature of its proposed employment and how costs were to be apportioned between ship and charterer. In July 1758 captain Julián de San Llorente was charged with a cargo belonging to a San Sebastián merchant, Juan Ignacio Ibáñez de Zabala. The latter had agreed to a charter party with shipowner Juan Antonio de Cardón to transport wine, cord and brandy to Dublin. The ship was not to 'receive cargo from anyone else', and as soon as it arrived in Dublin, Zabala's consignee would have eight days to unload the cargo, beyond which time he would have to pay the captain £2 sterling for every additional day's delay.[5] Although in theory a captain could

---

[3] *Nuestra Señora del Rosario* (1710), HCA 32/74 (1), fo. 1.
[4] *Nuestra Señora del Camino* (1739), HCA 32/137/9, doc. no. 5.
[5] For a copy of the charter party see *San Juan Bautista* (1758), HCA 32/208 (1), doc. no. 4.

sign a charter party only if he was in a port other than the shipowner's, in practice captains enjoyed considerable flexibility on this score.[6]

Since ship captains and merchants/shipowners were united in their desire for profitable voyages, it is no surprise that they enjoyed close relationships. When captain José de Ajeo received a letter from his mother in December 1778, he noted that 'it came by my merchant'.[7] Papers seized by the British reveal that shipowners and captains maintained an extensive correspondence. Captain Juan Bautista de Ajeo had thirty-eight letters at the time of his capture, while captain Juan Bautista de Artamóniz had twenty-one and captain Juan Bautista de Sarría eleven. Some of these were from wives, friends and relatives, but most were written by merchants and shipowners and were addressed to other merchants or to the captains themselves. The only surviving eighteenth-century letter-book belonging to a Bilbao mercantile firm is for Goicoechea and Otero, owners of at least six ships. Fifteen of the 147 letters that it sent between May 1797 and February 1798 were addressed to the Basque captains of four of those ships in Morlaix, Barcelona, Santander and La Coruña (a Bilbao carpenter was minding two more ships moored in Lorient, France).[8] For Goicoechea and Otero, the captains' reliability was essential. Of captain José Manuel de Uruburu they had 'the best belief in his person',[9] and to captain Antonio de Zavala they openly wrote that 'we have blind trust in you'.[10]

Close relationships between merchants and ship captains were sometimes reinforced by joint ownership of vessels. In 1761 at least sixty-one of Bilbao's nearly 200 merchants were listed as shipowners or ships' 'husbands' (managing owners) with total holdings of 120 vessels, half of them with a capacity of less than 100 tons and most of the remainder between 100 and 150 tons (the largest ships were of 300 tons). In total they amounted to 13,050 tons, the average ship being 108 tons.[11] In the last third of the century those figures would not change much according to two list of ships and shipowners made in 1768–71 and 1789–93.[12] In addition, the neighbouring coastal villages had a large number of lighter merchant vessels. Between 1765 and 1770, the

---

[6] Ramón Fernández-Guerra, 'El fletamento en el litoral cantábrico durante el siglo XVIII', unpubl. PhD diss. Deusto 1992, 241.
[7] José Ajeo to María Arteaga, San Lucar, 21 Dec.1778, HCA 32/412/7, fo. 90.
[8] AFB, Consulado 602, pp. 23, 24, 40, 48, 62, 75, 98, 108, 115, 126, 129, 133, 153, 167, 180.
[9] Simón Antonio Goicoechea to José Antonio Suárez Valdés, Bilbao, 16 May 1797, ibid. 23.
[10] Goicoechea to Antonio Zavala, Bilbao, 23 May 1797, ibid. 40.
[11] Guiard, *Historia del Consulado*, ii. 426–32.
[12] Ibid. 432–42. See also Ana María Rivera Medina, 'Paisaje naval, construcción y agentes sociales en Vizcaya: desde el medioevo a la modernidad', *Itsas Memoria* ii (1998), 49–92. The reason why Bilbao did not have larger ships was partly because of the importance of its coastal trade and partly because its port up the river Nervión was inaccessible to ships of large tonnage. The average tonnage of the merchant fleet of Bilbao contrasted sharply with that of Cádiz. In the period 1717–78 only 14% of the ships setting sail from

Bilbao *consulado* granted passports to 317 such ships, their tonnage ranging from ten to 110 tons (thirty-seven tons on average).[13] It is likely that many of them were also included among the ships owned by the merchants of Bilbao, for it was common for merchants and captains to share ownership. Even though there is no systematic study on the subject, several historians working on the merchants of Bilbao provide telling examples. In January 1754, for instance, five *bilbaínos* created a marine company that lasted for nine years and managed eight ships. The shares were equally divided among the partners.[14] Likewise, in 1758 captain Valentín de Artaza (from Plencia, Vizcaya) and the Bilbao merchants Nicolás de Zabala, Gregorio de Achutegui and Francisco Antonio de Nougaro shared equal parts of the ship *Nuestra Señora del Rosario*.[15] Captains' depositions before the British High Court of Admiralty suggest that shared ownership was widespread particularly in the case of ships with a capacity of less than 100 tons. Between 1778 and 1782 the British captured thirty-eight Basque prizes (from both Bilbao and San Sebastián). Thirteen of the twenty-four ships under 100 tons were partially owned by captains (54.1 per cent), eight were owned exclusively by merchants (33.3 per cent), while no information is available for the other three (12.5 per cent). Thus, over half of the captains had a share in the ships they commanded. Captains were less likely to have an ownership share in a larger vessel. Of fourteen Basque vessels greater than 100 tons captured in the same period, only one captain was a co-owner of his vessel (7.14 per cent).[16]

In the eighteenth century, shipowning was not a full-time occupation. In Bilbao most shipowners were merchants, and most merchants were at some point shipowners. In 1761 most shipowners (62 per cent) owned only one ship, whereas only a few of them (6 per cent) owned five or more ships. Furthermore, Bilbao merchants did not necessarily stay in the shipowning business on a long-term basis. Of the sixty-one names listed as shipowners in 1761 only twenty-two – just over a third – would appear among the fifty-three listed in 1768–71.[17] A possible motivation for entering the shipowning business at least once in their commercial career might have been the advantages of having a close relationship with a ship captain.

Cádiz for the colonies were less than 100 tons, while 57% were substantial vessels of over 200 tons: García-Baquero, *Cádiz*, i. 253.

[13] Guiard, *Historia del Consulado*, ii. 448–64.

[14] Elena Alcorta Ortíz de Zarate, 'Negocios familiares y circuitos laneros en Bilbao en la segunda mitad del siglo XVIII', in Agustín González Enciso (ed.), *El negocio de la lana en España, 1650–1830*, Pamplona 2001, 195–6.

[15] Basurto, *Comercio*, 236.

[16] For a full list of the 1778–82 Basque prizes, their tonnage, captains and owners see Xabier Lamikiz, 'Basque ship captains as mariners and traders in the eighteenth century', *IJMH* xx/2 (2008), 106–9.

[17] Guiard, *Historia del Consulado*, ii. 426–42.

Although details of captains' ownership shares are rare, the available evidence suggests that they never owned more than a one-third interest. In 1779, captain Juan Bautista de Ajeo owned one-third of *Nuestra Señora de Begoña* (fifty tons), the other two-thirds belonging to two Bilbao merchants.[18] The following year, Ajeo commanded the forty-five-ton *Santa Úrsula*, later captured by the British. This time his share was one-quarter, the other three-quarters belonging to San Sebastián merchant Fermín de Aizcorbe.[19] Similarly, in 1778, captain Juan Bautista de Artamóniz owned one-quarter of the fifty-ton *Nuestra Señora del Carmen*, while San Sebastián merchant Juan de Bousignac owned three-quarters.[20] Pierre Vilar has described a similar situation in Catalonia, although captains there were always partial proprietors of their ships, which for them constituted a second source of income, rather than sometimes being share-holders as was the case in Bilbao.[21] Yet although Basque captains did not universally participate in shipownership, it was common enough. Moreover, the Bilbao *consulado*'s 1737 Ordinances stipulated that once a captain took command of the ship he was to act as though he were its owner.[22]

Captains also assisted shipowners in purchasing vessels, since this was an area in which their professional judgement was as obvious as it was welcome. In June 1758 captain Juan Bautista de Artamóniz bought the sixty-five-ton brigantine *El Constante de Bayona* from two French-Basque captains in Bayonne. In typical *bilbaíno* fashion, Artamóniz renamed the ship *Nuestra Señora de Begoña y Ánimas* (*Our Lady of Begoña and Souls*). He then set sail for Bilbao, where the merchant Gregorio de Achutegi would later purchase three-quarters of the vessel.[23] Occasionally, captains also chose the ship even when they did not intend to own any part of it. In December 1778 captain Agustín de Butrón travelled to London to buy a second-hand ship of between 200 and 250 tons for £2,000 sterling. He had been commissioned by the Bilbao merchant Juan Antonio de Gana and was assisted by a Basque merchant established in London, named Pedro de Atristain; but the choice of ship was ultimately his.[24]

In addition to owning shares in smaller vessels, Basque captains tended to eschew fixed schedules or routes. By contrast, larger ships crossing the Atlantic usually operated as pre-arranged charters and followed direct routes. Such charters were the norm in the Spanish colonial trade. Simon Ville has already observed that captains with shares in their own ships did not

---

[18] *Nuestra Señora de Begoña* (1779), HCA 32/412/7.
[19] *Santa Úrsula* (1780), HCA 32/469/9.
[20] *Nuestra Señora del Carmen* (1778), HCA 32/414/3. Bousignac was a French merchant naturalised in San Sebastián in 1752: AHN, Consejos, leg. 28585/exp. 3.
[21] Vilar, *Catalunya*, iv. 225.
[22] [Bilbao *consulado*], *Ordenanzas ... de 1737*, 222.
[23] *Nuestra Señora de Begoña y Ánimas* (1762), HCA 32/227 (1).
[24] Juan Antonio Gana to Pedro Atristain, Bilbao, 30 Dec. 1778, AFB, Corregimiento 1763/013.

necessarily perform more efficiently.[25] Nevertheless, the need for loyalty and reliability was reason enough for shipowners to offer captains an ownership stake, and there can be little doubt that shared ownership reinforced mutual dependence. The greater suitability of smaller ships to flexible trade might be another reason why their captains so often had shares in such vessels, since this would have given them greater independence in decision-making. It is no coincidence that the only ship that Goicoechea and Otero shared with a captain was a 100-ton brigantine, in which captain Adrián Larrabeiti owned one third.[26] Ships with crews of less than ten – which needed considerably less time to load and discharge – could trade almost continuously from one port to another, following a complicated pattern that linked dozens of ports along the Iberian Peninsula, western France and northern Europe. Sometimes the captains of these ships bore passports from the Bilbao *consulado*, which explicitly limited their operations to the north coast of Spain and the Basque Country ('from Bayonne in France to Bayona in Galicia and no more') and obliged them to obtain pilots if they wished to go beyond it. Many captains, however, ignored such regulations. Others, like captain Ajeo, had a two-year royal passport enabling them to sail anywhere from Cádiz to England.[27] From January 1777 to February 1778, for example, captain Sarría's ninety-ton vessel visited, in order, San Sebastián, Liverpool (where he stayed for forty-three days), Cádiz, Málaga, Liverpool, Dublin (accidentally, due to bad weather), Liverpool, Bilbao and finally back to San Sebastián. In the process, Sarría amassed a grand total of 13,889 *reales* in freight, roughly equally to the value of the vessel itself, which was welcome news for the San Sebastián firm of Ruimes, Burgue and Company, the ship's husband.[28]

There were several reasons for shared ownership. First and foremost, it was a means of raising the necessary capital. This probably did not apply to most merchants, especially the wealthiest ones, but it gave minor investors (artisans, shopkeepers, captains and even mariners) a chance to invest in a potentially lucrative venture. Shareholding was also an effective way to spread risk, which had an obvious appeal to merchants, since owning quarter shares in four different vessels was less risky than owning a single ship outright.[29] Finally, shipowning offered the merchant another advantage that was related to his commercial networks. It is clear that most vessels plied

---

[25] Simon P. Ville, *English shipowning during the Industrial Revolution: Michael Henley and Son, London shipowners, 1770–1830*, Manchester 1987, 85.
[26] Goicoechea to Adrián Larrabeiti, Bilbao, 3 June 1797, AFB, Consulado 602, p. 62.
[27] *Nuestra Señora de Begoña* (1779), HCA 32/412/7, doc. no. 5.
[28] *Nuestra Señora del Carmen* (1778), HCA 32/414/5, fos 89–90. For captain Ajeo's ship accounts see *Nuestra Señora de Begoña* (1779), HCA 32/412/7, fo. 137.
[29] Simon Ville, 'The growth of specialization in English shipowning, 1750–1850', *EcHR* xlvi (1993), 717. Still, it is likely, as Ralph Davis suggested, that the increasing use of marine insurance throughout the eighteenth century progressively reduced the importance of shareholding as the predominant structure of ownership: *The rise of the English shipping industry in the seventeenth and eighteenth centuries*, London 1962, 87–9,.

routes that did not always include their home ports but instead embraced Spanish, European and even North American harbours. For the merchant, this diverse and complex web was reason enough to enter the shipowning business and to share ownership with his captain. Ralph Davis has noted that shipping gave the merchant an opportunity to exploit his contacts, but the implications were broader than that. According to Davis, 'it was trade that gave assistance to shipowning, rather than vice versa'.[30] Joint ownership enabled the merchant not merely to exploit his connections but also to maintain, augment and monitor them through trustworthy partners who happened to be captains.

Ship captains as overseas agents

The captain's roles were not restricted to seafaring and shipowning. When a ship left its home port, the captain usually knew only his first destination, and a return cargo was not always guaranteed. Naturally, instead of returning with ballast it was more profitable to find another cargo, and as soon as that cargo had been delivered, there were new options to consider. Although merchants relied on their contacts to obtain additional cargoes, this was not always possible. In July 1757 *Espíritu Santo* left Cádiz for Nantes with a cargo consigned to the Spanish merchant Francisco de la Villa. After delivering his cargo, the ship's Basque captain, Juan de Goitia, was under instructions from the shipowner 'to proceed to Morlaix, Hamburg, Ostend or to such other port for which the said don Francisco de la Villa shall have a cargo'.[31] Shipowners did not always give the captain a letter of instruction. Particularly when the captain had been commanding a ship for several years and knew the shipowner's contacts well, it was assumed that he would act for the best. However, captain Goitia was further instructed:

> If by any means you ... should arrive or touch at San Sebastián your consignee shall be don Juan de Michelena and in the absence of him don Nicolás de Guilisasti. At London shall be don Pedro de Errecarte and in the absence of him Mess James and Thomas Tierney. At Amsterdam Mess Wernier and Harsigk. At Marseille don Diego Solier and his brother don Marcos Solier. At Genoa Mess don Alexo and Amado Regni.[32]

Moreover, nothing in the instructions would 'bar the said captain in other places from acting according to his own prudent management, giving through the whole proof of his real and good conduct in observing the interest of the ship'. If a contact could not secure a freight, or if the ship docked at a

---

[30] Davis, *Rise of the English shipping industry*, 99.
[31] *Espíritu Santo* (1758), HCA 32/188 (2), doc. no. 73.
[32] Ibid.

port where neither the shipowner nor the captain knew anyone, the captain could resort to a shipbroker (*corredor de navíos*). Indeed, the number of these professional intermediaries, who secured freights on commission and acted as interpreters for foreign captains, grew greatly in the eighteenth century.[33] Alternatively, the captain himself could act as an overseas agent, a role that was sometimes agreed upon in advance by means of a notarised contract (*comenda*).[34] Still, letters intercepted by the British show that informal methods based on mutual understanding were widespread. Often it was enough simply to include the captain's name as consignee on the bill of lading or to give him a note with some instructions; indeed, for the smallest cargoes a verbal agreement would suffice.

The *comenda* (whether formal or informal) was especially useful for merchants who lacked contacts in places where their goods were to be sold or where new ones were to be purchased. It enabled the captain to act as an agent not only for the merchant but also for lesser investors such as craftsmen, shopkeepers and the like. In October 1778 José Blas Ruiz (possibly a Bilbao shopkeeper) asked captain Artamóniz to purchase six barrels of salt in Landernau (in the harbour of Brest, France) but only if the price were good. Ruiz also asked Artamóniz to pay for these and, if this proved impossible, to 'indicate to me a merchant of your satisfaction who could serve me in the future'.[35] Shipowners themselves were also very keen on appointing their captains as agents, particularly when the cargo was to be sold in some remote place where the merchant/shipowner knew nobody. Thus, the captain was instrumental in forging new connections and in disposing of cargoes himself.

However, contrary to what is usually assumed, the presence of a comenda did not always mean that the shipper was lacking in contacts, since merchants with extensive networks of correspondents also entrusted ship captains to sell their goods. They did so because they knew that their captains could usually find a port with better prices in far less time than it would take them to contact their own external correspondents. The captain had the advantage of superior and dynamic intelligence in different ports, which he could easily amass during the course of his voyages, either from public sources (such as newspapers) or from private ones (such as fellow captains and traders). In

---

[33] Davis, *Rise of the English shipping industry*, 161–2; Ville, 'Growth of specialization', 716–17. The Bilbao *consulado* regulated the shipbroker's occupation in its 1737 Ordinances where it was specified that there should be no more than four such brokers in Bilbao. They had to know at least Spanish and one foreign language among French, English, Dutch and Flemish, and were not allowed to trade on their own: [Bilbao *consulado*], *Ordenanzas ... de 1737*, ch. xvi. In addition, captains could also receive help and advice from their country's consuls.

[34] See José Martínez Gijón, 'La comenda en el derecho español, II: La comenda mercantil', *Anuario de Historia del Derecho Español* xxxvi (1966), 379–456.

[35] José Blas Ruiz to Juan Bautista Artamóniz, Bilbao, 21 Oct. 1778, HCA 32/414/3, fo. 32.

October 1778 San Sebastián merchant Juan Bousignac loaded his own ship with a cargo of iron to be sold along the French Atlantic coast, where he had many correspondents. He left it to captain Artamóniz, however, to seek out the best price between La Rochelle and Nantes. If he chose to go beyond Nantes he would 'have to get a better price'.[36] Moreover, if prices were good, Artamóniz was to buy sardines and butter beans for transportation back to San Sebastián, otherwise he would have to contact Bousignac's French correspondents (the names of nine merchants were provided in the letter of instruction) to secure a cargo elsewhere. To finance these transactions and to avoid the risk of carrying specie, Artamóniz was instructed either to secure a bill of exchange or to leave the money with one of Bousignac's contacts.

Captains also facilitated commercial exchanges between merchants who did not know one another, as demonstrated by the case of captain Nicolás de Aldecoa and Bilbao merchant Luis Des Essartz, co-owners of the ninety-ton *San Joseph y San Joaquín* in which their respective shares were one-quarter and three-quarters.[37] 'Beyond the Canary Islands', said Des Essartz in his letter of instruction, 'you will avoid any encounter, but if you have to talk to any foreign ship, you will say you are on your way to Campeche [on the Yucatán Peninsula in México]; but if the ship were Spanish, you would tell them you are heading to the united America [i.e., the US].'[38] The vessel's true destinations were Maryland, Virginia and Carolina, where the captain was to sell the ship's cargo (rum, nails, linen, brandy and salt belonging to the Bilbao firm Juan de Villabaso and Company, in which Des Essartz was also a partner) and to buy rice and tobacco for the return leg. This venture was conceived in Bilbao in January 1778 when Des Essartz met an American merchant named John Emery, who provided reference letters for four merchants in Charleston, Baltimore, Edenton and Williamsburg.[39] Despite the references, Des Essartz was more inclined to trust his captain, to whom he also wrote in his letter of instruction that '[y]ou have reference letters for some individuals of those provinces, but before leaving any money or goods in their hands, you shall find out about their circumstances and solidity, and if they are satisfactory you shall ask them for help and advice'.[40] Finally, captain Aldecoa was ordered to buy rice and tobacco only if prices were

---

[36] Ibid. fo. 77.
[37] Luis Des Essartz was born in Bragelogne (Champagne-Ardenne, France) but was naturalised in Bilbao around mid-century. He married María Lorenza de Villabaso, sister of the important local merchant Juan de Villabaso: Mauleón, *Población*, 284.
[38] *San Joseph y San Joaquín* (1778), HCA 32/377/8, fo. 11.
[39] Ibid. fos 12–15. The merchants were Henry Crouch of Charleston, Samuel and Robert Purveyance of Baltimore, Haves, Smith and Allen of Edenton and Norton and Beal of Williamsburg. The reference letters included a few lines in French written by Des Essartz himself.
[40] Ibid. fo. 11.

good; otherwise he was to sell the ship in America and return with his crew aboard a merchant ship.[41]

In the course of fostering and maintaining mercantile networks, captains became well-connected men. The personal papers of captain Juan Bautista de Sarría, for example, include a letter of 26 December 1777 from English merchant Thomas Rexford, who declared in Spanish and in the most friendly terms that he looked forward to 'celebrating your arrival in Liverpool and if the weather is fine, I shall see you next week. My wife is already with me, and I will take her with me to Liverpool. We shall appreciate it very much if you have time to stay a couple of days in my house'.[42] It seems clear that captains built their own networks, but did they aspire to become merchants themselves? They certainly possessed much of the required knowledge, including the use of bills of exchange, an instrument of credit that avoided cash losses if a ship fell into enemy hands. Thus, in June 1779, while his ship was anchored in Ponthieu, France, captain Ajeo received word from the Bilbao merchant Luis Viollet that English privateers were allegedly cruising off the French coast. As a result, Viollet asked Ajeo to find a reliable local merchant to draw a bill of exchange on Paris or Bordeaux. 'The bill of exchange', stressed Viollet, 'has to be drawn up by someone very dependable and entirely satisfactory.'[43]

Although captains had much of the requisite knowledge, there was still a social gap between them and many of the merchants. This can be inferred from shareholding patterns and from letters that passed between captains and merchants/shipowners. In 1778 captain Artamóniz owned one-quarter of *Nuestra Señora del Carmen*, while San Sebastián merchant Juan Bousignac owned three-quarters. The imbalance not only gave greater authority to Bousignac but also reflected a patron-client relationship. In December 1778 Bousignac's correspondent in Nantes informed him that, instead of following his advice and proceeding to Bordeaux, captain Artamóniz had gone to Brest, which was in the opposite direction. Manifestly upset by the news, Bousignac wrote to Artamóniz on New Year's Day 1779 in strong language questioning the captain's integrity. Artamóniz, who received two copies of the letter through Bousignac's correspondents, replied that the complaint was unfounded and that he had written to San Sebastián and Bayonne explaining the decision to go to Brest. 'You should know', he emphasised, 'that I have never been a cheat nor do I intend to be one.'[44] According to his own account, Artamóniz had left Nantes with every intention of going

---

[41] In fact, his ship never reached America; it was captured by the British fleet near Baltimore on 29 October 1778. An identical plan had been intended by the Bilbao ship *El Begoña* (170 tons) a few months earlier: *El Begoña* (1778), HCA 32/282/13–14.
[42] Thomas Rexford to Juan Bautista Sarría, Manchester, 26 Dec. 1777, HCA 32/414/5, fo. 86.
[43] Luis Viollet to Juan Bautista Ajeo, Bilbao, 2 June 1779, HCA 32/412/7, fo. 70.
[44] Artamóniz to Juan Bousignac, Brest, 19 Feb. 1779, HCA 32/414/3, fo. 26.

to Bordeaux but had changed course due to contrary winds. It was only after he had returned to Nantes that he was offered a cargo for Brest, '[s]o it seems to me that I have not deceived you', he pleaded in his defence.

Trust was a *sine qua non* between merchants and their captains, but it was based on a vertical relationship. Trust existed not only between equals but also within social hierarchies, something that Artamóniz appreciated only too well when he replied to Bousignac's complaints:

> Until now I have been a prudent and trustworthy man, and I hope to be so from now on. But I can see that you do not trust me, and I would never have imagined you would tell me such things ... But, as I understand, your anger is a signal that you want to expel me from your house, and I am confused because you are like a father to me, because you have done many favours for me, that not even my relatives would have done.[45]

Artamóniz was a captain with over twenty years of experience, yet Bousignac assisted and protected him like a father; in return, he wanted a prudent and trustworthy captain.

Despite their impressive knowledge and all the services they could render, ship captains had limitations as overseas agents. They could fulfil certain commercial functions if the goods were ready at dockside, but not otherwise. Captains seldom spent enough time in a particular port to carry out the time-consuming tasks that a resident agent could perform. The importance of having a resident agent overseas to cooperate with ship captains can be clearly seen in the account books of the London merchants John Richards and his nephew John Rooke (1716–36).[46] They recorded the names of both the captains and the ships that carried the wool from Bilbao to London, and sometimes even the name of the shipowner. Captain Cosme de Umaran, for instance, commanded Diego de Allende Salazar's *Nuestra Señora de Begoña*, and captain Nicolás del Barco was in charge of Miguel Antonio de Jussué's *San Joseph*. The Basque captains Umaran, del Barco, Menchaca, Revilla, Llosa and Escarza, all of them repeatedly mentioned in Richards's accounts, were a continuous channel of communication between the merchant in Bilbao and Richards, and could, therefore, monitor Richards's (and other agents') performance. However, there were two crucial tasks with regard to the wool/cloth trade that only resident agents such as Richards could perform. Firstly, he dealt face-to-face with the English cloth purveyors, and sold the Bilbao merchants' wool in London, allowing the buyers to pay in between three and six months;[47] and, secondly, he arranged in the coffee houses for marine

---

[45] Ibid.
[46] LGL, MSS 19017/1, 19017/2.
[47] For example, the fifty-nine sacks of wool sold to Wallington and Smith on 21 May 1716 were to be paid in three months, and the twenty-seven sold to John Greenhill on the same day in six months: ibid. p. 55.

insurance for the Bilbao ships.[48] In addition, Richards assisted the captains themselves. In June 1721, for example, Richards got some carpenters, rope makers and blacksmiths to repair Cosme de Umaran's ship.[49] He also lent cash to the captains – cash which was charged in the shipowner's account current – and even paid salaries to the crews.[50]

Not only were certain tasks time-consuming but there was also the matter of proficiency in foreign languages. Virtually all the intercepted correspondence belonging to Basque and other Spanish captains during the eighteenth century was written in Spanish, with only a couple of letters in French. With conversational skills in French, Dutch and English, a captain could manage to gather information and to sell a bulk cargo of iron, salt or oranges, but he would be hard-pressed to perform other important functions that only a resident merchant could offer.

Ship captains and crews

In the perilous maritime world, trust was not merely restricted to captains and merchants; it also extended from captains to crews. Ordinary seamen were renowned for their nautical skills in the treacherous Bay of Biscay, where sudden storms made for notoriously dangerous sailing. In Vizcaya, it was the Bilbao *consulado* that granted certificates of captaincy for merchant vessels. It also specified how much formal education captains required. Candidates had to provide certificates signed by known captains testifying that they had at least six years of experience at sea (four as mariner and two as pilot). After that, candidates had to pass an examination.[51] It was therefore vital for a captain to have quite a high degree of literacy and numeracy. Interestingly enough, Basque captains always commanded the merchant ships of Bilbao and San Sebastián.[52] Of the twenty-four Basque ships of less than 100 tons captured by the British between 1778 and 1782, their captains came mostly from the coastal villages of Vizcaya. Fourteen of the twenty-four captains (58.3 per cent) were from Plencia and the adjacent villages of Barrica, Górliz and Lemóniz; six were from Bilbao (25 per cent) and its immediate surroundings (Deusto, Abando and Olabeaga); and the remaining four were from Bermeo and San Sebastián (16.7 per cent). By contrast, of the twenty-four known shipowners (excluding captains), thirteen resided in Bilbao (54.1 per

---

[48] For example, on 4 February 1717 he agreed an insurance policy with seven underwriters for the value of £700 sterling. The ship insured was the *San Francisco*, captain Cosme Umaran, which set sail from London to Bilbao by order and on account of Martín de Jussué. The premium was 1.25%, and Richards' commission 0.5%: ibid. p. 30.
[49] Ibid. p. 269.
[50] For example, in September 1719 he paid captain Pedro Escarza and his crew their salaries: ibid. p. 189.
[51] [Bilbao *consulado*], *Ordenanzas ... de 1737*, ch. xxiv, arts ii to iv, 222–3.
[52] Aingeru Zabala, 'Notas sobre el cabotaje vasco en el siglo XVIII', *Ernaroa* i (1985), 112.

cent) and six in San Sebastián (25 per cent).⁵³ There was a similar pattern for ships greater than 100 tons, although there were fewer captains from Plencia and more from Santurce, Portugalete and Somorrostro, villages downstream from Bilbao on the Nervión River. Vessel ownership was almost entirely in the hands of Bilbao and San Sebastián merchants: of the nineteen shipowners (excluding a captain and his supercargo), thirteen were from Bilbao (68.4 per cent) and six from San Sebastián (31.5 per cent). Interestingly, three captains had moved from their birthplaces (Barrica, Somorrostro and Santurce) to Abando and Olabeaga, which were closer to Bilbao.⁵⁴

The repetition of Basque surnames among the captains suggests that certain families (probably somewhat wealthier than their neighbours) were specialising in ship captaincy. In the small town of Plencia in the late 1760s, three captains bore the surname Andraca, four Ajeo, four Artamóniz and six Arrarte.⁵⁵ Other captains, such as Villabaso and Sarachaga, were members of well-known Bilbao merchant families. Given the level of trust required of captains, the owners' frequent employment of sons, brothers, nephews or cousins is not surprising: '[n]epotism was by no means a wholly discreditable and absurd practice'.⁵⁶

In addition to captains, the merchant marine required cooks, pilots, surgeons, carpenters and ordinary seamen. According to the Bilbao *consulado*'s 1737 Ordinances, it was the captain's duty to choose the necessary number of officers and mariners. If the ship was moored in the owner's home port, then the captain had also to agree the choice of the crew with the ship's other owners.⁵⁷ According to most mariners' testimonies at the HCA, however, it was captains who were responsible for most of the hiring. As the pilot Juan Antonio de Arriaga declared in 1780, 'the said seamen or mariners were shipped or hired by the said master, Atanasio Sertucha; and the said master (as he believes) was hired by the said don Juan Bousignac', the shipowner.⁵⁸

Coastal villages such as Santurce, Portugalete and Plencia in Vizcaya; Pasajes and Fuenterrabia in Guipúzcoa; and Hendaye and Biarritz in Labourd (in the French Basque Country) were essential labour sources for the merchant vessels of Bilbao, San Sebastián and Bayonne. In the province of Guipúzcoa, the Royal Guipuzcoan Company of Caracas (which traded with Venezuela via Cádiz) had an enormous impact. In its lifetime (1728–82) this chartered company had sixty-two ships (up to nine working every year), seventeen of

---

⁵³ Lamikiz, 'Basque ship captains', 106–9.
⁵⁴ Ibid.
⁵⁵ Guiard, *Historia del Consulado*, ii. 448–64.
⁵⁶ Davis, *Rise of the English shipping industry*, 159.
⁵⁷ [Bilbao *consulado*], *Ordenanzas ... de 1737*, ch. xxiv, art. xi, 225–6.
⁵⁸ *Nuestra Señora de la Antigua* (1780), HCA 32/412/4, fo. 5.

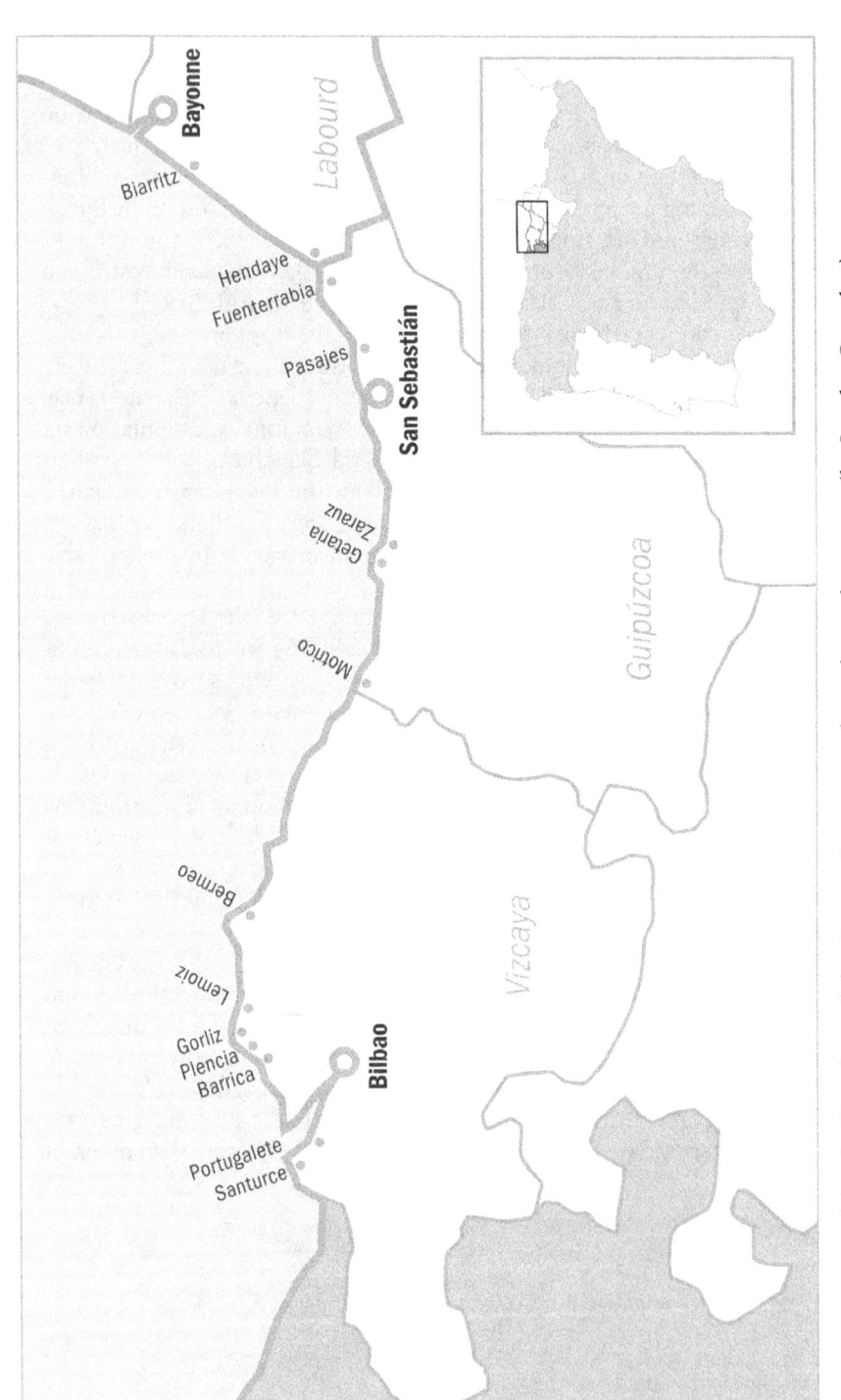

Map 2. Coastline of the Basque Country in the eighteenth century (by Lander Gurtubai)

which were of over 500 tons.[59] In 1754 one priest, Manuel de Larramendi, noted that virtually all mariners of the company were from the province and that as a result the coastal villages lacked people to fish.[60] In 1764 there were 800 people waiting to be employed by the company, although not all as mariners. In those instances where the names and geographical origin of crews are recorded, they are all from Guipúzcoa, particularly from San Sebastián, Pasajes, Rentería and Fuenterrabia.[61] The employment of the *guipuzcoano* seamen in the Company of Caracas might be partly the reason why the majority of small Basque ships captured by the British were from Vizcaya.

Vizcaya's population was similar to that of Guipúzcoa (around 100,000 in the mid-eighteenth century), but since Vizcaya had no chartered company, most of its mariners were employed either in the merchant marine of Bilbao or in the small vessels of the coastal trade. The only document that provides specific data relating to the seamen of Vizcaya is a list made in 1794, according to which Vizcaya had 1,005 mariners (including fishermen), constituting 4 per cent of its adult male population.[62] Although the exact number of mariners is difficult to establish, a crude estimate can be offered for the period 1765–70. It is known that, for the small ships captured by the British during the American Revolution, there was a ratio of one crewman for every 9.4 tons.[63] If the same ratio is applied to the 317 Vizcayan merchant vessels of 1765–70 for which tonnage figures exist (these ranged from ten to 110 tons), the result is a figure of 1,280 seamen, or 5 per cent of the entire male population. Although this estimate must be used with some caution, it is likely to be closer to the minimum than the maximum. It is also probable that some of those ships were seasonally engaged in fishing.

Historians of the Dutch, English, Irish and North American merchant marines have pointed to the likelihood of crews being recruited from the same regions as their captains.[64] Although the Basque case appears to reflect

---

[59] Montserrat Garate Ojanguren, *La Real Compañía Guipuzcoana de Caracas*, San Sebastián 1990, 128–30.
[60] Manuel Larramendi, *Corografía de la muy noble y muy leal provincia de Guipúzcoa* [1756] (Barcelona 1882), Buenos Aires 1950, 214.
[61] Garate, *Real Compañía*, 198–218; José Garmendia Arruebarrena, 'La Compañía de Caracas y familias donostiarras (1784–1798)', *Boletín de Estudios Históricos sobre San Sebastián* xxi (1987), 517–40.
[62] Fernández de Pinedo, *Crecimiento*, 381.
[63] According to the sources in the HCA, the number of mariners in larger ships appears to have varied more substantially. In order to make ships both navigable and profitable, the 1737 Ordinances advised that each ship should have 'the necessary number of them': [Bilbao *consulado*], *Ordenanzas ... de 1737*, ch. xxiv, art. xi, 225. For the Vizcayan merchant vessels in 1765–70 see Guiard, *Historia del Consulado*, ii. 448–64.
[64] Ville, *English shipowning*, 92–3; John Mannion, 'Waterford and the south of England: spatial patterns in shipping commerce, 1766–1777', *IJMH* vi/2 (1994), 130; Paul C. van Royen, 'Manning the merchant marine: the Dutch maritime labour market about 1700', *IJMH* i/1 (1989), 14–17; Murielle Bouyer, 'L'Aire de recrutement des gens de mer, par le commerce nantais au XVIIIe siècle', in G. Saupin (ed.), *Le Pouvoir urbain dans l'Europe*

this broader tendency, the fact remains that very little is known about mariners' geographical origins or about relationships between captains and crews, or between crews and their families in the Basque Country and elsewhere. This unmapped territory of social history can nevertheless be explored by using material in the HCA collection, which tends to support the assumption that Spanish Basque ship captains recruited their crews locally. Take the example of captain Juan Angel de Múzquiz, who in 1782 commanded *La Amable Josefa* (230 tons): Múzquiz and all of his sixteen shipmates came from Santurce or its environs.[65] A similar picture emerges for the French Basque Country. The 110-ton *Saint Nicholas* of Hendaye, captured in November 1743 *en route* to the Cape Verde Islands, yielded papers showing the crewmen's names, ages and hometowns. Apart from the surgeon and the son of a Béarn merchant, the other nine mariners were all from Hendaye.[66]

There are three main reasons why Basque merchant vessels tended to be manned by local mariners. First, Bilbao's merchant fleet was not large enough to exhaust the local supply of seamen. In fact, many other Basque seamen found employment in Cádiz's colonial trade and in the Spanish navy. Secondly, the Basque language also played a part. While it was essential for captains to speak Spanish, this did not apply to crews, most of whom spoke only Basque. Although the use of written Basque was extremely rare in the eighteenth century, there is no doubt that Basques spoke their mother tongue; indeed, when outside the Basque Country they defined themselves as *nación bascongada*, or 'nation of Basque speakers'.[67] The Bilbao *consulado* distinguished between *los puertos del Romance* (the ports of the Spanish language) and *los puertos Bascongados* (the ports where Basque or euskera is spoken).[68] The line between the two was the Nervión river and Bilbao itself. The population along the west coast (Portugalete, Santurce) was Spanish-speaking, whereas the east coastline as far as Bayonne (including Plencia, Bermeo, San Sebastián, Hendaye and Biarritz) was the territory of the Basque language. In November 1778 the Oviedo merchant Bernardo de Llanos offered captain José de Zaldumbide a competent Asturian pilot for his ship. 'After some consideration,' he specified days later, 'I presume you would be happier with a *paisano* [countryman] than with a stranger.'[69] Captain Zaldumbide and his five shipmates were all from Plencia, where most people only spoke Basque. Indeed cases like that of the mariner Juan de Suxeda (from Mallorca), who moved to Bilbao in 1777 (four years before his

atlantique du XVIe au XVIIIe siècle, Nantes 2000, 172; Daniel Vickers and Vince Walsh, *Young men and the sea: Yankee seafarers in the age of sail*, New Haven 2005.
65 *La Amable Josefa* (1782), HCA 32/266/15, fo. 19.
66 *Saint Nicholas* (1743), HCA 32/138 (2), fo. 9.
67 For examples of written Basque in the correspondence belonging to eighteenth-century colonial traders see p. 124 below.
68 Allende to Mendieta, Bilbao, 21 June 1751, AFB, Consulado 539, fo. 398r.
69 Bernardo Llanos to José Zaldumbide, Oviedo, 27 Nov. 1778, HCA 32/414/6, fo. 26.

ship was captured by the British), were very uncommon.[70] No doubt a shared language gave cohesion to the crew and improved efficiency by facilitating fast and easy communication.

The third reason why Basque ships were manned by local mariners was their common geographical origin, an additional source of unity for the crew and a tendency seen elsewhere in Europe. In a navy, the chain of command is the surest guarantee of cohesion aboard ship. This was also true for Basque (and other) merchant ships, but there was more to it than that. Pierre Vilar argues that on Catalan merchant ships the captain was similar to a gild master, and the crew were like journeymen and apprentices, thus establishing a type of patriarchal authority founded on familiarity.[71] The relationship between captain and crew on Basque ships was much the same, although familiarity occasionally caused economic inefficiencies. For example, in October 1775 Luis Viollet wrote to captain Ajeo that he was 'surprised that your crew have not wanted to follow you to Hamburg. You would not have regretted it, for [in Hamburg] you would have found a good freight for the return. This will teach you to find appropriate mariners in the future'.[72] On the whole, however, familiarity – based on common geographic origins – tended to promote cohesion. Thus, in August 1777, Magdalena de Zinza complained to her husband, captain Juan Bautista de Sarría, who was then in Liverpool, that '[y]ou have remembered everything in your letter except for saying something about your cousin and the rest of the shipmates; you know that I have to inform their families every time I receive a letter from you, so next time tell me how they are'.[73]

Since most captains were married, the communication system extended from the captain to his wife and, through her, to the mariners' families. Literate wives could relay written information verbally to the men's families, many of whom were doubtless illiterate (mariners frequently signed a simple cross at the end of their sworn testimonies before the HCA). No less important, captains' wives also funnelled advance payments to the men's families. In October 1778, for instance, María de Arambalza reported to her husband, captain Artamóniz, that she had given 'eight reales to Josefa de la Rentería, your shipmate Josepe's wife, so do not tell him anything until payday, and do not show this letter to him till then'.[74] Since most shipowners and ships' husbands resided in Bilbao or San Sebastián, they had little direct contact with mariners' families in the coastal villages. It was the captains' wives who kept crews and families in touch.

Captains' communication networks also included other captains and crews, all of whom invariably originated from the same stretch of coast.

---

[70] *Nuestra Señora de los Remedios* (1781), HCA 32/415/11.
[71] Vilar, *Catalunya*, iv. 349.
[72] Viollet to Ajeo, Bilbao, 2 Oct. 1775, HCA 32/412/7, fo. 96.
[73] Magdalena Zinza to Sarría, San Sebastián, 8 Aug. 1777, HCA 32/414/5, fo. 76.
[74] María Arambalza to Artamóniz, Plencia, 18 Oct. 1778, HCA 32/414/3, fo. 27.

Captains were, in a sense, the seagoing postmasters of the eighteenth century. In January 1775, while his ship was moored on the Thames, captain Juan Bautista de Sarría received a letter from his wife indicating that she had received his letters through captain Pedro de Ormaza, 'who has given us the little packet with socks and shoes, and I have complimented him as you ordered in your letter'.[75] Captain Sarría's papers also contained petitions from mariners' wives who were trying to locate their husbands. María Ignacia de Miner's husband was known to have sailed from Hamburg to Málaga with captain Antonio de Murrieta, and she therefore begged captain Sarría for advice as to where she might find him.[76]

Captains were a conduit of information for shipowners, merchants (local and foreign), other captains and crews and their families. To know a captain was a convenience for any merchant, and familiarity was heightened if merchants also functioned as shipowners, which often made them partners with captains. Because captains had such extensive networks, knowing even one captain gave access to many. Thus, the merchant Luis Viollet ordered captain Ajeo on 11 October 1777 to send money from his freights 'with some known captain of yours'.[77] As Viollet well knew, Ajeo was more than likely to be able to find such a captain. A week later Viollet wrote again to Ajeo:

> Captain Antuñiano, who arrived here from Santander the day before yesterday, has told me that you carried a cargo to Santander last Wednesday; so you could have written to me or at least sent me the money with the said captain. You could also have done it with captain Villabaso who came from Havana and stopped there on its way to Bilbao. I hope that you will not miss the opportunity of sending it to me with [captain] Juan Bautista de Sarachaga. ... I have also sent you a letter with captain Arambalza.[78]

It is well worth noting that the four captains mentioned in the preceding quote – Antuñiano, Villabaso, Sarachaga and Arambalza – were all from Vizcaya, and that the last three possessed distinctly Basque surnames. The common geographical origins of captains and crews provided the merchants of Bilbao with multiple sources of information, thus engendering trust and minimising the risk of cheating.

Amongst the records of the HCA are papers belonging to other Spanish masters, which suggest that their experiences and circumstances were very similar. What makes the Basque Country different within Spain is that no Spanish region (perhaps with the exception of Catalonia) had as many local seamen involved in the merchant marine. It is no coincidence that in 1740 Bilbao became the first Spanish port to have a school of pilots for merchant

---

[75] Zinza to Sarría, San Sebastián, 9 Jan. 1775, HCA 32/414/5, fo. 80.
[76] María Ignacia Miner to Sarría, San Sebastián, 30 Apr. 1776, ibid. fo. 75.
[77] Viollet to Ajeo, Bilbao, 11 Oct.1777, HCA 32/412/7, fo. 84.
[78] Viollet to Ajeo, Bilbao, 17 Oct. 1777, ibid. fo. 95.

vessels (the next school would be founded in Barcelona thirty years later).[79] Any merchant intending to hire a Spanish captain in the Atlantic coast of Spain knew that Bilbao was the most appropriate port to do it. 'I shall not be able to get a Spanish master at any other place', noted from Bilbao the English merchant Antony Gibbs in November 1788.[80] Furthermore, the small ships of Bilbao and the Basque coast were 'almost the only Spanish ships ever to appear in English harbours in peacetime'.[81]

The peculiar system of recruitment for the Spanish navy in Vizcaya and Guipúzcoa (a direct consequence of the *fueros*) also gave the Basques certain advantage over other Spanish mariners, though the Basques were not excluded from service in the navy, and indeed, the Spanish Armada relied heavily on them throughout the entire early modern period.[82] The difference lay in the system of recruitment. In Vizcaya and Guipúzcoa mariners were recruited by each provincial government with the assistance of the numerous *cofradías de mareantes* (brotherhoods of seamen). Both provinces were compelled to provide a certain number of seamen. Mariners were first asked to join the navy voluntarily and then, if the number of volunteers turned out to be insufficient, a ballot was made to meet the allocated figure. The Spanish government had no direct power over any Basque mariner, and was not even allowed to know their names.

By contrast, in the rest of Spain (with the exception of the village of Castro Urdiales in Cantabria, where the system was similar to their Basque neighbours) recruitment was conducted by resorting to the *matrícula de mar* (a census of all mariners), which was greatly reinforced after 1748. Outside of the Basque regions, mariners were divided into four *cuadrillas* (groups) by the *matrícula de mar*. One *cuadrilla* would be recruited every year, and the mariners listed in the next were not allowed to leave their residence for long periods which meant that Spanish mariners could only be employed on a merchant ship every two years. It is highly doubtful that a different recruitment policy would have improved the quality of the Spanish merchant marine,[83] but the system did not help to foster it. The three Spanish naval departments (Cádiz, Ferrol and Cartagena) listed 24,312 mariners in 1754–9, 31,637 in 1765 and 51,381 in 1786. Considering that 42,000 seamen were required to crew the Spanish navy in the second half of the century, the immediate consequence

---

[79] See Itsaso Ibañez and José Llombart, 'La formación de pilotos en la Naútica de Bilbao, siglos XVIII y XIX', *Itsas Memoria* iii (2000), 747–72.

[80] Antony Gibbs to Dolly Gibbs, Bilbao, 9 Nov. 1788, LGL, MS 11021/3, fo. 135.

[81] Davis, *Rise of the English shipping industry*, 233. Apart from the Basques, at the HCA there are indeed few examples of Spanish ships going to northern Europe. One exception was that of the Catalan captain Pedro Jaime Rabassa, which was captured on its way to London: *Santa Rosalía* (1779), HCA 32/443/10.

[82] Angel O'Dogherty, 'La matrícula de mar en el reinado de Carlos III', AEA ix (1952), 347–9. See also José Manuel Vázquez Lijó, *La matrícula de mar en la España del siglo XVIII: registro, inspección y evolución de las clases de marinería y maestranza*, Madrid 2007.

[83] O'Dogherty, 'La matrícula de mar', 369.

was unsurprising.[84] In a country so severely lacking seamen, and in which the navy was always given priority, it was practically impossible to have both a strong navy and a large merchant fleet. No wonder that repeated royal decrees aimed at securing the Spanish origin of the crews in the merchant marine (particularly in colonial trade) never achieved their goal.

When in 1763 the members of the Bilbao *consulado* appealed to the crown to end the support given to the northern Spanish town of Santander, they stressed that they had built ships and employed a large number of Basque mariners. To take the wool trade away from Bilbao, therefore, meant undermining the only Spanish merchant fleet that competed with foreign ships – or rather, it meant leaving the wool trade entirely in foreign hands.[85] It is revealing that the merchants of Bilbao saw their fates as being inextricably linked to those of their captains and crews. They knew that their increasing participation in the trade with northern Europe and the north Atlantic had been possible thanks to a substantial supply of local captains and crews.

It seems clear that the reason why *bilbaínos* increased their participation in international trade was intimately connected to issues of trust. The Bilbao *consulado* actively improved its reliability and the education of its members, but, crucially, their efforts were accompanied by cultural factors such as the *fueros* and the Basque seafaring tradition that contributed enormously to the fostering of relationships of trust. In many ways their experience was unique and hardly comparable to that of most Spaniards. Nevertheless, the need for trustworthy connections was of paramount importance for any merchant involved in any type of trade, and especially for those who attempted to trade with places that were a few months away. Extreme distances posed a unique challenge that tested merchants' ability to build and to maintain robust relationships of trust. Nowhere was that more clear than in the colonial trade between Spain and the Pacific shores of viceroyal Peru, although this time it was the Spaniards who were at an advantage rather than the foreigners.

---

[84] Ibid. 358. According to Vázquez Lijó there were 38,967 mariners listed in 1754–9, 45,418 in 1764–5, 54,971 in 1785–7 and 47,285 in 1800: *La matrícula de mar*, 554.
[85] Bilbao *consulado*'s petition to the king, Bilbao, 28 Sept. 1763, AFB, Consulado 549, fo. 31v.

PART II

COLONIAL TRADERS: CÁDIZ AND PERU

3

Trading with Peru

The Spanish colonial trade operated under many more regulations and restrictions than that of Bilbao, but unlike the *bilbaínos* their merchants had to cope with the risks involved in trading with places three to six months away. Naturally this tested their ability to establish the trustworthiness of their correspondents, something that turned out to be highly problematic. Following the conquest of American territories in the sixteenth century, the Spanish crown handed over all commercial exchanges with the colonies to a community of individual merchants. Although in the eighteenth century some chartered companies were created to trade with certain areas (especially Venezuela, Havana and the Philippines), essentially Spain's trade with its colonies remained an individual endeavour. Uncertainties and risks arising from this long-distance trade were reduced by allowing a sole Spanish port to trade with America, and by organising the exchanges by means of periodical fleets. However, the eighteenth century saw the demise of this arrangement and the arrival of the so-called Bourbon reforms, which in turn brought about new challenges for the merchants on both sides of the Atlantic.

It was in the trade with Peru that the changes were most profound. Between 1717 and 1821 (the year of Peru's independence) trade was for the most part conducted by merchants established in Cádiz and Lima. In 1680 Cádiz became the official port for dispatching fleets to America, and in 1717 it was the administrative centre of the colonial trade, attracting merchants from all over Spain and Europe as well as mariners, bureaucrats, solicitors, priests, shopkeepers and many other professionals. As a result its population jumped from 23,000 in 1700 to 70,000 at the end of the century.[1] In the second half of the eighteenth century Cádiz had between 400 and 600 overseas merchants (*comerciantes al por mayor*), of whom around 40 per cent were foreigners.[2] Located on the Pacific coast, Lima was the second largest city in Spanish America after Mexico City. Its population rose from 37,000 in 1700 to 52,000 in 1790,[3] and at any given time it had around 200 merchants.

Until 1739 the commercial route that linked Cádiz with Lima went through the isthmus of Panama, but in the 1740s a new, more direct route was adopted via Cape Horn that compelled merchants to build up trans-

---

[1] De Vries, *European urbanization*, 277.
[2] García-Baquero, *Cádiz*, i. 462–5; Bustos, *Comerciantes*, 94–5; Fernández, *Rostro*, 10–1.
[3] María Pérez Cantó, *Lima en el siglo XVIII: estudio socioeconómico*, Madrid 1985, 43–71.

atlantic networks as never before. This chapter explores the difficulties in carrying out commercial exchanges over such a long distance and how those difficulties affected the building up of interpersonal trust. It also sets the scene by providing a diachronic view of merchants' experience of trading with Peru.

The *galeones* and the Portobelo fair

The history of Peru as a Spanish colony began in 1532 when Francisco Pizarro's conquering expedition captured the Inca emperor Atahualpa at Cajamarca. Within two years both the Inca capital of Cuzco and the important city of Quito were taken, and soon after, in 1535, the Spaniards founded their capital at Lima on the coast. In the years to come Peru and its capital were to attract large numbers of Spanish immigrants. The reason was simple: in the words of one observer, writing from Santo Domingo (in the Caribbean) in 1537, news had arrived from Peru about 'many millions of gold and silver, and ships loaded only of those metals'.[4] A succession of wars and rebellions followed the conquest, and would continue until the late 1550s. Despite the continuous turmoil and political chaos, important social and economic trends took shape during those years, and several social groups – including merchants – were able rapidly to establish themselves.[5]

Naturally the question of how to trade with the capital of the newly-created viceroyalties of Peru (which at the time constituted the entirety of Spanish South America) and New Spain (Central America and modern Mexico, which had been conquered by Hernán Cortés in the 1520s) became crucial for the Spanish crown. The creation in 1503 of the *Casa de la Contratación* (the House of Trade, which supervised the American trade for the crown) in Seville had been the first step towards putting colonial trade on an organised footing. Immediately afterwards 'regulations and restrictions upon ships, passengers and cargoes were to increase at an extraordinary rate'.[6] A system of fleets was soon regarded as the safest means of trading with both viceroyalties as they offered more protection than single ships and gave merchants the opportunity to diversify risks by loading their goods in several vessels. Of greater importance to the crown, however, was the fact that the fleet system made taxation a lot easier. It was that same motivation that prompted the crown to appoint Seville as the sole Spanish port allowed to send ships to America. As for the regularity with which the fleets should depart, a system was eventually established in the years 1564–6 that would remain in place

---

[4] Gonzalo Fernández de Oviedo to the king, Santo Domingo, 31 May 1537, in Raúl Porras Barrenechea (ed.), *Cartas del Perú, 1524–1543*, Lima 1959, 242.
[5] James M. Lockhart, *Spanish Peru, 1532–1560: a colonial society*, Madison 1968, 6.
[6] Clarence H. Haring, *Trade and navigation between Spain and the Indies in the time of the Hapsburgs*, Cambridge, MA 1918, 5.

until the eighteenth century: two separate fleets would leave for the colonies every year, one for each viceroyalty. In May the *flota* would set sail for New Spain, and in August the *galeones* (galleons) would depart for Tierra Firme, that is, the north coast of South America and the isthmus of Panama. Both fleets would winter in the Indies, then rendezvous at Havana and return together to Spain in March. This theoretical schedule was, however, only rarely adhered to.

The trade with New Spain was straightforward compared with the challenge posed by Peru, because the very inaccessibility and remoteness that made South America's Pacific coast so easy to defend was a liability when it came to establishing trade and communication. Thus, except for occasional single ships to Buenos Aires, all goods shipped to South America were required to travel via Panama, which effectively became the distribution centre for the Central and South American areas. In the sixteenth century, merchants and agents were positioned at the three key points on the long route to Peru, namely Seville, Panama and Lima. Usually the senior partner was established in Seville and the junior (whether partner or factor, often a ship captain) in the Indies.[7] The rapidly growing local economy, however, made it very complicated for this structure to survive successfully. In this respect, Daviken Studnicki-Gizbert's remarks on the commercial networks that linked Spain with New Spain from the sixteenth century onwards also apply to the trade between Spain and Peru: 'with the lines of communication stretched as thin as they were, there was relatively little a given [Sevillian] trading house could do to guarantee the loyalty or performance of their employees'.[8]

Both the difficulties for the Seville merchants in ensuring the loyalty of their agents in Peru and the growing Peruvian merchant community contributed significantly to the creation of two geographical areas of influence. Around 1575 an annual fair was established in the isthmus of Panama at Nombre de Dios to facilitate transactions. In 1597 the fair was moved to Portobelo, where it would remain until the 1730s. The fair was the result of a tacit agreement between the emerging Peruvian merchant community and the Seville *consulado* (founded in 1543). It was understood that neither the Sevillians nor the Peruvians would go beyond Portobelo. This division was accentuated by the creation in 1613 of the Lima *consulado* (twenty-one years after its Mexico City counterpart).[9] On the one hand the great increase in the amount of business conducted in Peru demanded a mercantile court to deal more efficiently with commercial disputes and bankruptcies; on the other the Lima *consulado* was created in order to to obtain reliable informa-

---

[7] Enrique Otte, 'Los mercaderes transatlánticos bajo Carlos v', AEA xlvii (1990), 95–121.
[8] Daviken Studnicki-Gizbert, 'From agents to *consulado*: commercial networks in colonial Mexico, 1520–1590 and beyond', AEA lvii (2000), 49.
[9] Rodríguez, *Tribunal*, 19–24.

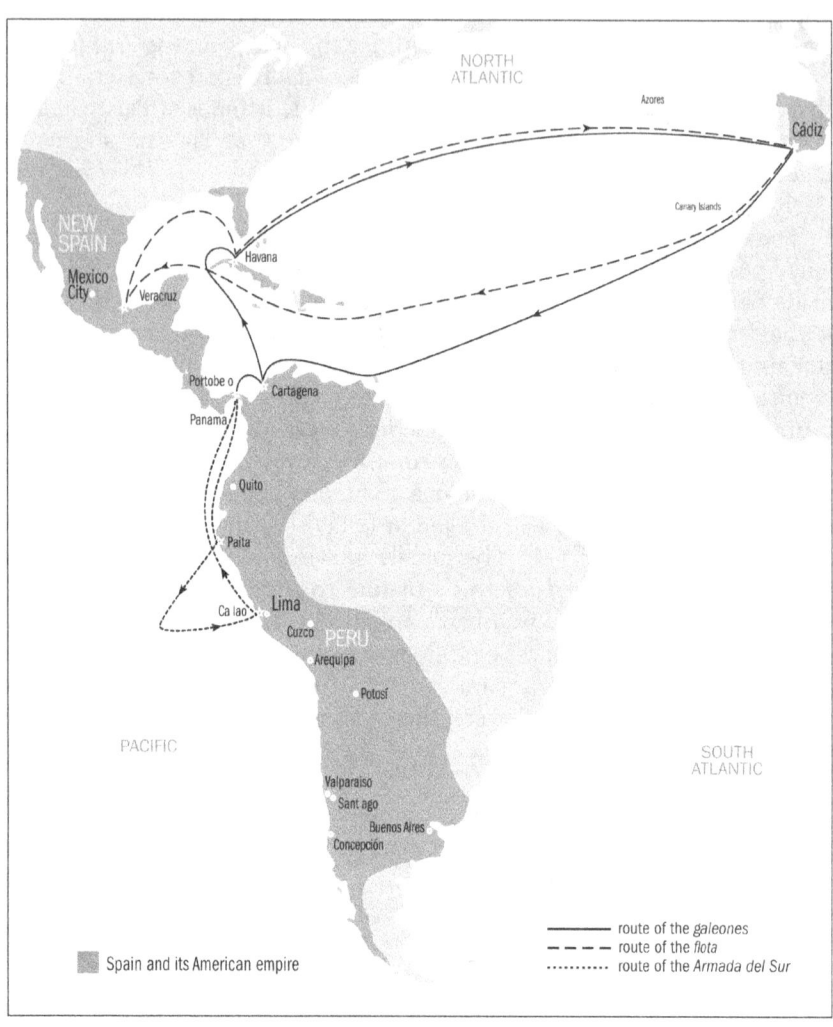

Map 3. Major trading routes between Spain and America before 1739
(by Lander Gurtubai)

tion about prices directly and officially from Spain, thus avoiding the extortionate prices that some Spanish factors were inclined to ask.[10]

Attending the isthmian fair was as awkward for the Lima merchant as it was hazardous for the Sevillian to cross the Atlantic. Another annual fleet, the so-called *Armada del Mar del Sur*, left Callao (Lima's seaport) for Panama to meet the galleons in September.[11] Thanks to the favourable Humboldt stream, navigation along the Pacific coast to Panama used to take about a month, but crossing the isthmus up the river Chagras to Portobelo was rough, perhaps taking another two weeks, and the return to Lima after the fair was even worse, as the Humboldt stream was now against the ships and they had to head towards open sea in order to avoid the current. It could take the *Armada del Sur* up to three months to get back to Callao. To make things worse, the isthmus was a dangerously unhealthy place: there were years when hundreds of mariners, soldiers and merchants died of fevers. For this reason the galleons always called first at Cartagena de Indias (in modern Colombia) instead of going straight to Portobelo. Only when it was known that the *Armada del Sur* had reached Panama did the galleons head west to the harbour of Portobelo.

At first the fair was supposed to last a fortnight, but in reality its duration depended on the amount of time it took for transactions to be completed successfully. In 1685, for instance, it lasted thirty days. The last Portobelo fair, in 1731, would last forty days.[12] There was little change in the goods traded over the centuries. In exchange for European commodities, large quantities of gold and silver were carried to Spain, especially after silver production began to expand rapidly in the 1550s in the seemingly inexhaustible mines of Potosí (in modern Bolivia). Before the opening of the fair, officials and representatives of the Spanish and Peruvian merchants met in order to fix prices for the various classes of merchandise carried by the galleons, the single largest item being fabrics such as linens, woollens, damask, canvas and sail cloth. The prices were then publicly announced, along with a statement of the merchandise carried by the fleet, and each merchant was expected to comply with them.[13] By fixing prices and reducing the distance and frequency of exchanges, the fleet/fair system made trade between Spain and Peru much less risky than it would have been otherwise.

The fleet/fair system also allowed the wealthy members of the Lima *consulado* to exercise control over the American end of the trade with Peru.[14]

---

[10] Ibid. 29.
[11] Emilio Pérez-Mallaina and Bibiano Torres, *La Armada del Mar del Sur*, Seville 1987, 189–202.
[12] Allyn C. Loosley, 'The Puerto Bello fairs', *HAHR* xiii (1933), 318.
[13] Ibid. 322, 329; Gervasio Artiñano y Galdacano, *Historia del comercio con las Indias durante el dominio de los Austrias*, Barcelona 1917, 140–1.
[14] Both the fair attendance figures and the following discussion on the Portobelo fair are taken from George R. Dilg, 'The collapse of the Portobelo fairs: a study in Spanish commercial reform, 1720–1740', unpubl. PhD diss. Indiana 1975, 12–15, appendix c.

In 1726 only sixty-two of the 180 colony-based merchants attending the fair at Portobelo were members of the Lima *consulado*, but in 1731 they were forty-six out of 117. However, despite the presence of a significant number of non-*consulado* merchants, the fleet/fair system strongly favoured the *limeños*. They had the power to negotiate prices with the *galeonistas* (the Spanish merchant travelling in the galleons), and could therefore influence the direction of trade. Merchants outside the corporation could freely attend the fair but had to comply with the rules and prices determined by the members of the *consulado*. Furthermore, the *limeños* were wealthier than the other American merchants – they consituted only 36 per cent of all the merchants attending the fairs of 1726 and 1731, but possessed more than 60 per cent of the wealth brought to the isthmus. And even among them, a few merchants such as Juan Antonio Tagle Bracho, Isidro Gutiérrez Cosío and Martín de Zelayeta stood out in terms of wealth. It was not only that purchasing a large quantity of goods at the fair compensated for the high costs involved in travelling to the isthmus; equally important was the fact that *galeonistas* preferred to sell their goods in bulk in their haste to return in the fleet. Hence the wealthier merchants could negotiate lower prices and reduce the choice of goods available to smaller competitors.

Illicit trade had been a pervasive characteristic of the fair since its early days, but it does not seem to have seriously affected the tonnage of goods carried to America, or the frequency of the fairs until the second half of the seventeenth century.[15] Table 1 shows, for the period 1550–1739, the number of fairs (each roughly corresponding to one fleet), the number of ships reaching Nombre de Dios and Portobelo and the tonnage of goods carried from Spain. The steady decrease in the number of ships, and in tonnage, until the 1650s was due largely to the fact that the Peruvian economy was gradually becoming self-sufficient in many of the goods that had been required in the early days of colonisation. The rapid decline after the 1650s, however, had more to do with the deterioration of the Spanish monarchy and a flourishing clandestine trade. As a result, by the 1680s the fairs became increasingly irregular. The Spanish merchants managed to delay the departure of the galleons following a simple logic: the longer the delay, the greater the demand for their goods at Portobelo. But this worked only to a certain extent, for once French and British interlopers began to offer the Peruvians cheaper manufactures, the whole system was brought to the verge of collapse. Between 1690 and 1739 there were fairs in 1691, 1696, 1708, 1722, 1726, 1731 and 1739 – only seven in five decades – and none seem to have been particularly successful. Since most manufactures carried in the galleons were foreign-made, in effect the foreigners' contraband trade meant the end of the *galeonistas*' role as intermediaries.

---

[15] According to Enriqueta Vila, in the first half of the seventeenth century only a third of the goods traded went through customs: 'La feria de Portobelo: apariencia y realidad del comercio con Indias', AEA xxxix (1982), 309.

Table 1
Galeones and isthmian fairs, 1550–1739

Years	Fairs	Ships	Tons	Tons/Fair
1550–9	9	252	52,930+	5,881+
1560–9	9	200	53,683	5,964
1570–9	8	178	60,906	7,613
1580–9	6	242	67,940	11,323
1590–9	6	186	52,264	8,710
1600–9	4	187	70,453	17,613
1610–19	7	169	66,870	9,552
1620–9	8	193	85,166	10,645
1630–9	9	160	70,096	7,788
1640–9	6	153	55,685	9,280
1650–9	7	56	28,070	4,010
1660–9	4	61	24,800	6,200
1670–9	5	57	25,300	5,060
1680–9	2	23+	9,000+	4,500+
1690–9	2	23	8,500+	4,250+
1700–9	1	15	3,542	3,542
1710–19	0	0	0	0
1720–9	2	31	5,174	2,587
1730–9	2*	23	5,753	2,876

Sources: Christopher Ward, *Imperial Panama: commerce and conflict in Isthmian America, 1550–1800*, Albuquerque 1993, 104–11. Data for period 1700–39 are taken from Walker, *Spanish politics*, 228–9.

* Due to the outbreak of the War of Jenkins' Ear, the second fair did not take place in Portobelo but in Quito (modern Ecuador).

+ Minimum figure.

Starting in 1698, the French were the first regularly to navigate around Cape Horn for the purpose of trade. At least 148 French merchant ships (mainly from St Malo) arrived on the Pacific coast between 1696 and 1725.[16] They supplied Peru and Chile with the same European merchandise as that carried by the galleons but at much cheaper prices. Around 1725 the French abandoned this trade due to both the determination of the French crown to stop illicit trade with the Spanish colonies, and the fact that it was safer for the French to concentrate on trading with the Spanish colonies through Cádiz rather than sending ships to Peru indiscriminately (something they learned after repeatedly glutting the Peruvian market). By contrast, the British, who

---

[16] Carlos Malamud, 'El comercio directo de Europa con América en el siglo XVIII', *Quinto Centenario* i (1981), 44. See also his *Cádiz y Saint Maló en el comercio colonial peruano (1698–1725)*, Cádiz 1986.

had attributed the decline of the Jamaican trade after 1708 to direct French incursions into the Spanish Pacific, adopted a different strategy to smuggling their merchandise into Peru. In 1713 they were granted an *asiento* (under the management of the South Sea Company) to supply the Spanish colonies with slaves, and permission to send a 500-ton ship (the so-called *navío de permiso*) to trade at the Spanish American fairs. On the face of it the South Sea Company was engaged only in the sale of slaves, but its contraband operations were an integral part of the business until war against Spain broke out in 1739.

However catastrophic the situation, few in Spain lost faith in the fleet/fair system. After much deliberation and several *proyectos* and decisions (such as transferring the monopoly of colonial trade from Seville to Cádiz in 1717), both fleets were reinforced in April 1720 with the publication of the *Proyecto para galeones y flotas*. Apart from a slight reduction in taxes, and the inclusion of individual ships to Buenos Aires, the *Real Proyecto* (as it was to be known) brought little novelty.[17] In spring 1720, just after its publication, the crown urged the Cádiz *consulado* to arrange new fleets for Tierra Firme and New Spain. The galleons (thirteen ships carrying 2,047 tons of goods) departed in June 1721, eight months behind schedule. The fair at Portobelo was a complete failure. The next fleet (eighteen ships carrying 3,127 tons of goods) set sail from Cádiz in December 1723. However, to the *galeonistas*' dismay, the *Armada del Sur* did not leave Lima until January 1726, and the fair at Portobelo did not open until June 1726, almost two-and-a-half years after the arrival of the galleons at Cartagena. Even so, the fair was a disaster, as was the last Portobelo fair in 1731.[18]

After those calamitous fairs, some *galeonistas* travelled on to Lima in the vain hope of selling their *rezagos* (remaining goods) in the 2,000 miles of jungle and desert that stretched between Portobelo and Lima. This had been achieved in the past by some Spaniards, but never *en masse*. According to the 1700 memoirs of Raimundo de Lantery (a merchant from Savoy established in Cádiz in the last quarter of the seventeenth century), *galeonistas* usually returned to Cartagena in order to sell their *rezagos* before leaving for Spain. The experience of the Basque Francisco Chanique, who in 1697 had travelled to Lima carrying the goods of many other Spaniards, was described by Lantery as 'a memorable case'.[19] But in 1726 and 1731 a large number of *galeonistas* went to Lima, an incursion into Peru that ruined many merchants and increased the existing rivalry between the Spaniards and the Peruvians.

It is important to stress that once it became irregular after the 1650s, the fleet/fair system did not encourage the establishment of transatlantic

---

[17] Anon., *Proyecto para galeones y flotas del Perú y Nueva-España, y para navíos de registro y avisos que navegaren en ambos reynos*, Madrid 1720.
[18] Walker, *Spanish politics*, 137–56, 177–88.
[19] Manuel Bustos Rodríguez (ed.), *Un comerciante saboyano en el Cádiz de Carlos II: las memorias de Raimundo de Lantery, 1673–1700*, Cádiz 1983, 320–1.

links between the Spaniards and the Peruvians. According to John Burnet, an agent of the South Sea Company who was stationed in Portobelo and Cartagena from 1716 to 1729, *galeonistas* never sold on credit at Portobelo.[20] In other words the merchants of Cádiz preferred to send their intermediary agents to Portobelo (and additionally to give loans to merchants attending the fair) rather than offer credit to the Peruvians. It also seems very unlikely that the Peruvians would order goods from Spain but then refuse to attend the Portobelo fair for more than two years. They had ordered merchandise from Spain in the past, especially before 1640, when the system functioned properly and fleets arrived in Portobelo almost yearly.[21] However, the difficulties in establishing trade between the Spaniards and the Peruvians in the first decades of the eighteenth century had a significant consequence. Speaking for the Lima *consulado* in 1737, Juan de Berría stated before the crown that if the fairs 'had been held near Lima, as those of the fleets are held near Mexico, the capital of New Spain, the Peruvian merchants could take advantage of the most appropriate means of establishing reciprocal and equal negotiations with *galeonistas*'.[22]

Little did Berría suspect that the road to reciprocity was about to be opened, although not through either fleets, or fairs. The Spanish efforts in the 1730s to halt British contraband in the Caribbean by means of *guardacosta* ships would eventually end up with Britain declaring war on Spain in 1739 – and it was this war, the so-called War of Jenkins' Ear (followed by the War of Austrian Succession until 1748) that forced the Spanish government to cancel the system of *flotas* and *galeones*, and to adopt a new system that instead encouraged merchants on both sides of the Atlantic to develop reciprocity and mutual trust as never before.

The Cape Horn route and the register ships

The Spanish government had both military and commercial purposes in mind when it took the decision to send *navíos de registro* or *registros sueltos* (single 'registered' ships) to Peru via Cape Horn. War had broken out in October 1739, and on 21 November the British admiral Edward Vernon destroyed the fortifications of Portobelo, thereby disrupting commercial exchanges between the Spaniards and the Peruvians. However, the new route was not adopted without opposition. In April 1740 the minister of the Indies, José de la Quintana, ordered the president of the House of Trade,

---

[20] Vera L. Brown, 'The South Sea Company and contraband trade', AHR xxxi (1926), 673.
[21] Margarita Suárez, *Desafíos transatlánticos: mercaderes, banqueros y el estado en el Perú virreinal, 1600–1700*, Lima 2001, 236–53; Studnicki-Gizbert, *Nation upon the ocean sea*, 94–107.
[22] Dilg, 'Collapse', 220.

Francisco de Varas, to approach some Cádiz merchants with a view to sending two ships directly to Peru. If no Spaniard was interested, then Varas was told to approach one or two reputable French merchants established in Cádiz.[23] Considering the problems at the isthmus, Quintana thought that Peru would be undersupplied and that the merchants of Cádiz would therefore be willing to undertake the project. Two weeks later Varas replied that the Cádiz *consulado* had found the idea 'repellent', exclaiming that 'any licence in the present circumstances would cause the total extermination of the trade of Spain and America'.[24] Many merchants had sent merchandise to Cartagena in 1737 in the galleons escorted by Blas de Lezo's squadron and were, three years later, still waiting for their goods to be sold. As a result the operation was cancelled. The year after, in 1741, two Cádiz *consulado* merchants, Juan Clemente de Olave and José de Guisasola, were granted a licence to send 600 tons of goods to the South Sea after payment of 153,000 *pesos*.[25] It was the representative of the Lima *consulado* in Madrid, Juan de Berría, who complained this time, using arguments similar to those of the Cádiz *consulado* months before.[26] Now, however, the Spanish government was determined to go ahead. Olave and Guisasola used their 600-ton licence in three French ships (from St Malo and La Rochelle) that left Cádiz for Peru in January 1742. Spanish merchants inevitably had to rely on French ships until they acquired sufficient knowledge about the Cape Horn navigation. The first Spanish ship to Peru would be the *Nuestra Señora del Rosario*, which set sail for the Pacific in 1748.

Two young naval officers, Jorge Juan and Antonio Ulloa, were among the first to foresee the beneficial economic effects that regular supply via Cape Horn would have on the trade with Peru. In a report commissioned by the minister of state, the marqués de la Ensenada, and drawing on their ten-year stay in Peru from 1735 to 1744, Jorge and Ulloa noted that despite the enormous difficulties of navigation the Cape Horn route was the best means of eliminating the Peruvian trade in smuggled European goods. They believed that register ships sailing directly to Peru would succeed 'in totally changing the course of things'.[27] There were two crucial points that the Spanish government would learn. First, for smuggling to take place, Juan and Ulloa observed that it had to yield larger profits than licit trade. Nobody would risk smuggling if profits were not particularly high. As trade rounding Cape Horn had no need of intermediaries, goods carried by that route were cheaper, making contraband less tempting as a result. Secondly, Juan and

---

[23] José Quintana to Francisco Varas, Madrid, 23 Apr. 1740, AGI, Lima 1521.
[24] Varas to Quintana, Cádiz, 8 May 1740, ibid.
[25] 'Expediente relativo a el permiso de 600 toneladas': ibid.
[26] 'El diputado del comercio del Perú don Juan de Berría', July 1742, ibid.
[27] Jorge Juan and Antonio Ulloa, *Discourse and political reflections on the kingdoms of Peru* [1748?], ed. and trans. J. J. TePaske and B. A. Clement, Norman, Ok 1978, 61 (first published in London in 1826 under the title *Noticias secretas de América*).

Ulloa stressed that for Peruvian merchants it was very important not to have their money lying idle, which was the inherent consequence of trade under the fleet/fair system. After completing their purchases at Portobelo and returning to Lima, the *limeño* merchant needed no more than six months to dispose of all the merchandise in Peru. The problem was that the cash he got from the sales did not produce any profit if he had to wait for the arrival of a new fleet, hence he had no other course but to obtain smuggled goods on the coast of Panama, in Buenos Aires, or even in New Spain. As engaging in smuggling was his sole option to ensure frequent provision of goods, the Portobelo fair could hardly suit his interests. 'If a great number of vessels of large tonnage did not appear all at once', concluded Juan and Ulloa, 'there would be money in Lima all the time, additional sums in the sierra, and supplies sold continuously in both areas.'[28]

But regular trade over such a long distance entailed risks that most merchants were unwilling to take. After having persistently refused to attend the Portobelo fair, the merchants of Lima now recommended that the old system be resumed. Unsurprisingly, the long-established merchants of Cádiz held a similar view. In 1750 the crown summoned five Cádiz *consulado* merchants to discuss the advisability of returning to the system of *flotas* and *galeones* now that the war was over. The merchants did not hesitate to stress the convenience of the old system,[29] as a result of which the fleet system was partially resumed in 1754: New Spain would be supplied by means of *flotas* (the first fleet would not set sail for Veracruz until 1757),[30] whereas the *galeones* and the Portobelo fair were both discarded for good.

Most register ships rounding Cape Horn after 1742 were vessels of over 500 tons, and in general were larger and carried richer cargoes than those bound for the Atlantic coast.[31] Four commodities constituted almost the entire cargo of Peruvian exports to Spain: silver, gold, cocoa and *cascarilla* (the bark of the wild *cinchona* tree, from which quinine was produced). Other commodities such as copper or *vicuña* wool were a long way behind. In terms of value, precious metals amounted to roughly 90 per cent of all exports. By contrast, the variety of commodities imported from Spain was much wider, for example including clothes, iron, steel, ironmongery, wax, paper, books, medicines, glass and spices. None the less, the main Spanish export in terms of both value and variety, was *ropas* – a collective term indicating both raw fabrics and finished clothing. In the mid-eighteenth century *ropas* amounted

---

[28] Ibid. 63.
[29] Andrés Loyo to Ensenada, Madrid, 26 Oct. 1750, BL, MS Add. 13976, fos 268–79.
[30] See Jeremy Baskes, 'Risky ventures: reconsidering Mexico's colonial trade system', *Colonial Latin American Review* xiv (2005), 27–54.
[31] In 1791, for example, the sixteen ships that set sail for Buenos Aires and Montevideo carried a cargo valued at 1.1 million pesos, whereas six ships bound for Callao carried more than 4.65 million: John Fisher, 'El impacto del comercio libre en el Perú, 1778–1796', *RI* xlviii (1988), 403.

to 65 per cent of the ships' tonnage, and their value to as much as 94 per cent of that of the entire cargo.[32] Most clothes and fabrics were first imported into Spain from France, England, Holland and Italy, as it was only after 1750 that the Spanish textile industry (especially in Catalonia and Valencia) grew significantly.[33] The share of Spanish products in total exports from Spain to Spanish America rose from 38 per cent in 1778 to 52 per cent in the period 1782–96.[34]

Trade with the Pacific coast of South America was the second most important colonial trade for Spain. In the period 1747–96, goods coming from New Spain amounted to 49 per cent of Cádiz's American imports, while Peruvian imports represented 19 per cent, the Caribbean islands 9 per cent, Carategena de Indias 7 per cent and Buenos Aires 7 per cent.[35] Similarly, in the years 1785–96 New Spain was the destination for 36 per cent of Cádiz's exports to Spanish America, Peru and Chile 22 per cent, Buenos Aires 10 per cent, Venezuela 10 per cent and the Caribbean islands 8 per cent.[36]

Trade via Cape Horn was constrained by the fact that the route was not navigable at certain times of the year. In order for register ships to avoid rounding the cape during the southern hemisphere winter they had to leave Cádiz in autumn or winter: in the period 1742–80, 90 per cent of them set sail between November and February, with the other 10 per cent leaving in September, October or March.[37] Register ships to Lima were therefore less unpredictable than those bound for the Atlantic coast. The merchants in Lima did not have any doubts about when the ships would come, but rather how many of them would arrive. More often than not they were reduced to speculation: 'We know nothing official about the situation of the merchant ships, nor how many of them are coming', reported a Lima merchant in April 1779, 'we think there will be four, because San Ginés will send his two ships at all cost, and it is already late to cancel the *Aurora* and the *San Pablo*.'[38]

Naturally, register ships rounding Cape Horn would pay higher premiums than the galleons. In 1688, from Cádiz to Cartagena, the galleons (that is, ships sailing in convoy) paid a 4.25 per cent premium, single ships 8.25 per

---

[32] Bernal, *Financiación*, 352.
[33] James C. La Force, *The development of the Spanish textile industry, 1750–1800*, Berkeley 1965, 7–27. For Catalonia see Marta V. Vicente, *Clothing the Spanish empire: families and the calico trade in the early modern Atlantic world*, Basingstoke 2006.
[34] John R. Fisher, *Commercial relations between Spain and Spanish America in the era of free trade, 1778–1796*, Liverpool 1985, 88.
[35] A. García-Baquero, *El comercio colonial en la época del absolutismo ilustrado: problemas y debates*, Granada 2003, 97.
[36] Fisher, *Commercial relations*, 55.
[37] AGI, Lima 1523; Parrón, *De las reformas*, 508–13.
[38] Antonio Elizalde to Matías Elizalde, Lima, 3 Apr. 1779, HCA 30/313/3, no. 1089.

cent and mail packet-boats 10.25 per cent.[39] It is worth noting that in 1688 the insurers of Cádiz (all them foreigners) did not contemplate insuring any ship or cargo beyond Portobelo. By contrast, in his 1791 dissertation on the commerce of Peru, José de Baquíjano noted that ships arriving in Peru in 1750 were insured in Cádiz at a 20 per cent premium. The year after it was reduced to 15 per cent, and from then on it continued to decrease down to 5 per cent.[40] For the merchants in Lima, however, getting insurance was especially problematic as there was no insurance market in Peru that could cover the riches shipped to Spain. As a result, register ships rounding Cape Horn and their cargoes were always insured in Europe. It is no wonder, therefore, that commodities could be shipped even before the letter ordering the insurance reached Spain. Unwilling to cope with such problems of coordination, there were merchants who only insured their goods if it was absolutely necessary. In March 1779, for example, the Lima merchant Pedro Celestino Fernández sent 25,191 *pesos* to his Cádiz correspondent, ordering that 'if there were war you will arrange an insurance in the terms of that place, but if there were not, not [sic], let it run the risk at sea on my account, as ever'.[41]

All in all, the difficulty of sailing to Peru had a more profound effect upon people than upon insurance rates. At the time of the galleons, the usual practice for the Spanish *encomenderos* (agents) had been to travel to Portobelo in order to dispose of their principals' goods, and when the fair was over they would return to Spain in the fleet. In the second half of the eighteenth century, register ships would also carry Spanish *encomenderos* but their experience was far harsher and in most cases they would not return to Spain for several years. After the mid-eighteenth century direct and regular trade gave rise to the consignment trade, making it unnecessary for merchants to travel back and forth as they had done during the time of the galleons. The long distance and terrifying voyage were additional factors in supporting this, as several dramatic examples demonstrate. When the *Gallardo* arrived in Cádiz in October 1776, the president of the House of Trade noted that most of the crew was suffering from scurvy.[42] When the warship *Pedro Alcántara* arrived in Callao on 17 June 1777, with a cargo valued at three million *pesos*, fifty-five men had died from scurvy during the voyage, nine more died upon arrival and 250 were sent to hospital.[43] Similarly, the warship *Santiago*, alias

---

[39] For insurance rates in Cádiz in 1688 see Manuel Ravina Martín, 'Participación extranjera en el comercio indiano: el seguro marítimo a fines del siglo XVII', *RI* xliii (1983), 502–10.
[40] José Baquíjano Carrillo, 'Disertación histórica y política sobre el comercio del Perú', in *Mercurio Peruano*, Lima 1791, facsimile 1964, i. 209–89 at p. 247.
[41] Pedro Celestino Fernández to Juan Vea Murguía, Lima, 29 Mar. 1779, HCA 30/314/3, no. 1297.
[42] Francisco Majón to José Gálvez, Cádiz, 20 Oct. 1776, AGI, Lima 1525.
[43] Manuel Guirior to Gálvez, Lima, 17 June 1777, ibid.

La América, lost ten crew members during the voyage and arrived in Callao in April 1779 with 150 sick.[44]

The problem of scurvy was caused by the length of the voyage and the fact that stopovers for taking on water, if they happened at all, were very short. At a time when the cause of the illness was unclear, such an ordeal could have an overwhelming effect both on body and mind. It is unsurprising, therefore, that few merchants travelled aboard the register ships – between 1757 and 1767, for example, only eighty-three went on register ships to Peru, contrasting sharply with the 300 or so merchants and *encomenderos* who went to New Spain in the *flota* of 1776.[45] The good news for ship captains and officials (if they survived the voyage), however, was that they were in a privileged position to engage in trade and build up their own networks.

The number of ships to be sent to Peru naturally became a crucial question after 1742. Early in the century the enormous success of the first French ventures to Peru had encouraged many merchants of St Maló, La Rochelle and even Marseilles to send ships to the Pacific coast. The ruinous consequences of the indiscriminate trade that followed were concisely described by the French seaman Le Gentil Labarbinais in his 1728 memoirs.[46] In the 1740s the Spaniards saw the French experience as a warning. The best way of assessing how many ships were sent in the 1740s and 1750s is by looking at the petitions for register ships that were rejected. For example, on 18 November 1754 the president of the House of Trade, Esteban José de Avaría, denied the request of one Juan de Fábregas because three register ships were still in the Pacific, one more was on its way to Spain and another two were in Cádiz about to set sail for Lima. Furthermore, three *permisos* had just been granted for the next year. President Avaría concluded that 'there is no reason to grant more *permisos* at least until there are news of the state of those provinces, for a multitude of them would be prejudicial to this commerce and to that of the Indies'.[47] However, even under such restrictions, trade between Cádiz and Lima kept growing. Writing in May 1767 the viceroy of Peru, Manuel de Amat, enthusiastically stressed the increase, noting that both the number of ships and the value of the gold and silver sent to Spain had risen from eleven ships (2.2 per year) and 16,640,875 *pesos* in 1757–61 to fifteen ships (3 per year) and 27,488,341 *pesos* in 1763–7. Amat was amazed

---

[44] Juan Casimiro Ozta to Jorge Araurrenechea, Lima, 29 Apr. 1779, HCA 30/313/2, no. 607.
[45] Stanley J. Stein and Barbara H. Stein, *Apogee of empire: Spain and New Spain in the age of Charles III, 1759–1789*, Baltimore 2003, 126, 378.
[46] Le Gentil Labarbinais, *Nouveau Voyage au tour du monde: enrichi due plusieurs plans, vues et perspectives des principales villes & ports du Perou, Chily, Bresil et de la Chine*, Paris 1728, ii. 40–1.
[47] AGI, Lima 1522.

by the 10.8 million increase, and recommended that the number of ships should keep growing.[48]

Amat's suggestion coincided with the government's new policy, from 1765, aimed at gradually liberalising the colonial trade. Although it would not directly affect Peru or most of the other colonies until the famous 1778 *comercio libre* (free trade), licences were now granted by ministers who were determined to make colonial trade grow. The effect upon the number of ships going to Peru was clear, with forty-one register ships setting sail for Lima in the period 1768–76 (4.5 ships per year). The rise in the number of ships had an unsurprising effect. On 6 July 1776 sixty-two members of the Cádiz *consulado* gathered in a *Junta general de comercio* to discuss 'the unhappy situation of the trade to the South [Sea] ... due to the free concession of registers in the last few years'.[49] The discussion that followed provides a good opportunity to see the Spanish monopoly from inside. The attendants claimed that the situation in Lima was so bad that the only way of selling their merchandise was either at the same prices paid in Spain or at a loss. Furthermore, things would get even worse with the arrival of four register ships and a warship that had set sail from Cádiz early that year. The Cádiz *consulado* therefore officially requested that the number of ships going to Peru be reduced. Thirty merchants considered it was sufficient to send one ship with 500 tons of clothes. Another eleven said that, if the number of tons they all intended to load turned out to be more than 500, a second ship would be necessary, or otherwise some merchants would be unfairly prevented from loading their merchandise. Eventually the minister of the Indies, José de Gálvez, decided that only a 500-ton register ship would set sail that year, the reason being that if there was not enough cargo to fill a second one, the foreign merchants established in Cádiz could be tempted into offering Spanish merchants lower prices in order to dispose of their merchandise.[50]

Clearly the Cádiz *consulado*'s petition was monopolistic, as was Gálvez's decision. However, it is important to stress that no merchant envisaged loading three, four or five ships – they actually doubted whether even a second one could be fully loaded. Indeed, by the 1770s the number of register ships had gradually come to reflect not only the market situation in Peru but also the risks merchants were ready to take. The government was well aware of this, and granted *permisos* accordingly.[51] It is therefore difficult to deter-

---

[48] Manuel Amat to Julián Arriaga, Lima, 8 May 1767, ibid. 1524. The increase in the official trade via Cape Horn coincided with a decrease in the amount of contraband passing through the Caribbean: Adrian Pearce, *British trade with Spanish America, 1763 to 1808*, Liverpool 2007, 28–9.
[49] Cádiz *consulado* to Majón, Cádiz, 8 July 1776, AGI, Lima 1525.
[50] Gálvez to Majón, Madrid, 10 Oct. 1776, ibid.
[51] In the 1770s the ministers of the Indies (both Julián Arriaga and his successor José Gálvez) were informed on a weekly basis about the vicissitudes of register ships' loading

mine whether merchants' decisions were driven by the risk-averse mentality that has repeatedly been attributed to Spanish colonial merchants or by a palpable risk that not even the most daring merchant was eager to take.

New pattern, new risks

The system of register ships was only one factor in shaping a completely new pattern of trade after 1739. The new system gave the trade the attribute of regularity, but the pattern of trade arising from it was greatly affected by geography, improvements in communication and the building up of trust. As a result the very nature of risk was transformed. Before 1739 risk was primarily associated with the good or bad functioning of the fleet/fair system and the effect of contraband, but afterwards the risks associated with agency and competition became more important. With the galleons, most competition occurred at Portobelo; with the Cape Horn route competition became transatlantic. The assertion, therefore, that after 1739 the only thing that changed was the trading route is clearly inaccurate.[52]

The Basque Andrés de Loyo was one of the five Cádiz *consulado* merchants from whom the crown requested advice in 1750. Like the other four, Loyo thought that the galleons should be resumed and the register ships to Peru cancelled. However, time was to prove that most of his arguments against regular trade via Cape Horn (increase in prices, monopolisation of the trade by a few merchants and perils of navigation) were either unfounded or surmountable. One argument spoke loudly of a new problem that would have critical ramifications. Loyo stressed that if register ships kept supplying Peru:

> the merchants of Lima will not want to buy large inventories, since they will have all they need on their doorstep, [whereas] the merchants of Spain will have to retail and sell on credit within the kingdom (which is very large and remote), experiencing long delays and maybe losses. For that reason, they will have to stay in the kingdom, and their debts and delays will cause further delays and bankruptcies back in Spain.[53]

---

in Cádiz: Juan Merida to Arriaga, Cádiz, 12 Jan. 1776, ibid.; Majón to Gálvez, Cádiz, 7 Nov. 1777, ibid.

[52] Carmen Parrón, 'Perú y la transición del comercio político al comercio libre, 1740–1778', AEA liv (1997), 469.

[53] Loyo to Ensenada, Madrid, 26 Sept. 1750, BL, MS Add. 13976, fo. 272. A comparable transformation occurred in the Portuguese colonial trade when the system of biennial *frotas* (fleets) to Rio de Janeiro (where a fair identical to that of Portobelo used to be held) were subsituted for single ships in September 1765. Four years later, similar to what Loyo stated for the Spanish case, the British Consul in Lisbon, William Lyttleton, reported that 'now that only single ships go [to Brazil], the miners content themselves with buying small occasional supplies from time to time by means of their agents at the Rio [de Janeiro] and other places leaving their old debts unpaid, which are very hard to

If the register shipping trade was to work, then the trust placed in correspondents and debtors in the colonies would have to be considerably greater than at the time of the galleons. As merchants worked hard to build up relationships of trust, they shaped a pattern of trade whose two main characteristics would be retailing and the use of credit. Due to the very long distance and the dangerous navigation, the new pattern of trade gave rise to the consignment trade. Though not an overnight transformation, by 1760 it was well established.

The main instrument of credit in Spanish colonial trade was the *escritura de riesgo* or *préstamo a la gruesa aventura* (sea loan). As the French historian Charles Carrière puts it, 'in the eighteenth century, among businessmen, *grosse aventure* meant, above all, Cádiz'.[54] The annual average value of the cargoes sent to Peru in the period 1760–80 was somewhere between 4 and 4.5 million *pesos*, of which an average of 1.8 million was financed by means of sea loans.[55] With this type of credit it was the lender who ran the risk during the voyage (rather like an insurer), and it was only when the ship reached its destination that the borrower took charge of the loan (usually in the form of *ropas*). In the contract the risk of the navigation was defined as that of 'sea, wind, land, fire, friends, enemies and other unfortunate maritime events'.[56] The reason why this archaic method of credit was widespread in Cádiz was intimately linked to the high risks that the Spanish colonial trade entailed, and to the main commodities it was meant to obtain: silver and gold. Interest rates were high as it was easy to lose the money. In the eighteenth century loans were usually given in *pesos sencillos* (8 *reales*) and borrowers had to redeem in *pesos fuertes* (10 5/8 *reales*) – which is to say the exchange rate (*cambio marítimo*) alone provided a profit of 33 per cent,[57] and on top of that the borrower had to pay interest (*premio de mar*). Since the interest rate was rarely mentioned in the contracts it is very difficult to follow its annual fluctuation, but some snapshots suggest that the interest rate for *escrituras de riesgo* in the trade between Spain and Peru declined as trade activities and competition increased. According to Alfonso Quiroz, in 1739 (when the war began) the premium was 130 per cent; in the period

---

be recovered': Lyttleton to Thomas Thynne, 2nd viscount Weymouth, Lisbon, 21 June 1769, SP, Portugal 89/69, fos 46v–47r.

[54] Charles Carrière, 'Renoveau espagnol et pret à la grosse aventure (Notes sur la place de Cadix dans la seconde moitié du XVIII siècle)', *Revue d'histoire moderne et contemporaine* xvii (1970), 237.

[55] For a complete list of ships and the value of *escrituras* they carried see Bernal, *Financiación*, 709–63.

[56] A copy of an *escritura de riesgo* for 6,840 *pesos* agreed in Cádiz on 23 January 1773 can be found in *La Carlota* (1781), HCA 32/288/3 (1), fo. 97.

[57] Bernal, *Financiación*, 328. In the second half of the eighteenth century the rate of exchange applied by the British to the Spanish-American *peso fuerte* was calculated at a precise £1 = 4.44 *pesos*: Pearce, *British trade*, p. xvi.

1751–65 it ranged between 30 and 65 per cent; in the years 1773–83 it was 16 per cent; and by 1790 it had decreased to 12 per cent.[58]

This form of credit has been thoroughly analysed by several historians, but virtually no connections have been made between its evolution and changes in the pattern of trade. In the second half of the seventeenth century borrowers were usually allowed eight, fifteen, twenty or thirty days to pay back.[59] There was an obvious connection between the time borrowers were given to clear debts and the duration of the American fairs, where most debts had to be redeemed. By contrast, during the eighteenth century the average time to clear debts increased significantly from twenty-five days in 1700–6 to ninety-eight days in 1775.[60] This gradual extension is worth stressing, for it suggests that, if only to recover their loans, merchants (and other creditors) were compelled to build up transatlantic networks. Moreover, in the case of Peru loans took much longer to recover. A merchant writing from Lima in 1779 reported to his correspondents in Cádiz that 'for many years now, few sales have been made for hard money, and even though the usual time to redeem debts is one year, those who go to the Sierra with clothes need two or three years'.[61] Moreover, it was precisely after the mid-eighteenth century that the use of the bill of exchange (*libranza* or *letra de cambio*) began to expand in the colonies and in the transatlantic trade,[62] although its importance as an instrument of credit in colonial trade remained much less than that of the sea loan.

Along with the credit terms and the increasing use of bills of exchange, the approach of merchants to colonial trade would also change dramatically after 1739. Before then, both *galeonistas* and *flotistas* (merchants travelling in the flotas to New Spain) carried a variety of commodities which they thought would be saleable in the colonies. Yet their knowledge of the market was fairly limited, and their chances of accurately meeting demand depended to a large extent on there being a situation of shortage. One example, the case of the Basque *flotista*, Pedro de Munárriz, provides telling evidence. In October 1702 the *flota* that had just returned from Veracruz was attacked by English and Dutch ships in the Bay of Vigo (north-west Spain). Historians have discussed the value of the precious metals captured on that occasion, which appears to have been much less than previously thought.[63] However,

---

[58] Alfonso W. Quiroz, 'Reassessing the role of credit in late colonial Peru: *censos, escrituras*, and *imposiciones*', HAHR lxxiv (1994), 214.
[59] Guadalupe Carrasco González, *Los instrumentos del comercio colonial en el Cádiz del siglo XVII, 1650–1700*, Madrid 1996, 91–3.
[60] Bustos, *Cádiz*, 429.
[61] Esteban Urrutia to Lecture and Gastambide, Lima, 27 Mar. 1779, HCA 30/312/4, no. 950.
[62] Pedro Pérez Herrero, *Plata y libranzas: la articulación comercial del México borbónico*, Mexico 1988, 222–5.
[63] See Henry Kamen, 'The destruction of the Spanish fleet at Vigo in 1702', *Bulletin of the Institute of Historical Research* xxxix (1966), 165–73.

it has gone totally unnoticed that in addition to silver and gold the English also seized the private correspondence of several Spanish merchants. That of Pedro de Munárriz, a set of 231 letters, covers most of the thirty-three months he spent in New Spain (from October 1699 to June 1702). Although he wrote little about his selection of goods to export from Spain, his letters do provide valuable information on how he managed to market the merchandise, and his relationship with Spain during his stay in New Spain.

Munárriz arrived in Veracruz on 6 October 1699, and soon after settled in Puebla, half way between Veracruz and Mexico City. From there he exchanged information on prices and markets with forty-four correspondents located in the main cities of New Spain (Mexico City, Veracruz, Oaxaca, Campeche, San Luis Potosí, Pachuca and Guatemala). Apart from Puebla, Munárriz's attention was mainly focused on Veracruz (eighty-one letters from seven senders) and on Mexico City (ninety-seven letters from nineteen senders). The latter was by far the largest market in New Spain, while the former was the main Atlantic port and hence the gateway to Europe. However, of the 231 letters only six came from Spain and another two were copies of letters sent by Munárriz to his principal in Seville. Such a low number may well have been caused by problems of communication with Spain due to the war. However, attention needs to be paid not to the quantity of letters but to their content, for Munárriz's letters to Spain contained little commercial information, apart from comments on how sales were going.[64] The point to emphasise is that merchants were caught in an extremely rigid system in which all the merchandise arrived at once, which inevitably led to a judgement of the market based on tonnage rather than upon consumer needs and tastes.

Another significant point emerges from Munárriz's correspondence. At the beginning of the eighteenth century the lists of market prices for goods seem to have circulated only within the colonies,[65] whereas the system of register ships shifted the competition to the Atlantic. Between 1740 and 1744 some 120 ships (many of them French) set sail from Cádiz for the colonies (mainly for New Spain and the Caribbean).[66] Rather revealingly, the mail sent from Veracruz, Havana and Cartagena to Cádiz in the 1740s included the prices of a considerable number of commodities. From Havana, for instance, Diego Morphy [sic] posted the Veracruz prices to his Cádiz principal and fellow Irishman Jacinto Butler, adding 'in case you want to send something there'.[67] From Veracruz, Francisco Vizcay did something similar, indicating to Lorenzo

---

[64] Pedro Munárriz to Juan Lamberto, Puebla, 5 Aug. 1700 and 12 Apr. 1701, HCA 30/231/1.
[65] For examples see Pascual Agesta to Munárriz, Mexico City, 13 July 1700, ibid.; Francisco Ferrari to Munárriz, Mexico City, 2 Aug. 1700, ibid.
[66] Walker, *Spanish politics*, 211.
[67] Diego Morphy to Jacinto Butler, Havana, 21 Sept. 1746, HCA 30/250/2. See also Nicolás Comino to Patricio O'Neale, Veracruz, 22 Aug. 1746, ibid.

del Arco that 'the following list, which a reliable friend has just sent me from Mexico [City], will inform you about the present prices of the articles from Europe in that city'.[68] He informed another correspondent that he had just requested from Mexico City 'the colours and drawings of the gold and silver fabrics that will bring more buyers and more appropriate for this Kingdom, and likewise of the more fashionable ribbons, noting their width and drawings'.[69] All this information was intended to ensure that merchants in Cádiz did not, as an agent writing from Cartagena remarked, 'act blindly'.[70] Naturally, in order for merchants in Spain to have access to that information, they required trustworthy correspondents in America. It is no wonder that in 1755 there were sixty Cádiz agents in Mexico City, some of whom had been there since the last *flota* of 1735.[71]

Commodity prices also began to be printed in New Spain in the 1740s. Printed in French, a *Prix courans des Mzes. á la Vera-Cruz*, sent to Cádiz, listed the prices of fifty-six European commodities in August 1746. The document, a rare surviving example of commercial ephemera, was compact (10.5cm by 32cm) and printed on one side of the page.[72] It also contained eleven 'articles quí manquent totalment' and eight 'articles sans demande'. The history of these commercial lists remains obscure. John McCusker rightly notes that these single-sheet serial publications deserve to be recognised as newpapers, pointing out that unfortunately many of them, being mere lists of names and numbers, have been studied only cursorily.[73] McCusker and Gravesteijn found a list similar to that of Veracruz (this one measuring 9cm by 15cm, and printed on both sides) in the Archive de la Chambre et d'Industrie at Marseilles: it is entitled *Prix courans au Mexique le 30 May 1745* and listed seventy-seven European commodities.[74] Understandably, they argue that the fact that it listed only European goods, was written in French and had its prices denominated in Spanish currency, is a strong argument for its having been published in Cádiz. However, the Veracruz list, which was intercepted in a ship coming from Veracruz itself, proves that both were actually printed in New Spain. Apart from testifying to the preponderance of the French in the Spanish colonial trade in the 1740s, these printed lists, along with a few handwritten ones, are telling evidence of the changes brought about

---

[68] Francisco Vizcay to Lorenzo Arco, Veracruz, 25 Jan. 1745, HCA 32/124/25.
[69] Vizcay to Esteban and José Gallart, ibid.
[70] Juan Bautista Arizón to Jacinto Arizón, Cartagena, 6 Oct. 1744, ibid.
[71] Walker, *Spanish politics*, 212.
[72] HCA 30/250/9.
[73] John J. McCusker, *European bills of entry and marine lists: early commercial publications and the origins of the business press*, Cambridge, MA 1985, 8.
[74] John J. McCusker and Cora Gravesteijn, *The beginnings of commercial and financial journalism: the commodity price currents, exchange rate currents, and money currents of early modern Europe*, Amsterdam 1991, 171–3.

by the register ships. These transformations are worth emphasising because historians say virtually nothing about them.[75]

With Peru the pattern of trade developed more slowly because trust between merchants was more difficult to establish, evidence of which was provided by the first register ships arriving in the Pacific. The Spaniards carried a well-assorted cargo but knew very little about the real demand – and certainly nothing had been ordered by any South American merchant. The sixth register ship departing from Cádiz to the Pacific in the 1740s, *El Henrique*, arrived in Concepción (Chile) in April 1744. Upon arrival its merchants rented the house that the *Marqués D'Antein*'s crew had used the year before. One of them, Pedro Hernández Dávila, reported that since their arrival, the local merchants had been preparing their inventories: 'They have not come yet to talk about business, neither unified nor divided, although for us it is the same.'[76] For him it did not matter whether the Chilean merchants acted individually or as a group: they were all just unknown people to whom nothing would be sold on credit. Indeed, a significant feature of the dealings between the Spaniards and the Chileans was the complete lack of trust. Hernández referred to the Chileans as *estos martagones* ('this canny lot'), stressing that the previous year they had played a dirty trick on José del Villar, a merchant travelling in the *Marqués D'Antein*. Eventually, on 26 May, they received some inventories. Resembling price negotiations at Portobelo, Hernández and his shipmates put each article's price in the margin of the document and then sent it back to the Chileans. But the Chileans were reluctant to buy anything because they were 'terrified of the ships arriving at Buenos Aires … and the uncertainty of more ships coming from the Cape'.[77] Seeing that they would not do any significant business in Concepción, Hernández and his colleagues decided to go to Lima.

Like their counterparts in Veracruz, the members of the first expeditions to Peru also sent lists of commodity prices to Spain. In May 1744, a month after *El Henrique*'s arrival in Concepción, Juan de Sobrevilla sent the prices of forty-six commodities in 'the coast of Lima and Concepción' to his Cádiz principal, the Frenchman Juan Behic, pointing out that 'you should not trust it much for [goods] are coming to this port via Brazil and via Portobelo when least expected'.[78] Lists of commodity prices would gradually disappear from the trade with Peru, but not due to the effect of contraband. In 1759 they were still being sent to Spain from Lima, as Juan Cranisbro's

---

[75] For example, the Steins make no mention of those changes in their chapter 'Changing patterns in the transatlantic system: *flotas* and *registros*, 1720–1759': Stein and Stein, *Silver, trade and war*, 180–99.
[76] Pedro Hernández Dávila to Diego José Miranda, Concepción, 19 May 1744, HCA 32/124/25.
[77] Ibid.
[78] Juan Sobrevilla to Juan Behic, Concepción, 24 May 1744, HCA 32/124/25.

1758–9 letter-book shows.[79] But, as retailing grew in importance, merchants stopped sending price lists in the 1760s. In 1779 none of the nearly 2,000 envelopes intercepted from the ship *La Perla* included a single list of prices. Merchants in Lima only mentioned prices in their letters in order to let their correspondents know about profits or losses. By the 1770s merchants used the so-called *nota de efectos aparentes* (inventory of articles in demand), a type of document that described *ropas* in much more detail than the earlier commodity listings. The proliferation of this document is a strong indication that, with the new pattern of trade, merchants discarded the idea of buying in bulk. The fleet/fair system had given an advantage to wealthier merchants over smaller competitors because they could buy in bulk, but the problems in ascertaining the number and date of arrival of the register ships, and the growing retail orientation of the trade, put an end to that advantage. That is why register ships rounding Cape Horn were loaded by many different merchants. As early as 1756, for instance, the ship *La Galga* carried to Peru a cargo of 250 tons belonging to 158 people.[80]

Indeed, the regularity of register ships gave Spanish merchants the opportunity to offer a wide variety of the most modern European cloths, and as a result American consumers began to play a decisive role in the Spanish transatlantic trade. At the turn of the century there was no mention of fashion in the correspondence generated by Munárriz and the other *flotistas*. In their letters, types of cloth were listed according to their generic name, with few references to colour and other distinctive characteristics apart from size. That is to say, European producers received little direct feedback from the markets where their cloth was ultimately sold. After the 1740s, however, an unprecedented amount of commercial information began to cross the Atlantic, compelling manufacturers to adapt their products to colonial taste. However, it is important to emphasise that European manufacturers and American consumers grew closer only because merchants on both sides of the Atlantic learned to trust each other. As the colonial trade diversified, the ability to judge the market became essential, leading to an increased stress upon a detailed knowledge of the market. It thus became extremely important for merchants to gather as much information as possible about their correspondents' performance and reliability. It is precisely this transatlantic communication that provides the subject of the next chapter.

---

[79] Juan Cranisbro to Pedro Cranisbro, Lima, 1 Mar. 1759, AGN, TC-GR1, caja 119, doc. 644, fo. 47.
[80] AGI, Contratación, leg. 1748.

4

Long Distance Communications

The more frequent and direct trade between Cádiz and Lima compelled merchants on both sides of the Atlantic to collaborate with each other. This process, which started off with the arrival of the first register ships in the 1740s and would gradually transform the pattern of colonial trade, was nevertheless the outcome of another equally important development. Following the establishment of regular commercial exchanges, an unprecedented flow of information began to cross the Atlantic. Daviken Studnicki-Gizbert states that, before 1640, and even if everything went according to plan, '[c]ommunicating across the Atlantic was generally restricted to the slow, biannual pulse of the Carrera fleets'[1] – and the situation deteriorated in the second half of the seventeenth century as the time lag between fleets increased. In stark contrast the register ships navigating the Cape Horn route would contribute significantly to improving communications, and this in turn would make the trade a lot more dependent on constantly updated information. The ameliorated communications played a crucial part in both shaping the trade and sustaining interpersonal trust across the ocean. Trust 'clearly depends ... on the availability of information about the object of one's trust'.[2] How much did the merchants of Cádiz and Lima knew about each other in the eighteenth century? How did that knowledge affect their ability to trust?

The mail between Spain and Peru

The significance of the mail in sustaining the Spanish colonial trade is a subject greatly neglected by historians. However, Spanish eighteenth-century bureaucrats such as the minister of state José del Campillo (1743) and the diplomat Miguel Antonio de la Gándara (1759), both supporters of the system of register ships, did not fail to stress the importance of improving communication with America in their reformist writings. In their eyes, trust, trade and communication were closely intertwined. In 1743, the year of his death, Campillo wrote that:

---

[1] Studnicki-Gizbert, *Nation upon the ocean sea*, 138.
[2] Anthony Padgen, 'The distraction of trust and its economic consequences in the case of eighteenth-century Naples', in Gambetta, *Trust*, 129.

Merchants' confidence is built upon experience of legality and good faith among them; but it has no effect upon their reciprocal interests unless fast and regular correspondence is provided; ... all the commerce that is left undone due to the interruption of correspondence is pure loss for the State.[3]

Even though their works would not be published until 1789 and 1811 respectively, they were circulated in manuscript form long before this, and their reformist ideas were shared by a growing number of high-level civil servants. It is revealing that the importance that they attributed to communication had been absent from the works of more traditional economists like Gerónimo de Uztáriz (1724) and Bernardo de Ulloa (1740), who thought that *flotas* and *galeones* were more appropriate than register ships.[4]

Campillo's economic postulates would be gradually adopted by Spain in the second half of the eighteenth century, breaking with the idea that the tonnage of goods for America should be fixed and dispatched from only one Spanish port. Naturally such innovations were to cause tremendous distress to the merchants involved in colonial trade, for they would require updated information about commercial activities in many American and Spanish ports. Campillo foresaw this problem, and suggested that information about both prices in America and ships sent from Spain should be published monthly in a *gazeta mercantil*, 'just like I have seen in other countries'.[5] However, his suggestion was totally ignored. In 1765 nine Spanish ports were allowed to trade with the islands of the Spanish Caribbean, and eight years later they were still complaining of the difficulty of finding out what was being sent to the colonies from other peninsular ports.[6] In fact, commercial newspapers that could have alleviated such problems (if only to a certain extent) did not develop in Spain until as late as the 1790s, and even then did not provide much information about the colonies.[7] In the eighteenth century Spanish colonial traders relied, not upon commercial newspapers (with the exception of the printed commodity price lists in the 1740s) but upon what their correspondents told them. After 1739 what those correspondents had to say became as important as the frequency with which they said it.

---

[3] Campillo, *Nuevo sistema*, 276–7. See also Miguel Antonio de la Gándara, *Apuntes sobre el bien y el mal de España* [1759] (Madrid 1811), Madrid 1988, 128. Campillo's work has also been attributed to Melchor Rafael de Macanaz, a Spanish bureaucrat in exile in France between 1715 and 1748: Stein and Stein, *Silver*, 222.
[4] Uztáriz, *Theórica*; Bernardo Ulloa, *Restablecimiento de las fábricas, tráfico y comercio marítimo de España. Segunda parte: que trata del comercio y tráfico marítimo que tiene España con las naciones y en la América: causas de su decadencia*, Madrid 1740.
[5] Campillo, *Nuevo sistema*, 274.
[6] See the petition of the merchants and manufacturers of Catalonia to Pablo Jerónimo Grimaldi, marqués de Grimaldi, Barcelona, 24 Apr. 1773. BL, MS Add. 13976, fos 139–51.
[7] See Luis Miguel Enciso Recio, *Prensa económica del XVIII: el correo mercantil de España y sus Indias*, Valladolid 1958.

For more than two centuries Spanish merchants had done their best to communicate with their transatlantic correspondents by either entrusting friends with their correspondence or sending it in the first ship bound for the other side of the Atlantic.[8] Letters were also sent along with the official mail in the *avisos* (mail packet-boats) which began to cross the Atlantic as early as 1525. Irregularity, however, remained a common problem. Transatlantic communication and trade being closely intertwined, *avisos* functioned well only when *flotas* and *galeones* were in the colonies. The various measures aimed at finding a solution in the seventeenth century were rather unsuccessful. In 1664 the Seville *consulado* was directed to send four annual *avisos* to the Indies (two for each viceroyalty), but the enterprise seems to have had poor results. It is therefore no surprise that in Josephe and Francisco Mugaburu's *Diario de Lima*, a chronicle of Peru in the second half of the seventeenth century, the arrival of a dispatch from Spain was recorded as a noteworthy event. In the forty-two years between November 1644 and December 1686 they recorded thirty-three dispatches.[9] Apart from the low number, the very fact that both father and son saw fit to note the arrival of news from Spain in their diaries says a great deal about communication between Spain and Peru in the period. It was naturally the case that such poor communication weakened the crown's control over the colonies. On 6 June 1713, just before his departure for Peru, the newly appointed viceroy, the prince of Santo Buono, was informed in Cádiz about 'the total lack of trade and delays of two and three years in obtaining a reply to the letters sent [to Peru]'. He was also told that many in Peru were interested in keeping things as they were because thus they could do as they pleased.[10]

It was in 1718 that the Spanish government considered sending eight annual *avisos* to the Indies instead of four. Two years later the first regulations on imperial mail were released, and the Cádiz *consulado*, rather reluctantly, was appointed to take on the project.[11] Immediately it began a programme of sending two packet-boats, one for each viceroyalty, four times a year, calling at Cartagena, Portobelo, Veracruz and Havana. Although this ordinance lasted for forty-three years it achieved disappointing results. The irregularity of the mail is particularly significant. The merchants, who theoretically would have had the greatest interest in regular and frequent communication with the colonies, seem not to have been particularly keen to achieve it

---

[8] Cayetano Alcázar, *Historia del correo en América (Notas y documentos para su estudio)*, Madrid 1920, 99–112; Francisco Garay Unibaso, *Correos marítimos españoles*, Bilbao 1987, i. 29–35.

[9] Josephe Mugaburu and Francisco Mugaburu, *Chronicle of colonial Peru: the diary of Josephe and Francisco Mugaburu, 1640–1697*, ed. and trans. R. R. Miller, Norman, OK 1975.

[10] Walter B. Bose, 'El proyecto sobre "correos marítimos" a las Indias, de 1713', *Anuario de Historia Argentina* ii (1940), 429.

[11] Antonia Heredia Herrera, 'Asiento con el consulado de Cádiz en 1720 para el despacho de avisos', in *La burguesía mercantil gaditana (1650–1868)*, Cádiz 1976, 167.

until the mid-eighteenth century. It was only when the register ships began to transform the colonial trade that the need for frequent and updated information became crucial.

Eventually, in 1764, transatlantic communication was significantly improved with the creation of the *Correos marítimos* (maritime mail). The reason for government itself undertaking this new initiative was clearly pointed out in the royal decree that established it: 'The trade of both dominions [Spain and the Indies] cannot be regularly carried on, neither can principals know about their merchandise from agents and factors.'[12] Historians have attributed the success of the *Correos marítimos* to the government's determination to make it work, but it was simultaneously a clear indication that the need for regular communication had increased dramatically. The Spanish government itself was struck by the success of the new project. A certain Pedro Antonio de Cossío was sent to Peru to find out more about the state of the mail in the viceroyalty, and wrote from Lima that 'on the matter of letters the extent of their production is incredible'.[13]

Under the *Correos marítimos*, one packet-boat sailed from La Coruña to Havana every month carrying the mail for the two viceroyalties.[14] Mail for Peru was then carried by land to the southern Cuban port of Trinidad, where it was shipped on again to Cartagena. From Cartagena there were two routes to Lima: by land via Santa Fe de Bogotá or by sea via Portobelo. Both were known as the *Carrera de Cartagena*. However, sending monthly *avisos* to Havana did not ensure that the mail would reach Peru without trouble. In September 1765, while waiting in Havana for his next assignment, Antonio Ulloa wrote on the situation regarding the mail between Spain and Peru via the Caribbean. He noted that since January that year only one shipment of mail had arrived from Panama, on 26 April, with letters from Lima dated 12 December 1764, and that the copies of those letters, sent via Santa Fe, did not arrive until June. He also pointed out the marked contrast between the two viceregal capitals: while there was no problem whatsoever with Mexico City, it usually took sixteen to eighteen months to get a reply from Lima. The problems were lack of efficiency (it was possible for mail boxes to sit for as long as five or six months in Panama before being dispatched) and the difficulty of the journey south from Cartagena and Panama.

Ulloa suggested a plan aimed at cutting the time needed to get a reply from Lima by more than half, but in order for it to work he stressed that more needed to be known about the Jívaro Indians, the rivers and their high waters, pumas, moorlands, roads, ports, currents and winds: 'Nobody

---

[12] Garay, *Correos marítimos*, i. 49–50.
[13] Pedro Antonio de Cossío to the directors of the Renta de Correos, Lima, 18 July 1767, AGI, Correos 102A.
[14] The choice of La Coruña as the port from which to dispatch all the mail packet-boats was the first of a series of measures intended to reduce Cádiz's control over colonial trade while stimulating the economy of northern Spain.

has that information in Spain because someone who knows part of the kingdoms of Santa Fe, Tierra Firme, Quito and Peru, does not know the rest, and someone who knows the inland roads knows nothing about the sea lanes.'[15] According to Ulloa the inland route from Cartagena to Lima via Santa Fe, Popayan and Piura, took too long and was too expensive. For him the sea lane from Panama was far more appropriate, but after the end of the *galeones* that route had virtually been abandoned. Only two ships per year sailed from Lima to Panama, in June and November, to carry the *situado* (money sent to the isthmus to pay the expenses of the army), in addition to a few small ships that sailed from Paita and Guayaquil with foodstuffs. Then there was the question of the seasonal Pacific winds: in order to avoid the strong winds that blew southwards between mid-December and April, Ulloa suggested that the mail from Lima should first be sent by land via Piura and Guayaquil to the seaport of Esmeraldas. From Esmeraldas the route to Panama was much easier and could be covered by three-mariner ships in eight days. Ulloa estimated that the mail could thereby travel from Lima to Cartagena in thirty-four days instead of the usual five months. He also made several suggestions for improving communications between Cartagena and the port of Havana, from which the mail was ultimately sent to Spain. If everything was carried out according to Ulloa's scheme it would still take the mail 'five and a half months to go from Lima to Spain, and as long as that from Spain to Lima'.[16]

In addition to the route via Cartagena, another mail service was created in December 1767 to reach Peru via Buenos Aires, the so-called *Carrera de Buenos Aires*, whereby between four and six ships per year would set sail from La Coruña.[17] From Buenos Aires to Lima there were different routes, each with its own problems. Writing on 20 February 1771, the viceroy of Peru, Manuel de Amat, noted that the fastest route was via Santiago de Chile, which took four and a half to five months to reach Lima. But the pass through the Andes was closed in winter due to the snow, and the alternative route, by land via Potosí, took no less than nine months. Amat saw the solution as a new route from Buenos Aires to San Juan (a lower passage in the Andes) and then to Coquimbo (north of Santiago on the coast), which would theoretically reduce the usual nine-month winter journey by two or three months.[18]

With the *Correos marítimos*, transatlantic communication became not only more regular and reliable but also more expensive. The year after its implementation, merchants ordered their correspondents to use as little paper as

---

[15] Antonio Ulloa, *Modo de facilitar los correos de España con el reyno del Perú*, Seville 2001, p. vii.
[16] Ibid. p. xxvi.
[17] Manoel Lelo Belloto, *Correio maritimo hispano-americano: a carreia de Buenos Aires, 1767–1779*, Sao Paulo 1972, 132–6.
[18] Amat to Grimaldi, Lima, 20 Feb. 1771, AGI, Correos 102A.

possible when writing their letters, and if they had to send something as heavy as an account book they were told to do so by using 'some person of confidence'.[19] Paradoxically, merchants were compelled to use little paper at a time when regular correspondence and detailed information were more necessary than ever. As a result letters in the second half of the eighteenth century had much narrower margins and were written in smaller handwriting than in the first half.

It is clear that the institution of the *Correos marítimos* improved communication between Spain and Peru significantly, but the key to its success had already been established by the system of register ships and the consignment trade that it had promoted. After all, register ships had carried mail before 1764 and would continue carrying it afterwards. Whichever means were used merchants were now able to receive and reply to letters on a continuous basis, as exemplified by a passage in a letter from Joaquín Lavena to the Cádiz merchant Juan Martín de Aguirre:

> Today is 30 April 1779. The above is a copy of the most substantial passages of the letter I sent you in the *Buen Consejo* [on 4 April]. The ship *La Perla* is about to depart, and I will take that opportunity to reply to yours of the 13th of November [1778] brought by the warship *Santiago la América*, which arrived at Callao the 26th current.[20]

From the mid-eighteenth century onwards, frequent communication between Lima and Cádiz had a decisive effect upon human relationships, bringing the communities closer together.

La Perla's mail

In the years after 1739 at least seven ships doing the Cape Horn route were captured by the British.[21] Usually, when their ships were about to be seized, Spanish captains would dispose of the ship's papers to ensure that potentially useful political, military and commercial information would not fall into enemy hands, generally by simply throwing them overboard. In June 1762, for example, the captain of *La Hermiona*, the Basque Juan de Zabaleta, declared in Gibraltar that 'two packets of papers or letters were thrown

---

[19] Lorenzo del Arco to Andrés Ramírez de Arellano, Cádiz, 20 Dec. 1765, IRA, ARA, Epistolario.
[20] Joaquín de Lavena to Juan Martín de Aguirre, Lima, 30 Apr. 1779, HCA 30/315/2, no. 965.
[21] Six of them were captured while coming from Peru: *El Héctor* (1747), HCA 32/116 (2); *La Hermiona* (1762), HCA 32/200 (1); *El Buen Consejo* (1779), HCA 32/413/8; *San Francisco Xavier* (1779), HCA 32/334/9 (1); *Santiago Apóstol* (1792), HCA 32/834 (1, 2); and *El Vigilante* (1807), HCA 32/1124. Only one ship was captured while sailing to Peru: *El Antélope* (1808), HCA 32/1123.

overboard at the time of the capture'.[22] Usually captains only kept the bills of lading so that owners could demand their cargo during the subsequent trial at the British High Court of Admiralty. Fortunately for historians, however, the British managed to seize the *San Francisco Xavier*'s entire mail.

The *San Francisco Xavier*, alias *La Perla*, set sail from Callao for Cádiz on 12 May 1779. It was captured by two British privateers near the Azores almost five months later, on 9 October, then taken to Falmouth. There, when asked about the mail and the ship's papers (question sixteen in the interrogation), its captain, the Basque José Pérez del Muente, declared that 'none of them were burnt, torn, thrown overboard, destroyed or cancelled, concealed or attempted to be concealed by any person or persons whatsoever'. Indeed, several bags – containing a total of almost 2,000 envelopes – were seized.[23] Only nine of those envelopes would be delivered to the addressees during the subsequent trial.[24] Apart from numerous official documents sent by the colonial authorities, *La Perla*'s mail included 1,529 main envelopes (franked) containing 402 under-cover envelopes, 2,269 letters, 470 bills of lading, 308 sales accounts, 87 notarial documents (contracts, powers of attorney and last wills and testaments), 54 inventories, 44 bills of exchange, 23 account currents and 14 textile samples. The 540 principal writers and the 926 main addressees were mostly members of the aristocracy, colonial officials, churchmen and women and, above all, merchants. The value of this extremely synchronic source (virtually all the letters and documents were written between late March and early May 1779) lies in both its quantity and quality. For example, fourteen envelopes were addressed to Matías de Landaburu, one of the most prominent Cádiz merchants of the eighteenth century, and his name was mentioned in at least another nine sent to other Cádiz merchants. Twelve envelopes were addressed to Juan Francisco de Vea Murguía, and his name appeared in at least another seventeen. The evidence provided by *La Perla* clearly demonstrates the importance of key concepts such as trust, reputation and social behaviour.

Almost 98 per cent of *La Perla*'s letters had been sent from Lima; the remaining 2 per cent had been posted from Callao, Arequipa, Valparaiso, Lambayeque, Jauja and Cañete. The reason for this was the sudden departure of *La Perla*, which gave people from outside Lima no time to post their letters. Besides, provincial towns south of Lima such as Arequipa, Arica and Potosí sent most of their mail via Buenos Aires instead of via Lima. Likewise, cities north of Lima such as Trujillo, Loja and Guayaquil would send most of their mail via Cartagena. However, even if the commercial mail from

---

[22] Almost inexplicably, one of the packets would reach the beach of Santa María (near Cádiz) two months later and the mail would be delivered to the addressees: Roque Aguado to Arellano, Cádiz, 3 Dec. 1762, IRA, ARA, Epistolario.
[23] Apart from the ship papers (HCA 32/334/9), there are eight boxes containing the entire mail: HCA 30/275, 30/276, 30/311, 30/312, 30/313, 30/314, 30/315, 30/316.
[24] HCA 32/334/9 (1), fo. 80.

Table 2
La Perla's mail destinations

Destination	Envelopes	Percentage
Cádiz	1,052	54.47
Madrid	409	21.18
Seville	74	3.83
Isla de León	28	1.45
Puerto de Sta. María	19	0.98
Rome	12	0.62
Pamplona	11	0.57
Bilbao	10	0.51
Ferrol	10	0.51
Santander	10	0.51
Málaga	7	0.36
Valladolid	7	0.36
Cartagena	6	0.31
Córdoba	6	0.31
La Coruña	6	0.31
Lequeitio (Vizcaya)	6	0.31
Valencia	6	0.31
Escorial (Madrid)	5	0.26
Limpias (Cantabria)	5	0.26
Jerez de la Frontera	4	0.20
Hernani (Guipúzcoa)	4	0.20
Oñate (Guipúzcoa)	4	0.20
Barcelona	3	0.15
Bayonne	3	0.15
Burgos	3	0.15
Elgoibar (Guipúzcoa)	3	0.15
Genoa	3	0.15
Llodio (Alava)	3	0.15
Salamanca	3	0.15
San Sebastián	3	0.15
Toledo	3	0.15
123 destinations with fewer than three envelopes	216	11.18
Total	1,931	100

important cities such as Cuzco or Arequipa had been carried in *La Perla*, it would certainly have represented only a small proportion, for the commercial preponderance of Lima in the period was unquestionable. Furthermore, the correspondence shows that provincial merchants were supplied and monitored by merchants resident in Lima.

The destinations to which the mail was sent were far more varied, however. The 1,529 franked envelopes were addressed to 111 cities, towns and villages scattered throughout Spain and Europe, and the 402 under-cover envelopes added a further forty-three destinations. In total, therefore, *La Perla*'s mail was intended for 154 destinations. Unsurprisingly, most of the addressees were in Cádiz and Madrid: 1,052 of the 1,931 envelopes (54.47 per cent) were sent to Cádiz (910 main envelopes and 142 under-cover) and 409 (21.18 per cent) to Madrid (304 main and 105 under-cover), meaning that together the two cities accounted for 75.65 per cent of the whole. Far behind in third place was Seville with seventy-four envelopes (3.83 per cent); fourth and fifth were Isla de León and Puerto de Santa María (both in the Bay of Cádiz) with twenty-eight and nineteen envelopes respectively (1.45 and 1 per cent); the other destinations with ten or more envelopes were Rome (twelve), Pamplona (eleven), Bilbao (ten), Ferrol (ten) and Santander (ten). Destinations with three or more envelopes are recorded in table 2. The remaining 216 envelopes were sent to 123 destinations – an average of fewer than two envelopes per destination. There were only eight destinations outside Spain: Rome (twelve envelopes) and Genoa (three) in Italy; Bayonne (three), Paris (two), Auch (one) and Asparren (one) in France; Lisbon (one) and London (one).

Apart from Cádiz, Isla de León, Puerto de Santa María, Seville and Madrid, the other destinations did not play any commercial role in the trade with Peru. The merchant houses of important trade centres such as Bilbao, Santander, Málaga, Valencia and Barcelona did not take part in trade with Peru, not even through factors resident in Cádiz. Addressees in Madrid were mainly members of the elite, officeholders or clergymen rather than merchants. Among the merchant companies there was, of course, Madrid's *Cinco Gremios Mayores,* a joint stock company which had also been established in Cádiz since 1763, and played a very active role in the trade with Peru after 1784.[25] The low number of Seville merchants confirms the gradual decline in Seville's participation in colonial trade after both the House of Trade and the *consulado* were moved to Cádiz in 1717. Overall, the merchants involved in the trade with Peru were, to an overwhelming extent, those established in Cádiz.

The correspondence was conducted almost entirely in Spanish. Only ten individuals wrote letters in other languages: French (five letters from Esteban

---

[25] See, for example, Jorge Pinto Rodríguez, 'Los Cinco Gremios Mayores de Madrid y el comercio colonial en el siglo XVIII', *RI* clxlii (1991), 292–326.

de Urrutia and one from Pedro Dionisio de Gálvez); Italian (three, from Filipo Porcel, Giovanni Miretti and Antonio Vaccarezza); Latin (three from Fr Manuel de Quintanilla, Petrus Julius Rospiglioso and Antonio Jiménez); English (two by the Irish-Spanish Charles O'Reilly); Portuguese (one by Bernardo Lopes); and Catalán (one by the widow of Cristobal Mora). Of these only the Basque Esteban de Urrutia, the Genoese Antonio Vaccarezza and the Portuguese Bernardo Lopes were merchants.

Writing about mercantile culture in eighteenth-century Europe, Francesca Trivellato contends that, long after the appearance and diffusion of printed periodicals containing economic information, 'merchants' letters remained uniquely valuable for circulating information about the aptitude and trustworthiness of distant agents'.[26] No doubt this was also true with regard to the Peru trade. When a register ship was about to set sail for Spain, many people hurried to write their letters. The mail constituted a veritable wave of information crossing the Atlantic and reaching the same city at the same time. Merchants therefore knew that hundreds of addressees would discuss their letters in the numerous coffee-houses and *tertulias* of Cádiz. In other words merchants were very aware that their conduct – their day-to-day lives, indeed – was being monitored, either formally or informally: whatever they did was sure to have a profound effect upon their reputation on the other side of the Atlantic. It is no wonder, therefore, that in the correspondence numerous remarks were made about other merchants' reputations. Alfonso de Losada, for instance, had good news for his Cádiz correspondent José de Ramos: 'your brother keeps his good reputation among the public, and is married to a woman of much discernment'.[27] In contrast, Simón Babil de Úriz was informed of the 'bad conduct' of Xavier de Huizi, one of his debtors.[28] Naturally, the greater the number of correspondents, the more numerous the opportunities to contrast and monitor the honesty and good faith of one's contacts and debtors. Likewise, the more correspondents, the more chances to have access to all the gossip that circulated in Lima. In February 1783 the *visitador* José Antonio de Areche, who had been sent to Peru to inspect the viceroyal administration (including the activities of the Lima *consulado*), provided a telling description of the atmosphere of gossip and secrecy reigning in Lima: '[T]he minds of this country are very fertile' and they have such a habit of dissimulation that it is not easy to penetrate the subterfuges when they wish their thoughts to be concealed.'[29]

---

[26] Francesca Trivellato, 'Merchant letters across geographical and social boundaries', in F. Bethencourt and F. Egmond (eds), *Correspondence and cultural exchange in Europe, 1400–1700*, Cambridge 2007, 81.
[27] Losada to Ramos, Lima, 8 May 1779, HCA 30/316/12, no. 1065.
[28] José Joquín de Sos to Simón Babil de Úriz, Lima, 5 Mar. 1779, HCA 30/314/7, no. 146.
[29] Eunice J. Gates, 'Don José Antonio de Areche: his own defense', *HAHR* viii (1928), 30–1.

The merchant of Cádiz who had access to those confidences was more likely to succeed in the Peru trade.

Merchants did their best to ensure that their contacts would get the information that they required. That is why, along with fresh letters, they also sent copies of letters that had previously been posted by other routes. To make sure that they would reach their destinations, letters were usually posted twice or three times. In the first paragraph the author always informed the addressee about the correspondence that he had recently received from him, referring to each letter by its date. This information was absolutely essential in order to establish a dialogue with someone who was nearly six months away. Then the addressee would check his letter-book and remind himself of what he had written six months before. In eighteenth-century Peru, of course, six-month-old information from Spain was considered fresh and up to date.

Merchants in Lima also ordered newspapers from Spain. Their preference was for *La Gazeta de Madrid*, which was published every Tuesday and Friday and had eight to twelve pages containing general news from Spain and Europe. The issue of 24 October 1780, for instance, reported on events in Smyrna, Warsaw, Stockholm, London, Amsterdam, Bilbao and San Sebastián, all of them related to the war against Britain.[30] *La Gazeta de Madrid* was by far the most common newspaper to reach the Spanish colonies in the 1770s: between 1769 and 1780 the mail packet-boats to Buenos Aires carried 43,677 copies in total.[31] Once in Lima the gazettes circulated among networks of friends. In the postscript of his letter to Sebastián de Zumaran, Manuel José de Amándarro noted that 'I have just received from Sarraoa's house the eleven gazettes brought by Sarralde.'[32] Other newspapers such as 'gazettes from Holland' were also mentioned in the correspondence, though less frequently.[33]

The importance of letter-writing increased alongside the development of the new pattern of trade. Letters sent from Mexico City to Seville at the beginning of the century referred to *cartas vivas* (living letters), an expression conspicuously absent from *La Perla*. In July 1701, for example, Lorenzo de Mendoza avoided reporting to Juan Martínez de Alzaga on some recent events because Alonso de Armentia, who was a *carta viva*, was to travel to Seville and could tell him in person.[34] Likewise, in August 1701, the merchant Alonso de Ullívarri replied to Juan Piñero Vellorino's complaints

---

[30] BL, MS Add. 13988, fos 87–94.
[31] Lelo, *Correio*, 263.
[32] Manuel José de Amándarro to Sebastián de Zumaran, Lima, 8 May 1779, HCA 30/315/1, no. 1577.
[33] Manuel de Erasun to Juan Francisco de Vea Murguía, Lima, 31 Mar. 1779, HCA 30/314/3, no. 1129.
[34] Lorenzo de Mendoza to Juan Martínez de Alzaga, Mexico City, 15 July 1701, HCA 30/230/1.

about his meagre letters, claiming that he did not write more 'because *cartas vivas* are going there who will tell you all'.[35] The fact that that expression is absent from *La Perla*'s mail reflects a telling difference between the two patterns of trade. At the time of *flotas* and *galeones*, many Spanish merchants travelled to the colonies in order to dispose of their merchandise. They would later return to Spain in the same fleet with news about the very place where their principals' goods had been sold. Back home, they could also talk about those who had not been able to sell their merchandise and had therefore been obliged to stay in America. By contrast, the trade with Peru by means of register ships demanded regular communication that could not always be secured through oral transmission. Ships' crews could perform that role, and indeed did so, but only to a certain extent. The correspondence shows that some merchants did rely on members of the crew and passengers as long as they were known and trustworthy. Most merchants, however, preferred to write down what they had to say – and furthermore, given that the long distance and the hazardous journey meant that they had few opportunities to speak face to face, they were inclined to write profusely.

In many cases merchants dictated their letters to an assistant. Those who had access to their employers' business records and correspondence were considered reliable and loyal. The merchant would add his own handwriting in the postscript, or when it was essential to keep some information as secret as possible. For example, in his envelope to Lorenzo de Asunsolo, the merchant José Antonio de Lavalle included three letters, several accounts, a bill of lading and an envelope with the note *reservada*. This envelope contained a letter written by Lavalle himself in which he requested Asunsolo's help in securing the post of director of the *Renta de tabacos*.[36] Likewise, the count of San Isidro sent a *reservada* letter to Miguel Izquierdo with a plan for an illegal business.[37] However, few of the 402 under-cover envelopes sent in *La Perla* were in the *reservada* category.

The main reason merchants (and other authors) included other envelopes along with their letters was to save money. Friends and assistants were also given the opportunity to include their correspondence in the merchant's mail as a favour. It was the franked envelope's addressee (usually in Cádiz) who would deliver those envelopes. It is important to stress that the reason for sending envelopes under-cover had nothing to do with the identity of the addressee: *La Perla*'s mail included correspondence for several foreign merchants established in Cádiz, but despite the fact that foreigners were legally banned from the Spanish colonial trade, most of their correspondence was directly addressed to them, with their name clearly written on

[35] Alonso Ullívarri to Juan Piñero Vellorino, Mexico City, 29 Aug. 1701, ibid.
[36] José Antonio de Lavalle to Lorenzo de Asunsolo, Lima, 10 May 1779, HCA 30/314/1, no. 278.
[37] Isidro Abarca y Gutiérrez, 4th count of San Isidro, to Miguel Izquierdo, Lima, 10 May 1779, HCA 30/313/19, no. 326.

the franked envelope. This suggests that merchants considered the *Correos marítimos* a reliable means of communication, without any vetting of the recipients.

Most of the several types of letters described in the letter-writing manuals of the period (letters conveying advice, recommendations, complaints, excuses and so forth) do appear in *La Perla*, although they were often included in general letters dealing with many other issues.[38] The letter of recommendation is particularly relevant for it was an assurance of trustworthiness. Apart from personal ties, the ebb and flow of credit upon which the merchants' business depended derived precisely from such recommendations. Those sent in *La Perla* all concerned people who were on their way to Spain, which means that those who had been recommended were due to meet the intended recipients of the letters face to face. The historian Gabriela Dalla Corte states that this type of letter was also an instrument of credit with legal value, for the author became the guarantor of the person he recommended.[39] However, her interpretation is based on a few examples that do not account for the flexibility with which merchants used this type of letter. In fact, the *La Perla* letters show that recommendations were often a mere formality, and that their real value could vary enormously from case to case. That is not to say that recommendations were granted to anyone, but they were often a product of social convention. Manuel José de Amándarro recommended Melchor de Alarcón (*La Perla*'s steward) to his Cádiz correspondent Sebastián de Zumaran. If necessary, Zumaran was told to make sure that the merchants of Cádiz knew about Alarcón's honesty and good conduct, 'so that they confide in him'.[40] But Amándarro sent another letter to Zumaran (the recommendation had probably been written in the presence of Alarcón himself) clarifying the implications of the recommendation: 'I have not been able to refuse Alarcón's petition for recommending him to you', noted Amándarro this time, and although he acknowledged that Alarcón was truly an honest man he also stressed that 'all the sentences and adulations with which such petitions are embellished must never be taken at face value'.[41] It was up to Zumaran to make his own judgement and to act accordingly.

---

[38] See, for example, the only eighteenth-century manual of commercial letters in Spanish: Ignacio Palomba, *El secretario de banco, español y francés, en que se contiene el modo de escrivir en estas dos lenguas las cartas de comercio, en todo genero de negocios y trafico*, Paris 1768.
[39] Gabriela Dalla Corte, 'Recomendaciones y empeños en la sociedad colonial y postcolonial: garantías jurídicas, poder y red social', in M. Bertrand (coor.), *Configuraciones y redes de poder: un análisis de las relaciones sociales en América Latina*, Caracas 2002, 133–65.
[40] Amándarro to Zumaran, Lima, 8 May 1779, HCA 30/315/1, no. 1838.
[41] Ibid. no. 1577.

Judging the market

Economic historians working on the Spanish colonial trade have paid a great deal of attention to the quantitative side of imports and exports. Charts, however, do not indicate the wide range of colours, shapes and qualities of the cloths sent to America. This information was of paramount importance to the merchant, for sales were not only affected by the number of register ships arriving in the colonies; equally important was the selection of merchandise they contained.

The fact that so little is known about the transatlantic flow of commercial information is only partly explained by the lack of private records. The other reason for merchants' ability to select articles that were in demand being overlooked is that, despite its bureaucratic reputation, the Spanish crown was generally unable to put on record exactly what was being sent to the colonies. Cargoes were packed in bales wrapped in sacking, and only the owners knew the contents. This, of course, was a major problem when it came to taxation. Up to 1629 merchants paid according to the declared value of their goods (the duty was called *almojarijazgo*), but this controversial system severely delayed the departure of both *flotas* and *galeones* because tax collectors did not trust merchants' declarations and merchants never allowed tax collectors to unpack the merchandise. After 1629 an equally unsuccessful system was adopted, and then in 1680, for a few months, it was decided that taxation would be based on volume rather than value or weight. The 1720 *Real Proyecto* was to confirm this principle with the establishment of a duty called *derecho de palmeo*,[42] which not only encouraged merchants to ship expensive goods but also left no record of the exact content of the cargoes.

However, the true impact of the register ships upon the colonies can only be understood by examining both the cargoes and the information on the basis of which they were selected. This is particularly important because lower prices and regular supply gave more consumers the opportunity not only to dress *a la moda* but actually to dictate the *moda* (fashion) itself. In 1761 the viceroy of Peru, José Antonio Manso de Velasco, 1st count of Superunda, remarked that, thanks to the register ships, 'those who could not afford it in the past wear exquisite silks at present'.[43] Likewise, in 1791 the creole José de Baquijano stressed that, after the mid-eighteenth century, 'custom, taste and commodity that came from Europe spread: prices decreased allowing families to wear the most exquisite fabrics at prices that previously would not have allowed them to buy the rough manufactures of this country'.[44] Furthermore, the impact of fashion upon colonial society seems to have been particularly great in Lima. Writing in 1784, an anonymous merchant stressed

---

[42] García-Baquero, *Cádiz*, i. 197–203.
[43] Alfredo Moreno Cebrián (ed.), *Relación y documentos de gobierno del virrey del Perú, José A. Manso de Velasco, conde de Superunda, 1745–1761*, Madrid 1983, 284.
[44] Baquíjano, 'Disertación', i. 246.

that consumption in Lima was far more sumptuous than in Mexico City. Lima had half the population of Mexico City, but its inhabitants consumed twice as many European articles – and all 'because of the powerful reason that in the latter, as it is well known, the lower orders live naked, whereas, in the former, craftsmen, Indians and black people dress splendidly'.[45] He also stressed that the merchandise had to be sold in less than a year simply because European manufacturers changed colours and drawings constantly, showing the women of Lima 'the road to the inconsistency of fashion'.[46] From the mid-eighteenth century, therefore, the ability to judge the colonial market became essential for the merchant (and the manufacturer in Europe). As the anonymous author himself put it, 'those who buy in Cádiz with equity and profound knowledge of what is in demand in that kingdom [Peru] make very large profits'.[47]

But in analysing the importance that knowledge of the colonial market acquired after the mid-eighteenth century, a distorting element must be considered: the *repartimiento de mercancías*, or forced distribution and sale of goods.[48] Until 1784 Peru was divided into seventy-four provinces, each of which had a *corregidor* who was appointed for five years. There were differences between the development of the *corregimiento* in Spain and its colonies during the sixteenth and seventeenth centuries: while *corregidores* in Spain operated in urban centres along with municipal authorities (as in Bilbao), in the colonies they ruled Indian communities as representatives of colonial hegemony, and as such had judicial and executive powers. More important, due to their low salary in the colonies, *corregidores* used to take advantage of their position by making use of the *repartimiento*, that is to say, forcing Indians to buy goods. The *repartimiento* functioned informally for most of the seventeenth and eighteenth centuries, but in 1751, in an attempt to improve the situation of the Indians, it became legal and was officially regulated. Even so, abuses were widely reported throughout Spanish America. Eventually, in 1784, the administrative structure of Peru was replaced by the 'intendant' system and the *repartimiento* was nominally (but not in practice) abolished.[49] Since the *corregidores* of Peru were often supplied by the merchants of Lima, it is essential to consider the possible connection between the *repartimiento* and transatlantic trade after the mid-eighteenth century.

Few aspects of Spanish rule in America are more controversial than the *repartimiento*, and it is unsurprising that the controversy also affects the trans-

---

[45] 'Noticias del comercio del Perú dirigidas a los 5G Mayores de Madrid', BL, MS Add. 13981, fo. 25.
[46] Ibid. fos 25–6.
[47] Ibid. fo. 24.
[48] The system was also known as *repartimiento*, *repartimiento de bienes* or simply *reparto*.
[49] John R. Fisher, *Government and society in colonial Peru: the intendant system, 1784–1814*, London 1970, 1–28; David Cahill, 'Repartos ilícitos y familias principales en el sur andino, 1780–1824', *RI* xlviii (1988), 449–73.

atlantic trade. Javier Tord and Carlos Lazo show that the increase in income obtained from the *alcabala real* (the main commercial tax in Peru) after the mid-eighteenth century was due to a higher consumption of European goods, whereas the income from the *alcabala de tarifa* (the tax on *repartimientos*) gradually decreased.[50] By contrast, and following a more traditional view, Carmen Parrón argues that the *repartimientos* and the growth of transatlantic trade from the middle of the century were closely interconnected, for the decrease in the tax on *repartimientos* did not account for *corregidores*' abuses.[51] The problem is that the real extent of those abuses is unknown. The picture arising from *La Perla*'s mail is clearly in accordance with the former interpretation, and Parrón's suggestion that merchants relied to a great extent on selling their European merchandise to ruthless *corregidores* is mistaken.

It is important to note that the traditional depiction of the *repartimiento* as a coercive method totally disregards the possibility that trust (or more precisely, lack of trust) may have had something to do with the very existence of the *repartimiento* (and with the fact that it survived its nominal abolition). That is precisely what Jeremy Baskes argues in his study of the *repartimiento* in Oaxaca, a province of New Spain devoted to the production of cochineal. He stresses that traditional depictions of the *repartimiento* are simplistic, mainly because the commercial role of Indian peasants, who were trading long before the arrival of the Spaniards, has been overlooked. For him it is unclear how a single *corregidor* and a couple of *tenientes* (lieutenants) were able to subjugate whole communities, forcing them to trade against their will. Moreover, if the *repartimiento* was no more than robbery, why did the *corregidor* deliver expensive and valued items such as livestock and money to the Indians, and always on credit? For Baskes, such inconsistencies can only be explained if the *repartimiento* is regarded as an institution of credit which developed under colonial conditions of high risk. He concludes that 'by reducing transaction costs, the costs of assessing creditworthiness and collecting the debts, the *repartimiento* made profitable (and less risky) the provision of credit'.[52] That is to say, the *corregidor* could hardly force whole Indian communities to trade, but did have sufficient leverage to ensure that individual loans (which were orally arranged with farmers living in remote areas) were repaid. This interpretation does not fully account for the widely reported abuses (particularly in the case of Peru), but shows that the *repartimiento* had a reason to exist other than mere coercion.

Nevertheless, coercion does seem to have been widespread in the provinces of Peru. In 1778 the crown sent the *visitador* José Antonio de Areche (who previously had been appointed to New Spain) to inspect the func-

---

[50] Javier Tord Nicolini and Carlos Lazo García, *Hacienda, comercio, fiscalidad, y luchas sociales (Perú colonial)*, Lima 1981, 135–9.
[51] Parrón, *De las reformas*, 307–8.
[52] Jeremy Baskes, *Indians, merchants, and markets: a reinterpretation of the repartimiento and Spanish-Indian economic relations in colonial Oaxaca, 1750–1821*, Stanford 2001, 92.

tioning of the colonial administration. A few months after his arrival in Lima he concluded that the situation of the Indians was much worse than in New Spain.[53] Two years later, in 1780, a force of 60,000 Peruvian Indians revolted against Spanish rule under the leadership of José Gabriel Condorcanqui, who adopted the name of an ancestor, the Inca Túpac Amaru. The possibility of the *repartimiento* being the direct cause of the uprising is the subject of further debate. According to Jürgen Golte, the connection between the two is incontestable, for the provinces most inclined to rebel carried the heavier burden of *repartimiento* debt.[54] Other historians, however, consider Golte's conclusion too simplistic. Scarlett O'Phelan, for example, argues that the rebellion was caused not by the *repartimiento* but by the increasing competition between *hacendados* (landowners), *obrajes* (textile manufactories), *corregidores* and priests for control over local communities and their economic resources.[55]

La Perla's mail strongly suggests that the transatlantic trade was not affected by the abusive use of the *repartimiento*. On the eve of the Túpac Amaru rebellion, merchants residing in Lima did not count on the *repartimiento* system to dispose of European imports. The Indians were not the customers that they had in mind when they ordered silk stockings and fur hats. If they resorted to using a *corregidor* when merchandise turned out to be unsaleable, they did not mention it in their letters. Instead, the correspondence provides a picture of fierce competition between merchants. Their comments on their inventories were similar to those of Juan Bautista de Gárate, who stressed to one of his Cádiz correspondents that the articles he had just ordered were 'in demand and are necessary for the commerce of my shop'.[56] Along with describing what was in demand, merchants also provided information about the reliability of potential buyers. For example, the merchant Antonio de Elizalde pointed out to his brother Matías that his inventory would be promptly sold 'for some trustworthy merchants are coming down from the sierra'.[57] The picture of competition provided by *La Perla* is consistent with the fact that, along with Peruvian commodities, register ships returning to Spain also carried 'articles from Castile that are sent back because they are not saleable'.[58]

---

[53] Gates, 'Don José', 22.
[54] Jürgen Golte, *Repartos y rebeliones: Túpac Amaru y las contradicciones de la economía colonial*, Lima 1980.
[55] Scarlett O'Phelan, *Rebellions and revolts in eighteenth-century Peru and Upper Peru*, Cologne 1985, 118–26.
[56] Juan Bautista de Gárate to Fermín Ramón de Barrera, Lima, 9 May 1779, HCA 30/313/2, no. 50.
[57] Antonio de Elizalde to Matías de Elizalde, Lima, 3 Apr. 1779, HCA 30/313/3, no. 1089.
[58] 'Extract of the cargo carried by the register ship *Gallardo*', 24 Apr. 1776, AGI, Lima 1525.

As might be expected, several *corregidores* are mentioned in *La Perla*. Two had arrived from Spain in April in the *Santiago*: Juan Casimiro de Ozta (a member of the Cádiz *consulado*, appointed to the province of Cotabamba) and Vicente Hore (appointed to Lampa and whose wife did not survive the voyage). Both had received sea loans in Cádiz and had brought merchandise to Lima. But for all their alleged power over Indian communities, *corregidores* like Ozta and Hore did not constitute totally secure business for their creditors. For example, one of the most important creditors in Cádiz was the merchant Matías de Landaburu, who was also one of the Cádiz merchants with better connections in Lima: in May 1779 his five bad debts in Peru included that of the *corregidor* of the Andean province of Huanta, Gregorio Xalavera, who was unable to repay 2,992 *pesos*.[59] Even more telling is the example of the six bad debts that the French firm Verduc, Kerleguen, Payan and Co. had in Peru: one debtor had been somewhere in the sierra since 1774, another had given up commerce and disappeared, one had gone bankrupt and the remaining three were *corregidores*.[60]

Crucially, *La Perla* shows that transatlantic merchants were involved in much more intense competition than previously thought. It also demonstrates that register ships had a spectacular impact on the flow of commercial information across the Atlantic. Increasing sales and product diversification were stimulated by the combined effect of consumer demand, the ongoing development of transatlantic networks and improvements in communication. Peruvian consumers and European manufacturers were therefore brought closer together than ever before. This development was epitomised by a type of document that appears nowhere in the historiography on Spanish colonial trade: the so-called *nota de efectos aparentes* (inventory of articles in demand), or, more commonly, the *nota*.[61]

Fifty *notas* were sent to Spain in *La Perla*'s mail,[62] and in addition the ship's captain had another thirteen *notas* among his personal papers.[63] Considering that in May 1779 there were at least 188 transatlantic merchants in Lima

---

[59] Juan Bautista de Orobiogoitia to Matías de Landaburu, Lima, 8 May 1779, HCA 30/313/1, no. 485.
[60] Juan Sabugo to Verduc, Kerleguen, Payan and Co., Lima, 3 Apr. 1779, HCA 30/312/10, no. 1529.
[61] Less commonly, terms such as *razón*, *factura*, *ancheta* and *memoria* were also used to name inventories.
[62] HCA 30/312/2, no. 1070; 30/312/3, no. 1506; 30/312/7, no. 784; 30/312/13, no. 172; 30/313/1, nos 16, 44; 30/313/2, nos 50, 1072; 30/313/9, no. 831; 30/313/16, no. 1093; 30/313/17, nos 1054, 1069; 30/314/2, no. 589; 30/314/4, no. 1505; 30/314/5, no. 368; 30/314/7, nos 625, 849 (two *notas*), 1298; 30/314/8, no. 996; 30/314/11, nos 972, 975; 30/314/13, no. 521; 30/314/17, nos 770, 774; 30/314/20, no. 629; 30/315/1, nos 162, 331, 517, 701 (three *notas*), 1577; 30/315/4, 21, nos 1046, 1075, 1106; 30/315/10, no. 1027; 30/315/13, nos 380, 394; 30/315/14, no. 1116; 30/315/18, envelope without number; 30/316/1, no. 844; 30/316/2, no. 166; 30/316/4, no. 1198; 30/316/5, no. 700; 30/316/12, no. 501; 30/316/13, no. 344; 30/316/15, nos 658, 659.
[63] HCA 32/334/9, fos 90, 91, 93, 95, 96–7, 99, 104, 107–9, 113, 119, 121.

and that by then Peru and Spain were connected by a monthly mail, sixty-three *notas* is truly a remarkable number. Each consisted of between one and five folios, with long, carefully crafted lists of articles followed by detailed instructions. The astonishing number of names of types of cloth, and the variety of different colours and designs, was matched only by the extreme intricacy of the language used. Sending patterns was an additional way of providing precise information. In the *La Perla* mail ten envelopes contained one or more textile swatches.[64] Gregorio de Sarasa, for example, informed Juan Miguel de Aguerrebere that he would take care of 'sending *notas* and samples in advance so that you may have time to get the articles'.[65] *Notas* and samples provided invaluable feedback for the European manufacturers. Antonio and José Matías de Elizalde assured their brother that 'some dozens [of stockings] that came last year from [the Royal factory of] Talavera are well produced, and only the colours and their *colocación* [fitting] seem to be defective, which will be easily solved with the samples that have already been sent from here'.[66]

Some merchants not only described what they wanted but also indicated where and from whom the articles should be purchased. Silvestre Amenábar, for instance, sent to his brother Xavier Ignacio a *nota* divided into four sections: *sedas* (silks), *lienzos* (linens), *lanas* (woollens) and *surtimiento de algunos de los efectos puestos en la nota* (assortment of some of the articles listed in the *nota*).[67] The specifications for colour and design were followed by precise instructions. Two winter dresses: 'you will find them in the house of Lostaud, Martínez, or other warehouses of articles from Valencia'. Eighty dozen *virretes*: 'in Juan de Andas street, you will select the better ones'. Superior lingerie from Naples: 'Those from Alfonso di Mayo's workshop are usually good.' *Estameñas*: 'in the house of White and Fleming'. Twenty-five pieces of *sarazas*: 'They should be from China.' He also wanted twenty dozens of silk handkerchiefs 'such as those sent by José de Madariaga to Manuel Ignacio de Erasun last year'.

For the merchant, putting what he wanted into precise words was a challenge that not only required knowledge of trade and fashion but also specialised vocabulary and language skills not possessed by the lay person. Writing from Madrid in the summer of 1778, Francisco de Obregón asked his friend Gaspar de Orúe whether it would be more profitable for him to send clothes to Lima or to lend money *a riesgo de mar*. If the former was

---

[64] HCA 30/312/3, no. 837; 30/312/9, nos 549, 1032; 30/312/13, no. 172; 30/313/1, no. 947; 30/313/17, no. 1067; 30/313/18, no. 1044; 30/314/11, no. 972; 30/315/1, no. 701; 30/315/6, no. 1576.
[65] Gregorio Sarasa to Juan Miguel de Aguerrebere, Lima, 3 Apr. 1779, HCA, 30/314/7, no. 849.
[66] A. Elizaldes to M. Elizalde, Lima, 26 Apr. 1779, HCA 30/313/3, no. 1089.
[67] Silvestre de Amenábar to Xavier Ignacio de Amenábar, Lima, 8 May 1779, HCA 30/312/2, no. 1070.

the better option, Obregón wanted Orúe (who was not a merchant) to tell him which clothes were in demand in Peru. In his reply, a year later, Orúe included a *nota* for Obregón at the end of which he wrote: 'Here you have a list made by somebody who knows this commerce well. I am not a merchant to express an opinion, and if you decided to send some inventory, you will do it to somebody else, for I do not understand this *farándula* [blarney].'[68] The reason why Obregón had chosen Orúe was because he trusted him and because he knew Orúe was a well-positioned colonial official with close friends in the merchant community. However, merchants were not always so keen to help others through their ability to judge the market. When a certain María Andrea de la Cantolla asked the merchant Juan Bautista de Gárate to arrange a small *nota* for her (worth only 300 *pesos*), he confided to Fermín Ramón de Barrera that 'although my desire is to please her, I am so perplexed by this matter that I do not know what to do'.[69]

The merchant in Lima could send the *nota* either to buy goods on his account or to provide updated information for his Cádiz correspondent. In the latter case the merchant in Lima would be the future consignee and would sell the merchandise for a commission. In either case, however, merchants stressed that their *notas* had to be followed carefully. For example, José Antonio de Lavalle warned Lorenzo de Asunsolo that if he wanted to send clothes to Lima and get a quicker return, the merchandise should be 'well assorted and better purchased' than the last time, and 'as close as possible to the *notas* I have sent you until now'.[70] Unlike Lavalle, Juan Bautista de Irigoyen ordered the merchandise for himself. 'Make sure that this *nota* comes as I request, not differing at all in its details', he stressed to Sebastián de Zumaran.[71] In order to avoid misunderstandings, merchants in Lima tried hard to be precise in their specifications, but knew only too well that their Cádiz correspondents would inevitably have the last word. Mutual understanding and trust were therefore essential. It was not only that the Cádiz correspondent would have to select the right articles, but he would also have to buy them at good prices. How much should he spend on the whole *nota*? For this the merchant in Lima assigned an approximate budget, and then asked his Cádiz correspondent to buy the articles as cheaply as possible. Manuel José de Amándarro, for example, wanted Pedro de Ibarrola to spend between 30,000 and 40,000 *pesos* on his *nota*, 'reducing [prices] proportionally to all its articles'.[72]

Despite all the details that they contained, *notas* were based on individual perception and their subjective nature engendered competition. 'Amándarro

---

[68] Gaspar de Orúe to Francisco de Obregón, Lima, 8 May 1779, HCA 30/316/15, no. 659.
[69] Gárate to Barrera, Lima, 30 Mar. 1779, HCA 30/313/2, no. 50.
[70] Lavalle to Asunsolo, Lima, 29 Mar. 1779, HCA 30/314/1, no. 278.
[71] Irigoyen to Zumaran, Lima, 3 Apr. 1779, HCA 30/315/1, no. 162.
[72] Amándarro to Ibarrola, Lima, 8 May 1779, HCA 30/313/2, no. 1072.

has shown me a draft of an inventory of articles he is sending to you', wrote Silvestre de Amenábar to Pedro de Ibarrola; 'he has much experience of this city's commerce, but although mine is lesser, I think otherwise.'[73] Naturally, only close friends were allowed to see one's *nota*. Gregorio Sarasa, for example, relied on the Cádiz merchant Juan Miguel de Aguerrebere. Sarasa pointed out that if there was any problem with his inventory, 'you will try to purchase other articles following the *notas* you will receive from here'.[74] Instead, Amenábar wanted Ibarrola to purchase his *nota* 'on the condition that it is not disclosed'. The point to emphasise is that, despite a forthcoming glut of European fabrics (predicted by virtually all merchants writing in *La Perla*), merchants could still do good business if they were accurate and also fortunate enough to provide fashionable articles. As Joaquín Xavier García pointed out to Simón Babil de Úriz, 'all in all, the merchant who guesses correctly the taste of these *madamas* [ladies] will sell promptly, for luxury is on the increase day by day'.[75] For all their efforts, merchants knew only too well that the element of guesswork in trading was an inevitable part of the game.

Register ships and improvements in communication transformed the pattern of the Peru trade. But what was the impact of the new pattern of trade upon the merchants themselves? How did it affect their participation?

---

[73] Amenábar to Ibarrola, Lima, 8 May 1779, HCA 30/316/2, no. 166.
[74] Sarasa to Aguerrebere, Lima, 3 Apr. 1779, HCA 30/314/7, no. 849.
[75] García to Úriz, Lima, 8 May 1779, HCA 30/314/7, no. 483.

5
Merchants and Networks

It is clear that the new pattern of trade on the Cádiz-Lima route and the significant improvements in the system of communications which accompanied it contributed to the fostering of transatlantic networks. However, very little is known about these networks, or about the identity of the merchants who created them. Understanding has been shaped by almost exclusive attention to documents emanating from the *consulados* and the crown, which largely ignore merchants' individual experiences. According to Alfonso Quiroz, Carmen Parrón and Patricia Marks, after the mid-eighteenth century there were two divergent merchant groups in Lima: Cádiz *consulado* merchants on the one hand, and Lima *consulado* merchants on the other. A non-reciprocal relationship existed whereby metropolitan merchants dominated the two poles of trade by excluding the Peruvians, meaning that consignments from Cádiz to Lima were only made to members of the Cádiz *consulado*.[1] *La Perla*'s mail, however, paints a very different picture, showing that when it came to transatlantic trade, merchants cared little about consular affiliation but were very concerned with the trustworthiness of their correspondents. It was clearly the case that the frequent arrival of register ships and the improvements in communication led to collaboration between merchants of both sides of the Atlantic for the purpose of trading, but they also had other things in common that helped to foster mutual understanding.

The merchants

The terms used for merchants involved in the trade between Spain and Peru (*gaditanos*, *galeonistas*, *encomenderos* or Spaniards in the case of those operating from Cádiz, and *limeños*, Peruvians or simply Americans in the case of those functioning from Lima) are conventional in the historiography of colonial trade. However, they conceal other identities that played a crucial part in building up transatlantic networks. Again, *La Perla*'s mail provides a unique insight into merchants' individual experiences. Amongst the letter-writers in the ship's mail were 188 merchants (including three foreigners),

---

[1] Alfonso W. Quiroz, *Deudas olvidadas: instrumentos de crédito en la economía colonial peruana, 1750–1820*, Lima 1993, 103–4; Parrón, *De las reformas*, 165–72; Patricia H. Marks, *Deconstructing legitimacy: viceroys, merchants, and the military in late colonial Peru*, University Park, PA 2007, 55–105.

whilst the addressees comprised 292 individuals (forty-six of whom were foreigners).

It is easier to uncover the names and geographical origin of the merchants of the Cádiz *consulado* than of their Lima counterparts. The most useful source for identifying the Cádiz merchants is the *consulado*'s *libro de matrícula* (membership book), which was created in 1730 when the Spanish government was trying to revitalise colonial trade. The previous year the Cádiz *consulado* had agreed its new ordinances. The *libro de matrícula* was intended to strengthen the monopoly of Spanish merchants, making it clear who was Spanish and who was not.[2] From 1743 to 1823 this book recorded the names and birthplaces of 3,094 new members (in addition to providing the names of another 158 merchants without specifying their birthplace).[3] It shows that the members of the Cádiz *consulado* came almost equally from northern Spain (45 per cent) and Andalusia (43 per cent). In the north, the Basque region (Vizcaya, Guipúzcoa, Alava and Navarra) had the largest share (21 per cent of the entire membership), while in Andalusia the province of Cádiz had the largest share (also 21 per cent of the total). However, whilst the *libro de matrícula* gives names and birthplaces, it says nothing about how long merchants remained in the trade. This is crucial, given that many members traded only for a very short period of time. In 1753, for instance, a list of Spanish merchants resident in Cádiz was compiled in preparation for a new unified tax, the *única contribución*, which contained 286 names. A 1762 revision recorded 221 merchants, whereas a new attempt to establish the same tax in 1771 recorded 422 names. These three figures all included *consulado* (two-thirds) and non-*consulado* (one-third) members.[4] It would therefore appear that the 246 Spanish merchants who were the addressees of *La Perla*'s mail is a good representative sample.

The geographical origin of the Spanish merchants is significant because to a great extent it determined their partners and connections. Among the 246 Spanish addressees in the correspondence were 179 members of the Cádiz *consulado*, and sixty-seven who never joined it. Of the former group a very significant 54 per cent came from northern Spain (Basques or *vasco-navarros* alone amounted to 30 per cent), whereas the Andalucian share was 27 per cent (Cádiz alone made up 21 per cent). The rest of Spain accounted for a mere 6 per cent. Spaniards or Americans whose birthplace was not recorded in the *libro de matrícula* represented 6.7 per cent of the total, naturalised foreigners 4 per cent, and Peruvians 1.7 per cent. The presence of three Peruvians is significant (José de Santiago, Juan Manuel de Sarría and

---

[2] Julián Bautista Ruiz Rivera, 'Patiño y la reforma del consulado de Cádiz en 1729', *Temas Americanistas* v (1985), 16–21.
[3] For the complete membership see Ruiz, *Consulado*, 113–216.
[4] Antonio García-Baquero, 'Permanencia y renovación en la matrícula mercantil gaditana del siglo XVIII: el componente español, 1749–1773', in A. García-Baquero (ed.), *Comercio y burguesía mercantil en el Cádiz de la Carrera de Indias*, Cádiz 1991, 75.

Francisco de la Barreda) because they demonstrate that *criollos* (creoles) could and did become members of the Cádiz *consulado*.⁵ In fact, fifty-five American-born merchants (ten of them from Peru) joined the Cádiz *consulado* between 1744 and 1806.⁶

In addition to the individual merchants listed, among *La Perla*'s addressees there were also forty-six foreign firms, forty of which were French, five Irish and one Genoese. The historian Didier Ozanam provides a list of French merchants residing in Cádiz in 1777 (most of them came from south-west France). Seventy firms are depicted as *Maisons de commerce et négociants en gros* (trading houses and wholesalers).⁷ Thirty of these were addressees of *La Perla*'s mail.

Finding out the names and the geographical origin of the merchants of Lima is much more problematic. Carmen Parrón states that the term *criollo* included both Peruvian and Spanish merchants who had settled in Peru around the mid-eighteenth century: 'The term [*criollo*] must be always understood in that relative way.'⁸ But she does not say who the *criollos* were, except that they were white and members of the Lima *consulado*. Patricia Marks concludes that after the mid-eighteenth century, 'commerce, firmly in the hands of new (and constantly renewed) cadres of metropolitan merchants, had been reduced to something resembling an extractive industry'.⁹ However she acknowledges that both the number and the identity of the new merchants trading with Lima are difficult to ascertain and, surprisingly enough, one of the few merchants she mentions, the count of San Isidro, whom she depicts as 'peninsular-born but *acriollado*', seems to weaken her interpretation: apparently San Isidro was leader of the *limeño* faction in 1787, but three years later was acting on behalf of the metropolitan sector.¹⁰

The question of the *peruleros* is equally controversial. The term was used most commonly in the first half of the seventeenth century, but it also appears in *La Perla*'s mail. According to most historians *peruleros* were agents sent to Spain in the *galeones* by the merchants of Lima, along with their money for the purchase of specific merchandise to be transported in the next fleet. However, in the first dictionary of Castilian, published in 1611, the term *perulero* is defined rather differently as 'he who has come rich *from* the Indies of Peru' (my italics).¹¹ Who, then, were the *peruleros*? Pierre Chaunu states

---

⁵ The term *criollo* had no particular pejorative connotations. In the Spanish American colonies the concept was adapted into a context of racial hierarchy based on racial 'purity'. Those to whom the label *criollo* could be applied would have been of proven unmixed Spanish ancestry.
⁶ Ruiz, *Consulado*, 49–50.
⁷ Didier Ozanam, 'La Colonie française de Cadix au XVIII siècle d'aprés un document inédit (1777)', *Mélanges de la Casa de Velázquez* iv (1968), 311–24.
⁸ Parrón, *De las reformas*, 167–8.
⁹ Marks, *Deconstructing legitimacy*, 104.
¹⁰ Ibid. 69–71.
¹¹ Sebastián Covarrubias, *Tesoro de la lengua castellana o española*, Madrid 1611, 586.

that in the early seventeenth century 'the creole merchants of Seville were called *peruleros*'.[12] Enriqueta Vila suggests that they were mainly merchants from Seville who had returned to Spain after spending many years in Peru.[13] Margarita Suárez finds Vila's assertion to be an 'odd conclusion' but does not provide any evidence to the contrary.[14] Only Lutgardo García provides precise information about some of them, showing that between 1580 and 1630 at least 10 per cent of the *peruleros* were born in the Basque Country.[15]

Clarifying the question of identity is very important, because along with information it was pivotal in generating trust. In order to understand the networks linking Spain and Peru, it is thus crucial to elucidate the controversy over *criollos* and *peruleros*. To do so, attention must be paid to a phenomenon that applied not only to Peru but to the whole of Spanish America. In his 1971 seminal work on miners and merchants in late colonial Mexico, David Brading proposed a compelling hypothesis. Although he warned that the evidence for his theory was literary rather than statistical, he argued that colonial trade could not be fully understood without discussing what he called 'the unusual sociology' of its structure: 'All our evidence', he argued, 'suggests that generation by generation, from the Conquest until Independence, immigrant Spaniards dominated colonial trade.'[16] Subsequent research has confirmed that for Mexico and Buenos Aires in the second half of the eighteenth century Brading's hypothesis is incontestable.[17] Peru was no exception. By coincidence, the only surviving list of the Lima *consulado*'s membership for the second half of the eighteenth century was made in January 1779, four months before the departure of *La Perla*. It listed those who were present at the Consular elections of that year, and contains the names of 160 merchants.[18] Of those, at least 108 figure in *La Perla*'s mail. Notably, of the 160 listed, forty-eight had previously been members of the Cádiz *consulado*. An examination of the list of those present at the election, *La Perla*'s mail and the Cádiz *consulado*'s *libro de matrícula* makes it possible to identify the geographical origin of the transatlantic merchants residing in Lima. The content of *La Perla*'s mail shows that in May 1779 there were at least 188 transatlantic merchants living in Peru. Of these the origin of 124 has been located. The data speaks for itself: 114 were born in Spain, nine in Peru, two in Portugal (Bernardo Lopes and Juan Lopes Acunha)

---

[12] Pierre Chaunu, *Séville et l'Amérique aux XVIe et XVI et siècles*, Paris 1977, 187.
[13] Vila, 'Feria', 295–301.
[14] Suárez, *Desafíos transatlánticos*, 8.
[15] Lutgardo García Fuentes, *Los peruleros y el comercio de Sevilla con las Indias, 1580–1630*, Seville 1997, 153.
[16] Brading, *Miners*, 104.
[17] See, for example, Christiana Borchart de Moreno, 'Los miembros del consulado de la ciudad de México en la época de Carlos iii', *JbLa* xiv (1977), 135–6; Kicza, *Colonial entrepreneurs*, 235; Socolow, *Merchants*, 16–18; and Félix E. Converso, 'Españoles y americanos, agentes de un mercado regional', *AEA* xlvii (1990), 280.
[18] AGN, TC-GO2, caja 6, leg. 10, cuaderno 145.

and one in Genoa (Antonio Vaccarezza). Even if the remaining sixty-four merchants (all of them with Spanish surnames) were *criollos*, which is very unlikely, it would still mean that 66 per cent of the merchants involved in transatlantic trade and residing in Lima were born in Spain. Furthermore, like those of Cádiz, most of the merchants of Lima came from the mountainous seaboard of northern Spain. Of the 114 peninsular-born merchants residing in Lima whose letters were carried in *La Perla*, sixty-one came from the Basque Country, thirty-seven from other northern areas of Spain, twelve from Andalusia and only four were from the rest of Spain. In other words, 86 per cent of the peninsular-born merchants of Lima came from northern Spain.

It is true that this analysis is only valid for 1779. Many of those merchants might well be from the 'new cadres of metropolitan merchants' depicted by Patricia Marks – the consequence of the opening of the Cape Horn route and the regular arrival of register ships. However, further evidence suggests that the pattern of peninsular predominance also applied to the previous decades. Jesús Turiso has recently shown that between 1688 and 1764, 80 per cent of the heads of the Lima *consulado* were born in Spain (36 per cent were Basques and 18 per cent *montañeses*), the origin of 12 per cent is unknown, and only 7 per cent were born in Peru.[19] In short, since at least the 1680s, long before the adoption of the Cape Horn route, most members of the Lima *consulado* had been Spanish-born.

The reason why so few *criollos* were involved in trading is not easy to discern. They certainly occupied most of the positions of power and responsibility in the colonial administration (bureaucracy, clergy and army) – often to an overwhelming extent. In 1777, for example, ten of the twelve judges in the Lima *Audiencia* (the high court for civil and criminal cases, and the most prestigious political institution in South America) were *criollos*.[20] When it came to commerce, however, they were only a small minority. It seems that, in general, they found trade less attractive than peninsular emigrants did. This is a controversial argument that the post-colonial period seems to corroborate: independence did not give rise to a *criollo* merchant class. In fact, after the 1820s foreigners replaced peninsular merchants, and so the pattern of foreign numerical domination, inherited from the colonial period, was perpetuated throughout the nineteenth century. Eugene Ridings states that, in the century following independence, 'the persistence and strength of values associated with the landowning aristocracy was probably the chief reason why so few creoles became overseas traders'.[21] Furthermore, in the nineteenth century, foreign merchants would consistently choose their

---

[19] Turiso, *Comerciantes*, 96–100.
[20] Leon G. Campbell, 'A colonial establishment: creole domination of the Audiencia of Lima during the late eighteenth century', *HAHR* lii (1972), 3.
[21] Eugene W. Ridings, 'Foreign predominance among overseas traders in nineteenth-century Latin America', *Latin American Research Review* xx/2 (1985), 18.

assistants from among their own countrymen, and few of them would pass control of their business to their own sons, whether born in the colonies or not. Eighteenth-century Spaniards did exactly the same.

Emigration and cohesion

A staggering 85 per cent of all the merchants figuring in *La Perla*'s mail were born neither in the city or the province of Cádiz nor in Peru. Furthermore, 69 per cent of the Spaniards whose geographical origin is known came from the mountains of northern Spain. This fact, along with the cultural diversity of Spain, is crucial to an understanding of the structure of the networks that linked Spain and Peru.

Though the recruitment of northerners had some peculiar characteristics, in general most Spaniards who were not born in Cádiz joined the colonial trade in similar circumstances. The first significant feature is that the great majority of northerners came from peasant families with no mercantile background. They came from villages such as Limpias in Cantabria, Vinuesa in Soria or Irurita in Navarre – where the small family farm was the characteristic form of enterprise and where most peasants were owners of the land they cultivated. But the small size of plots meant that the land could not be divided if it was to be profitable. As a result, the property was passed on to a single heir. Throughout the colonial period, inheritance practices and the high population density of the region led northern families to consider emigration as the main opening for offspring who were not due to inherit. For women, the best options were a good marriage or a convent. For men, the Army, the Church, the imperial administration and colonial trade all offered the prospect of a promising career. It was no wonder, therefore, that younger sons were encouraged to leave their home town. In general the people of the region shared a sense of social equality, the majority regarding themselves as *hidalgos* (lesser nobility) even though they came from rather humble backgrounds. Generation by generation, emigration became part of daily life in the villages of northern Spain, and not even the economic revival experienced by the region in the eighteenth century would change that. Population growth exceeded economic expansion and the northern rural area saw the departure of even more people. The main destinations were Madrid, Seville, Cádiz and the colonies (America and the Philippines). In fact, the extensive participation of northerners in colonial trade was replicated in the Spanish capital: in the period 1765–1800, 82 per cent of merchants established in Madrid had been born in northern Spain.[22]

---

[22] Juan Carlos Sola Corbacho, 'El papel de la organización familiar en la dinámica del sector mercantil madrileño a finales del siglo XVIII', *Historia Social* xxxii (1998), 5.

Kinship ties in colonial trade involved uncles, nephews, brothers and cousins, but seldom fathers and sons.[23] Successful merchants viewed other occupations (government service, clergy or army) as being more promising and less risky for their children. Moreover, the inheritance laws of central and southern Castile, which governed both Cádiz and the colonies, favoured a constant dispersal of accumulated capital, dividing the merchant's earnings between his widow and children.[24] Since the typical figure in the Hispanic commercial world was the individual trader (great corporations and financial institutions were non-existent in the Indies and fairly rare in Spain), investing in share-holding was seldom an option. The merchant could prevent the division of his fortune by investing his capital in land and establishing a *mayorazgo* (an entailed estate), which was exempted from the usual process of division and could be therefore bequeathed to a sole heir. But if he wanted to pass his trading house to the next generation, he would consider marrying his daughter to a capable merchant or to a promising assistant, either of whom was often a nephew brought from his home town.

Most future merchants left their homes as teenagers. No doubt the network of relatives and *paisanos* (countrymen) that would either employ or find a position for such youngsters also acted as surrogate families. This is a feature worth emphasising, for the future career of these young men would feature these same people. The implications of emigration are illustrated in the case of Luis José de Echevarría. On 4 October 1745 Echevarría left Rentería (Guipúzcoa) as a teenager for Cádiz with the intention of going to Buenos Aires, where his uncle Pedro de Iribarren and a fellow Basque, Miguel Antonio de Ezcurrechea, had a trading house. Because of Luis José's youth he was accompanied to Cádiz by Pedro de Arrambide, a Basque ship captain who had returned from Buenos Aires in July 1741 and was now on his way back to America. Two months later Juan Bautista de Lacoa, a young man in his early twenties also from Rentería, would join Luis José in Cádiz. Together the young Luis José and Lacoa were to spend ten months in Cádiz waiting for the next ship to Buenos Aires. The correspondence that they received from Rentería during those months (a set of fourteen letters that were intercepted by the British) shows that a whole network of relatives and *paisanos* was required to incorporate them into the colonial trade. In Cádiz, they were assisted by Andrés de Loyo, Santiago de Irisarri and Juan de Garay y Leániz, three Basque merchants and renowned members of the Cádiz *consulado*. The arrangements for Luis José's journey were perfectly described by his godfather Luis de Echevarría in a letter to Iribarren:

---

[23] Late colonial Veracruz is the only place where sons emigrating to help fathers has been documented as a common practice: Booker, *Veracruz*, 36.
[24] Paloma Fernández Pérez, 'Bienestar y pobreza: el impacto del sistema de herencia castellano en Cádiz, el emporio del orbe, 1700–1810', *Revista de Historia Económica* xv (1997), 243–68.

You emphatically ordered Micaela to send her son Luis José to your company and that to do so she might contact Andrés de Loyo, which I immediately did by writing on your behalf to him; and the reply was a categorical no. Consequently I had to insist, this time in a personal capacity. And having written to him he replied that there were some obstacles as I had to pay 200 *pesos* for a passage and to get a licence from the Council [of the Indies] for the boy. I answered that you would pay any amount and that I would have no problem getting a licence since I have a cousin working at court. ... So he could not refuse this time and agreed to embark your nephew. ... He said we would have to wait until he calls Luis José over for he had many boys at home.[25]

Even though the process was customary, the problems encountered in sending the young Luis José to America were rather unusual. Indeed, his godfather was annoyed to find there were so many difficulties, claiming that 'in my time seventy thousand [*sic*] boys were sent to the realms of Peru and Mexico without so many obstacles'.

In *La Perla*, the number of letters in which merchants discussed the possibility of bringing in boys from their hometown is genuinely surprising. They all stressed that it was absolutely essential for young emigrants to acquire a basic level of literacy and numeracy before departure. Writing from Lima in May 1779, the Basque Miguel Ignacio de Otaegui stressed that he would support his nephew in whatever he might need, but in turn that the boy had to have 'good temperament and judgement ... and he must apply himself to reading as well as writing'.[26] Inevitably, however, the youngster's education had to be completed at his destination. Writing home to Oñate (Guipúzcoa), the Lima merchant Juan Bautista de Sarraoa noted that 'it is eight days now since Vicente de Lizarralde arrived in this city, where I already have five boys in my care, although they do not allow me any rest for I have to teach them as if they were schoolboys'.[27] Rather than employing all their nephews and *parientes* (relatives) themselves, merchants used their contacts to find jobs for them. In general these contacts were other *paisanos*, but they could also be from other regions of Spain. The Basque merchant Juan Bautista de Gárate wrote to his brother Pedro (at the time treasurer of the Army in Zamora) that the Cádiz merchant Jaime Fourrat would take on one of their young relatives as an apprentice. 'He is from Valencia', wrote Gárate on Fourrat, 'has his house of commerce in Cádiz and many connections, and is eager to please.'[28] Gárate asked his brother to choose a boy 'with good temperament and that has studied out of the country': that is a boy who could speak Spanish.

---

[25] Luis de Echevarría to Pedro de Iribarren, Rentería, 25 Jan. 1746, HCA 32/134 (2).
[26] Miguel Ignacio de Otaegui to Francisco Antonio Olloqui, Lima, 8 May 1779, HCA 30/315/6, no. 1290.
[27] Juan Bautista de Sarraoa to Manuel de Urmeneta, Lima, 8 May 1779, HCA 30/313/2, no. 1073.
[28] J. B. Gárate to Pedro de Gárate, Lima, 8 May 1779, HCA 30/312/1, unnumbered.

Indeed, those who came from the Basque Country, Catalonia and Galicia had to learn *castellano* (Spanish) before leaving their home town. While Catalan and Galician resemble Castilian (all three are Latin languages), Basque or *euskera* is unrelated to any other language. Despite the fact that most people in the Basque Country had Basque as their sole language, it was chiefly an oral culture and the use of written *euskera* was extremely rare. That is why a note in Basque in the margin of one of Luis de Echevarría's letters is such an important piece of evidence. He told Lacoa 'esaisu ea esten acordasen neregatic eta señoragatic eta besteacatic, baraqui senbat obligaci[o] badu don Luis jaunari, [eta] suc gure echeco gusiai' (ask him if he remembers me and my wife and the others, he knows how much he is obliged to don Luis, and you to all of our house).[29] And following that sentence, Echevarría added in Spanish 'Micaela, Luis [José's] mother, has asked me to write the sentence above so that you read it to him and let him understand well, well, well.' Naturally, Basque merchants were well aware of the problems that poor language skills could cause, and therefore insisted that youngsters learned *castellano* properly. It is clear, however, that emigrants whose first language was not Castilian found it much easier to socialise with their own *paisanos*. Moreover, *La Perla* shows that Basques wrote their letters in Spanish, but often added words of their native language when writing to other *paisanos*. They used words such as *goranciac* (regards), *adisquide* (friend), *jauna* (sir) and *agur* (goodbye). The use of these written words strongly suggests that Basques (and other Spaniards), when they had the opportunity to meet their *paisanos* in person, communicated with each other orally in their language or dialect. This had important consequences: in the 1770s, the Cádiz-born officer and renowned writer José Cadalso (himself the son of a Basque merchant) wrote in reference to 'all those who speak the Basque language' that 'when a Basque is absent from his country, in a sense he returns to it when he meets his *paisanos*. They have such unity between them that the best recommendation one may have for another is the mere fact of being Basque'.[30]

Young emigrants used to leave their home towns and travel to southern Spain and the colonies in a very similar fashion. Sometimes it was the merchant established in Cádiz or America who asked his family to send a young relative from his hometown, and sometimes it was the young man's own family who asked the merchant to take the youngster in. This 'nephew syndrome' was an extended social phenomenon in the Spanish empire, but its enduring effect on successive generations of merchants, and on their perception of themselves, has not been stressed sufficiently. The continuous flow of people from northern Spain to Cádiz and America left its imprint on the mentality of the emigrant: he was perfectly aware that he was part

---

[29] Echevarría to Juan Bautista de Lacoa, Rentería, n.d. 1746, HCA 32/134 (2).
[30] José Cadalso, *Cartas marruecas* (Madrid 1793), Tarragona 1984, letter no. xxvi.

of a long chain. In May 1779 Juan Bautista de Gárate (member of the Lima *consulado*) stressed to a fellow Basque (and member of the Cádiz *consulado*) that his attempt to send his nephews to Cádiz was 'intended to help some of them to leave the valley so that they can follow in our footsteps and help those that will come after them'.[31]

The fact that most merchants of Cádiz and Spanish America were emigrants explains why they were so eager to meet with their *paisanos*. Such encounters contributed greatly to the maintenance of the regional, ethnic and cultural identity of Basques, *montañeses*, Catalans, Galicians and other Spaniards wherever they decided to settle. Perhaps the most remarkable institutions for bringing together Spanish emigrants were their religious *cofradías* (brotherhoods). Cádiz, Mexico City and Lima each had a Basque *cofradía* founded by merchants. In Cádiz it was the *Cofradía del Santísimo Cristo de la Humildad y Paciencia*, which in 1626 was permanently established in the church of San Agustín. On its ceiling, the four shields of the three provinces and the kingdom of Navarra can be seen to this day. In Mexico City and Lima, Basques gathered around the *Cofradía de Nuestra Señora de Aránzazu*. In Lima, the members of the *cofradía* were buried beneath its chapel, which still remains intact in the church of San Francisco. Similarly, *montañeses* had their *Cofradía del Santo Cristo de Burgos* in Cádiz, Mexico City, Lima and many other places. These brotherhoods not only organised celebrations and helped their poorer members, but also exercised control over their behaviour, expelling those who regularly acted in what was deemed to be a disorderly or shameful way.[32]

It was naturally the case that the bonds between people from the same town or valley were even stronger. Without doubt the most striking example is that of the Navarrese valley of Baztán (near the French border, where a particular dialect of Basque was spoken).[33] Towards the end of the seventeenth century, people from Baztán began increasingly to occupy important positions in the Spanish empire. Among the first to stand out in Madrid were Gerónimo de Uztáriz himself and his friend the financier Juan de Goyeneche. In 1685 Goyeneche published a book in which he enthusiastically extolled his beloved Baztán. Although there were 'fewer than a thousand families' living in the valley, he stressed that 'by virtue of the union that makes them

---

[31] Gárate to José Antonio de Madariaga, Lima, 9 May 1779, HCA 30/314/2, no. 589.
[32] Elisa Luque Alcaide, 'Coyuntura social y cofradía: cofradías de Aránzazu de Lima y México', in P. Martínez López-Cano and others (coors), *Cofradías, capellanías y obras pías en la América colonial*, México 1998, 102.
[33] See Julio Caro Baroja, *La hora navarra del XVIII (personas, familias, negocios e ideas)*, Pamplona 1969; José María Imízcoz, 'Patronos y mediadores: redes familiares en la monarquía y patronazgo en la aldea: la hegemonía de las élites baztanesas en el siglo XVIII', in J. M. Imízcoz (dir.), *Redes familiares y patronazgo: aproximación al entramado social del País Vasco y Navarra en el antiguo régimen, siglos XV–XIX*, Bilbao 2001, 225–61.

share each one's risk, they act as if they were a numerous army'.[34] Between 1749 and 1796 at least eighty-one *baztaneses* joined the Cádiz *consulado*, a truly remarkable number when compared with all other valleys of Spain, and their presence in the Lima *consulado* was also very significant.

Trading networks

Andrés de Loyo's prediction in 1750 about Cádiz merchants having to retail, to sell on credit and to remain in Peru for several years was soon proved right. For years merchants would only communicate with their agents by mail, getting a reply to their letters a year after they were posted. This new context added a whole new dimension to the question of trust between merchants established on either side of the Atlantic. Naturally under such circumstances, kinship, common geographical origin and ethnicity played a central role in providing the context for trust. But if that was the case, why not trade reciprocally with the members of the Lima *consulado*, who also came from the same regions of Spain? In fact – despite some restrictions, and the Lima *consulado*'s complaints on the matter – that is precisely what happened. The reason why reciprocity between the two communities had not flourished under the fleet/fair system, and even now would take several years to achieve, can only be understood if the arguments discussed in chapters 3 and 4 are considered. That is, when the pattern of trade made transatlantic networks absolutely necessary and communication was sufficiently improved, sources of trust such as ethnicity and common geographical origin would bond merchants of both sides of the Atlantic together and these common links would override differences of formal consular affiliation.

The increasing complexity of trade did not lead to changes in the size of the average firm. Spanish colonial trade remained atomised in the second half of the eighteenth century, involving hundreds of individual merchants (helped by an assistant or clerk). In Spanish America, until independence, the typical business figure was the individual trader; partnerships continued to be rare and joint-stock ventures almost unknown. In Cádiz, although partnerships were more common, most merchants also operated individually. Joint-stock companies such as Madrid's *Cinco Gremios* and the Royal Philippine Company (founded in 1783), which entered the trade with Peru rather aggressively after 1784, were exceptions rather than the norm. It is worth noting that most of *La Perla*'s mail was addressed to individual Spanish merchants rather than to companies, whereas practically all the French addressees were partnerships. For Manuel Bustos, the fact that Spaniards preferred to trade individually, despite having exclusive access to the

---

[34] Juan Goyeneche, *Executoria de la nobleza, antigüedad y blasones del Valle de Baztán*, Madrid 1685, p. ii.

consulado, is clear evidence of their lack of maturity.³⁵ However, it can also be argued that partnerships did not proliferate among Spaniards precisely because they operated under the protection of the *consulado*.

In 1729, after several disastrous *flotas* and *galeones*, the Cádiz *consulado* agreed its new ordinances by the terms of which colony-based merchants were forbidden to involve themselves in the transatlantic trade (the minister of state José Patiño felt it necessary to approve those draconian statutes to offset the weakening position of the merchants of Cádiz). It is misconceived to argue that 'for the first time in the history of Spain's American commerce a distinction was drawn between peninsular-born and American-born Spaniards'.³⁶ Rather, a line was drawn between the members of the Cádiz *consulado* and the rest. A royal *cédula*, issued on 21 January 1735, ratified the condition that colony-based merchants were banned from buying merchandise in Spain, although this time they were assured that the *gaditanos* who traded via the *flotas* and *galeones* would not go beyond the American fairs of Jalapa and Portobelo. Tremendously unhappy with this resolution, the American merchants lodged an appeal. Three years later, on 20 November 1738, the crown granted them the right to order their merchandise from Spain, although under two strict conditions: first they could only consign their money and commodities to members of the Cádiz *consulado*, and secondly the merchandise bought with that money would have to be consigned to a Cádiz *consulado* member travelling to America, the so-called *encomendero*. The crown considered that in that way neither the American nor the *encomendero* was adversely affected.³⁷ But those decisions were taken on the eve of the cancellation of *flotas* and *galeones*, and the crown could not foresee the transformation that the trade was about to experience with the introduction of register ships.

In 1742 the ordinances of the Cádiz *consulado* were suspended. Two years later the merchants of New Spain demanded that the two conditions imposed on the Americans in 1738 should be lifted. The question of trust was now pivotal to their arguments. They claimed that the Spanish colonial trade would grow if they were not constrained to put their money and commodities 'in the hands of individuals whose faithfulness, application and conduct was unknown to them'.³⁸ What the Americans demanded was *recíprocas consignaciones* (reciprocal consignments) with merchants they knew and trusted. Furthermore, they stressed that, due to the lack of trust, circulation of credit between Spaniards (whether peninsular or creole) on both sides of the Atlantic was scarce. The American *consulados* argued that, if reciprocity

---

³⁵ Bustos, *Comerciantes*, 262.
³⁶ Walker, *Spanish politics*, 169.
³⁷ Rafael Antúnez Acevedo, *Memorias históricas sobre la legislación y gobierno del comercio de los españoles con sus colonias en las Indias occidentales*, Madrid 1797, appendix xxi, p. xcvi.
³⁸ Ibid. appendix xxii, p. c.

was supported, the merchants of Cádiz would not have to resort to foreign capital since they would find the funds they needed in America. On 20 June 1749 (the war having finished the previous year), the merchants of both New Spain and Peru were eventually granted the right to consign to any person of their choosing. Nevertheless, that decision did not end the controversy. Despite the *cédula* of 1749 the merchants of Cádiz were compelled to take an oath swearing that the merchandise consigned to Americans had been bought with American money. This method was initially intended to make sure that merchandise did not belong to foreigners, but it was also used by the House of Trade to restrict consignments on commission to the *encomenderos* travelling to Peru with a three-year licence. As late as the 1770s the Lima *consulado* kept complaining that its members were not allowed to receive consignments of goods to be sold on commission from Cádiz, and that they were forced to rely on *encomenderos* whom they did not know.[39]

However, neither the House of Trade's restrictions nor the Lima *consulado*'s complaints reflected actual practice. The irony was that dealings in Peru took so long to complete that many *encomenderos* would eventually settle in Peru and would become members of the Lima *consulado*. It is no wonder that merchants in Cádiz were ready to take a false oath rather than risk cutting links with those they trusted. Alternatively, they consigned their merchandise to *encomenderos* who, on arrival at Lima, endorsed the bills of lading to American merchants.[40] The situation was therefore less complicated than it might appear. The testimony of the *encomendero* Manuel Gato, who was accused in Lima in April 1764 of being a *testa* (front-man) for foreigners, shows that behind all the regulations and institutional confrontations lay a rather simple reality. When it was discovered that he was not a *testa* for foreigners but instead for Spaniards, he sarcastically claimed that he would like to be 'accused and sentenced by a merchant who is free of this offence'.[41] Rather revealingly, he called the cover-up *hacer confianza* (to formulate trust), stressing that it was an extremely frequent (*freqüentísima*) practice in both Cádiz and Lima. All that was required was *confianza*, that is to say, a combination of trust and confidentiality. La Perla shows that merchants did indeed use that method continuously, without even having to explain the reason to their correspondents. Silvestre de Amenábar, for example, sent six bags of *vicuña* wool to his brother Xavier Ignacio, using the Amándarro brothers as front-men. Manuel José de Amándarro would be the shipper in Lima and his brother Juan Antonio the consignee in Cádiz. Then Manuel José would send a letter (*carta orden*) to Cádiz declaring 'that the said wool belongs to me [Silvestre de Amenábar] despite having been

---

[39] Petition of José de Azofra on behalf of the Lima *consulado*, Madrid, 7 Mar. 1777, AGI, Lima 890.
[40] Aguado to Arellano, Cádiz, 24 Jan. 1761, IRA, ARA, Epistolario.
[41] AGN, TC-GR2, caja 127, doc. 731, fos 34–5.

shipped under his name'.[42] Even more telling is the case of Joaquín José de Arrese, one of the three heads of the Lima *consulado* between 1775 and 1777. He was asked by one of his correspondents in Cádiz to send a copy of all the accounts of the transactions made between the two from 1773 to 1779. Those accounts (which amounted to a very substantial 247,380 *pesos*) prove that the merchants of Lima received consignments from Cádiz by resorting to front-men.[43]

La Perla's mail certainly shows that the relationship between *gaditanos* and *limeños* was excellent, and that reciprocity between them was well established. But such reciprocity had not grown spontaneously: in fact, most senior merchants featuring in the *La Perla* documents had crossed the Atlantic at least twice in their twenties and thirties. Furthermore, using as a sample the forty-two Navarrese merchants appearing amongst the ship's papers, it is clear that there was a clear correlation between merchants' participation in one commercial route and the destination of their transatlantic crossings: the forty-two merchants made a total of seventy-two trips from Cádiz to America, and on sixty-four occasions (83 per cent) the final destination was Lima.[44] Crossing the Atlantic and attaining both commercial knowledge and a good reputation required much time and effort. It is hardly surprising that of the 252 current and former members of the Cádiz *consulado* appearing in the *La Perla* letters (among authors and addressees), 175 (69 per cent) had joined the *consulado* before 1770. That is, they had at least ten years experience in the trade. For example, Simón Babil de Uriz and Juan Francisco de Micheo became members of the Cádiz *consulado* in the 1740s. In the early 1750s the three of them were in Lima. In 1779, the year of his death, Micheo was long settled and married in Lima, whereas Uriz was established in Cádiz and maintained friendly correspondence with Lima *consulado* merchants like his cousin José Joaquín de Sos, Antonio de Elizalde, Isidro de Adana and Ignacio de Elola (head of the Lima *consulado* in 1756–9, and an active member until his death in 1786).

For such merchants it was often difficult to decide on which side of the Atlantic to settle. In 1773, leaving his wife and daughter back in Cádiz, Ignacio de Torres y Mato went to Peru to trade for several years, along with his brother Francisco. By 1779 their dealings were taking longer than expected, and therefore Torres thought about bringing his family to Lima. He told his wife that he had no choice but to stay with his brother, for if he went back to Spain and his brother died in Peru 'all our sales on credit

---

[42] S. Amenábar to X. I. Amenábar, Lima, 8 May 1779, HCA 30/312/2, no. 1070.
[43] Joaquín José de Arrese to Nicolás de Rojas, Lima, 8 May 1779, HCA 30/316/18, no. 1851.
[44] Xabier Lamikiz, 'Movilidad transatlántica: navarros en el comercio directo entre España y el Perú, 1739–1796', in Rafael Torres Sánchez (ed.), *Volver a la 'hora navarra': la contribución navarra al construcción de la monarquía española en el siglo* XVIII, Pamplona 2009, 343–86.

would be lost without remedy'.[45] But Torres was not absolutely sure about bringing his family. He asked his *compadre* (a term that refers to a very close family friend who is also in a quasi-fiduciary relationship as the godfather of someone's children) Agustín de Amenábar for advice:

> I have carefully considered that it is better gathering the entire family together rather than remaining in the situation we are at the moment; but if you thought that this consideration of mine may be prejudicial to me in order to work from now on, (I mean) that I might lose the concept of honesty among the residents there, and that they might not want to give me more credit because my family would not be there anymore, and I might delay the payment or commit any other dirty trick, in that case you will decide, as you are there, what is more convenient, for I do not want them to change the opinion they had about me.[46]

It is clear that, before settling down, merchants needed to build up a network that they trusted, and in which they themselves were trusted. 'I am glad you have decided to establish yourself in that city [Cádiz]', wrote Domingo de Lasquívar to his *paisano* José Antonio de Madariaga. 'It is a wise decision', he added, 'for with your knowledge of this commerce and your friends you can earn more staying there than risking your life in the dangerous navigation.'[47] Most likely, from then on Madariaga would be considered a *perulero*. In fact, after the mid-eighteenth century, the term *perulero* was used to refer both to the merchants established in Peru and to those established in Cádiz who had previously been in Peru for at least several years (and had, therefore, a robust network and extensive knowledge of the Peruvian market). The *perulero* could be a creole by birth like Juan Manuel de Sarría (member of the Cádiz *consulado* since 1772), but he was most commonly peninsular-born like Fermín Ramón de Barrera (Cádiz *consulado* member since 1775).

It is not difficult to imagine how sources of solidarity and cohesion impinged upon the transatlantic networks. For example, in May 1779 there were at least ten merchants from Baztán residing in Lima (Berindoaga, the Elizaldes, Aycinena, Larráin, Munárriz, Urrutia, Ozta, Legasa and Gárate). Some were members of the Cádiz *consulado*, some of the Lima *consulado*. In Lima they were in touch with one another. Martín de Legasa, an *encomendero* who had just arrived in Lima, wrote to Santiago de Iriarte that the house of their *paisanos*, the prominent Lima *consulado* merchants Antonio and José Matías de Elizalde, was his 'only visit in the morning and in the afternoon'.[48]

---

[45] Ignacio de Torres y Mato to María Badillo, Lima, 10 May 1779, HCA 30/312/2, no. 622.
[46] Torres to Agustín de Amenábar, Lima, 10 May 1779, ibid.
[47] Domingo Lasquívar to José Antonio de Madariaga, Lima, 6 May 1779, HCA 30/312/6, no. 125.
[48] Martín de Legasa to Santiago de Iriarte, Lima, 30 Apr. 1779, HCA 30/316/15, no. 675.

Unsurprisingly, most of their addressees in Spain were *baztaneses*, members of the Cádiz *consulado* like Uztáriz, Aguerrebere, Araurrenechea, the Iriartes, Gortari, Lacoizqueta, Echandía, Marticorena, Iraizoz and Ezpeleta.

Merchants did not build their networks exclusively around their *paisanos*. The most successful merchants in particular had many other contacts who were not only merchants from Peru and from other regions of Spain but also members of creole aristocracy, colonial officials and clergymen. However, at the core of a merchant's network there were always a few *paisanos* who were usually his oldest contacts. Furthermore, *La Perla*'s mail shows that merchants actively supported and relied upon their countrymen. For example the Basque Juan Bautista de Orobiogoitia wrote to the great Cádiz merchant Matías de Landaburu to reassure him following a serious delay in disposing of some merchandise, and did not hesitate to appeal to Landaburu's 'laudable inclination to favour immediate *paisanos*'.[49] Another Basque merchant, Joaquín de Tajonar, was in need of new merchandise from Spain: 'I can assure you', he wrote to a fellow Basque in Cádiz, 'that nobody is more concerned about receiving clothes promptly [than me]; because I have much consumption by myself as by other *paisanos* I supply.'[50]

One reason why merchants trusted (or distrusted) *paisanos* residing on the other side of the Atlantic was because they knew more about them. As most Spanish immigrants had come to Peru to enrich themselves, it was customary for merchants to include in their letters accounts of the good or bad luck of their *paisanos*. For example, after having talked about Bidegaray and Echegaray, Esteban de Urrutia informed Juan de Ezpeleta that 'the other *paisanos* [*baztaneses*] are doing well. They wrote to me a few days ago saying that Juan de Larrea had married a widower in the province of Huailar. Hugarte and Hiriarte keep paying doña Isabel 10,000 *pesos* every year; they still owe her 40,000'.[51]

Established merchants were usually supported by a group of close friends, headed by senior and experienced merchants such as Matías de Landaburu, Juan Miguel de Aguerrebere or Juan Agustín de Uztáriz. The Lima merchant Juan Bautista de Gárate, for example, referred to Aguerrebere (who had previously spent seventeen years in Peru) as 'my patron and dear friend'.[52] Gárate had not received a letter from Aguerrebere in the previous mail, but was not worried for 'in those [letters] you have sent to my *compadres* and friends I have had the satisfaction of seeing myself mentioned among those of your highest appreciation'. Aguerrebere could even decide who among his junior friends would receive a consignment. Gárate wrote to Fermín

---

[49] Juan Bautista de Orobiogoitia to Matías de Landaburu, Lima, 30 Mar. 1779, HCA 30/313/1, no. 485.
[50] Joaquín de Tajonar to Juan Francisco Vea Murguía, Lima, 10 May 1779, HCA 30/315/18, unnumbered.
[51] Urrutia to Juan de Ezpeleta, Lima, 9 May 1779, HCA 30/313/3, no. 17.
[52] Gárate to Aguerrebere, Lima, 30 Mar. 1779, HCA 30/314/7, no. 1300.

Ramón de Barrera that 'your efforts to get me the commission of the fabrics and stockings from León have not succeeded. They have been sent to these gentlemen our friends because our common patron [Aguerrebere] said so. I fully approve of his power to decide'.[53]

These networks prevailed even over the restriction on transatlantic shipping, which until 1796 was, at least theoretically, in the exclusive hands of shipowners based in Spain. In the company of José Antonio de Lavalle, Vicente de Corcuera, Miguel Francisco de Corcuera and Miguel de Sarralde (a copy of the nine-article company agreement was included in the mail), it was the Lima partners, Lavalle (a creole by birth) and Vicente de Corcuera, who ordered their Cádiz partners to buy a 450-ton ship in Bilbao.[54] Furthermore, rather than being a barrier between the two, transatlantic shipping actually brought the merchant communities of Lima and Cádiz closer, for the preponderance of a few shipowners such as the firm Uztáriz, San Ginés and Co., generated hostility on both sides of the Atlantic.[55]

Although the economic ramifications of the reciprocity between the Spaniards of both sides of the Atlantic are far reaching, they remain totally unexplored. Antonio Bernal suggests that in the second half of the eighteenth century the French firms of Cádiz were the largest creditors in the Spanish colonial trade because of their sea loans to the Spaniards of Cádiz.[56] However, he acknowledges that his hypothesis is unlikely to find empirical confirmation, for foreigners' names do not appear in the thousands of loan contracts held in the Spanish archives (there are no fewer than 65,000 contracts for the eighteenth century). Many Spanish lenders were mere front-men for foreign investors. However, *La Perla*'s mail suggests that the colony-based merchants, who are repeatedly celebrated in the historiography for the huge fortunes that they amassed, were also an important source of capital for the merchants of Cádiz. Through their Cádiz correspondents the merchants of Lima gave loans to *encomenderos* travelling to Peru. It was for the Cádiz correspondents to find 'individuals or houses of moral security'.[57]

Moreover, the Peru model also seems to apply to New Spain, a point worth stressing because it goes against almost everything that has been written about *gaditanos* and *mexicanos* in the period. In a fascinating thirty-one-page report written in March 1773, the *diputado* (responsible official) of the *flota* of 1772, José de Echea, assured the minister of the Indies that the recent Jalapa fair had been a farce characterised by false oaths, false endorsements and fake commissions, stressing that a large part of the cargo had

---

[53] Gárate to Barrera, Lima, 9 May 1779, HCA 30/313/2, no. 50.
[54] Vicente de Corcuera to Sarralde and Corcuera, Lima, 5 May 1779, HCA 30/316/1, no. 830.
[55] Joaquín Manuel de Azcona to Aguirre, Lima, 30 Mar. 1779, HCA 30/315/2, no. 279.
[56] Bernal, *Financiación*, 449–62. See also Bartolomei, 'La Bourse', 168–76.
[57] Jacinto de los Santos to Istúriz and Albizu, Lima, 8 May 1779, HCA 30/312/1, no. 612.

already been purchased by the *mexicanos* through their correspondents in Spain. For Echea, who was himself a merchant with much experience, things in New Spain were getting as bad as in Peru: 'more than three-quarters of the trade with Peru is in the hands of the merchants of Lima and its Sierra, for they send large amounts of money to Cádiz either to buy cloth or to give sea loans to be paid off in Lima'.[58] It was probably an exaggeration to say that three-quarters of the trade was in their hands, but Echea's report attests, once again, that behind the veneer of sound regulations and restrictions there was a hidden reality of mutual understanding between the two communities. It is clear that trade with Peru after the mid-eighteenth century demanded an enormous level of trust between merchants. But to complete that picture it is necessary to discuss the role of the foreign merchants established in Cádiz, who, despite being banned from trading with the Spanish colonies, were traditionally reputed to make much larger profits than the Spaniards.

Spaniards and foreigners

Foreign merchants in eighteenth-century Cádiz were remarkably numerous,[59] accounting for 75 per cent of the city's merchant community in 1713. Their numbers remained high throughout the century, amounting to some 200 merchants. However, after the *consulado* of Seville was moved to Cádiz in 1717 they were joined by greater numbers of Spanish overseas merchants, so that in the 1770s 40 per cent of overseas merchants established in Cádiz were foreigners. These traders supplied Spanish merchants with goods (mainly textiles) that Spain was incapable of producing in enough quantity and cheaply enough. Legally that was all they could do, for sending such goods to America was exclusively restricted to Spaniards. Foreigners could neither trade with nor settle in the Spanish colonies. Nevertheless, all contemporaries agreed that the real roles of foreigners made any notion of a Spanish monopoly completely fictitious.

Most foreigners residing in Cádiz did not apply for naturalisation and had little intention of integrating socially. They kept their nationality partly because they did not intend to settle in Cádiz and partly because they enjoyed a number of privileges. Foreign merchants were not under the jurisdiction of the Cádiz *consulado* but under a special jurisdiction, the *fuero militar*. Furthermore, they tended to partner and employ their compatriots, and in most cases married women of their own nationality. Using a sample of 127 merchants, Paloma Fernández shows that 80 to 90 per cent of the

[58] José de Echea to Arriaga, Mexico City, 18 Mar. 1773, AGI, México 2492, 7.
[59] See, for example, Ozanam, 'Colonie française'; María del Carmen Lario de Oñate, *La colonia mercantil británica e irlandesa en Cádiz a finales del siglo* XVIII, Cádiz 2000; and Ana Crespo Solana, *Entre Cádiz y los Países Bajos: una comunidad mercantil en la ciudad de la Ilustración*, Cádiz 2001.

French and Irish residing in Cádiz married the Andalusian-born daughters of their compatriots. The same percentage of Basques and *montañeses*, meanwhile, married the daughters of their own *paisanos*.[60] The boundary between Spaniards and foreigners was therefore noticeable but not rigid: on the one hand foreigners learned Spanish and lived with Spaniards in the same city, but on the other they had their own consul and meetings to discuss the interests of their separate community.[61] It is significant that if a foreigner applied for naturalisation, an important qualification was that he had to have cut links with his compatriots.[62]

In 1753, 1762 and 1773, estimates of the annual profits (*utilidades*) of all merchants residing in Cádiz were made in connection with the government's attempt to establish a unified tax, the *única contribución*. Merchants refused to open their books to public scrutiny, so their profits were roughly estimated and the resulting figures are therefore very unreliable (particularly for 1773).[63] They do show, however, something that contemporary testimonies seem to corroborate: foreigners' profits were much larger than those of Spaniards. In 1753, for example, the 284 Spanish merchants' average annual profit on trade was 917 *pesos* (ranging from eighty to 6,000 *pesos*), whereas that of the 108 French merchants was 6,578 *pesos* (ranging from 300 to 40,000). Spanish merchants were also surpassed by other nationalities: the forty-nine Italians averaged 3,057 *pesos*, the forty-four Irish/British, 5,411, and the twenty Flemish, 3,735. It is commonly accepted that the reason for the Spaniards' limited profits was their role as intermediaries and front-men for foreigners, who were the biggest merchants and investors.

However, from the mid-eighteenth century, the foreigners of Cádiz would themselves acknowledge that Spaniards increasingly began to trade on their own account instead of being mere intermediaries.[64] Although this phenomenon has not gone unnoticed, the explanations offered have been rather unconvincing. Manuel Bustos, for instance, suggests that the main reason for the more active participation of the Spaniards is to be found in their growing independence, but says nothing about why or how they became independent. More detailed but similarly incomplete is the viewpoint of Antonio-Miguel Bernal, who considers that the participation of Galicians and Catalans, soaring fiscal pressure and rising competition explain the Spaniards' expanding role.[65] Neither Bustos nor Bernal contemplate the

---

[60] Fernández, *Rostro*, 166.
[61] Pedro Collado, 'Los consulados extranjeros en el Cádiz de Carlos iii', in García-Baquero, *Burguesía de negocios*, 245–57.
[62] Juan Morales Alvarez, *Los extranjeros con carta de naturaleza en las Indias durante la segunda mitad del siglo* XVIII, Caracas 1980, 263.
[63] García-Baquero, 'Permanencia', 69–101; Bustos, *Cádiz*, 158–65.
[64] Robert Chamboredon, 'Une Societé de commerce languedocienne à Cadix: Simon et Arnail Fornier et Cie. (Novembre 1768–Mars 1786)', in García-Baquero, *Burguesía de negocios*, 39–40.
[65] Bernal, *Financiación*, 366–7; Bustos, *Cádiz*, 172–84.

possibility that the new pattern of trade might have encouraged Spaniards to depend less on foreigners and more on their transatlantic correspondents.

In the 1740s, when French ships were granted special wartime passports to trade with the colonies, numerous French merchants arrived in Spanish America to act as agents for their compatriots in Cádiz.[66] As the war was coming to an end, however, the French began to realise that the Spaniards were not going to allow them to remain in the colonies. In January 1747, the French firm Verduc, Vincent and Co stressed to Lazaro Cadious (their compatriot and agent in Veracruz) that there was much talk in Cádiz about restricting the activities of those merchants who were not members of the *consulado*. Nevertheless they asked Cadiou 'not to shorten your stay in that kingdom, for God knows that we will help you as much as we can'.[67] In fact, both the House of Trade and the Cádiz *consulado* were demanding that foreigners residing in the colonies should be sent back to Europe. The crown had issued provisions to expel foreigners from the colonies from time to time, alleging that their residence in America could be risky in case of war, and that it might increase contraband, but from the mid-eighteenth century such restrictions multiplied. In Peru, the Lima *consulado* repeatedly denounced foreign competitors, particularly from 1761 to 1776,[68] which explains why there were only two foreign merchants writing in *La Perla*'s letters.

The campaign to expel foreigners from Spanish America was closely linked both to mercantile interests and to mercantile agency. But there was also a connection between the growing anxiety about foreign merchants residing in the colonies after 1750, and the new pattern of trade.[69] Furthermore, if foreign merchants felt it necessary to send their agents to the Spanish colonies, then it seems reasonable to assume that their expulsion had a negative effect on their trade. In Cádiz everyone knew that the legal means of attempting to end foreigners' participation in the colonial trade, including the oath taken by merchants to ensure Spanish ownership of the merchandise shipped for America, were entirely futile. For example, in October 1743 the Bayonne merchant Leon Brethous asked the Spaniard Francisco Ortiz to be his front-man, adding that 'if you take a false oath you will get the

---

[66] See, for example, François Lassala to Lemoyne et Cie., Mexico City, 12 Aug. 1746, HCA 30/250/7; Michel Demoyrier to Jean Jolif, Mexico City, 20 Aug. 1746, HCA 30/250/8.
[67] Verduc, Vincent and Co. to Cadiou, Cádiz, 31 Jan. 1747, HCA 32/134/3 (1).
[68] Several lists of foreigners and their situation in Peru can be found in AGN, TC-GR2, cajas 124–7.
[69] See, for example, Carmen Gómez Pérez, 'Los extranjeros en la América colonial: su expulsión de Cartagena de Indias en 1750', AEA xxxvii (1980), 279–311; Carmen Parrón Salas, 'El nacionalismo emergente y el comercio: la expulsión de extranjeros de América (Perú), 1750–78', in *Actas del XI congreso de la AHILA*, Liverpool 1998, i. 200–18; and Tamar Herzog, *Defining nations: immigrants and citizens in early modern Spain and Spanish America*, New Haven 2003, 94–118.

customary commission'.⁷⁰ In 1780 a counsellor of the Indies, Pedro Rada, acknowledged that oaths could always be falsified, or indeed could simply be avoided by using an *encomendero* as a front-man.⁷¹ As *La Perla*'s mail strongly suggests, the campaigns of expulsion seem to have been a more effective method of stopping foreign participation.

La Perla's papers show that foreigners received American commodities and silver *en confianza* through Spanish front-men, just as the Cádiz *consulado* members sent consignments to their Lima counterparts. For example, the Lima *consulado* merchant Domingo de Larrea sent silver to the French company Lecture and Gastambide through his partner in Cádiz. 'On this occasion', noted Larrea to the French company, 'I have embarked on Jiménez's account and risk ... 5,640 *pesos* ... which go in this way because your name cannot stand, and it is understood that in reality [they go] on your account and risk.'⁷² Nevertheless, the correspondence shows that foreigners were very cautious when resorting to that method.

In fact, there were three crucial differences between foreigners and Spaniards in this context. First, most of the forty-six foreign firms had only one envelope addressed to them, and none more than three: Spaniards, by contrast, were the addressees of many more. Juan Francisco de Vea Murguía, for example, would get twelve, Matías de Landaburu, fourteen, Juan Antonio de la Fuente, fifteen, Juan Martín de Aguirre, twenty-one and José Ramos, twenty-four. Secondly, the envelopes addressed to Spaniards were not only sent by merchants but also by many other members of colonial society, who wrote on all sorts of subjects (gossip, colonial administration, politics, economy and culture). Foreigners only received letters from merchants, and in general those letters were much shorter and contained much less information. The Basque Antonio de Elizalde's envelope for his brother Matías, for example, contained (apart from a long inventory and two envelopes for other merchants) a 4,330-word letter.⁷³ José Antonio Lavalle's to Lorenzo de Asunsolo had 3,800 words (plus several accounts and a letter from one of Asunsolo's debtors).⁷⁴ None of the envelopes addressed to foreigners contained anywhere near that much information.

A final important difference between foreigners and Spaniards was that relatively few merchants were the authors of all the letters sent to foreigners, whilst Spanish merchants had a far greater diversity of correspondents. Six merchants (Juan Sabugo, Esteban de Urrutia, Raimundo Marrés, Juan de Eguino, the count of San Isidro and Antonio de Elizalde) were the authors of forty of the sixty envelopes addressed to the forty French firms appearing

---

⁷⁰ Leon Brethous to Francisco Ortiz, Bayonne, 28 Oct. 1743, HCA 30/250/1.
⁷¹ Pedro Rada to Council of Indies, Madrid, 11 May 1780, AGI, Lima 1548, fo. 3r–v.
⁷² Domingo de Larrea to Lecture and Gastambide, Lima, 31 Mar. 1779, HCA 30/315/5, no. 1564.
⁷³ A. Elizalde to M. Elizalde, Lima, 8 May 1779, HCA 30/313/3, no. 1089.
⁷⁴ Lavalle to Asunsolo, Lima, 7 May 1779, HCA 30/314/1, no. 278.

in *La Perla*'s mail. Sabugo, Urrutia and Marrés alone sent twenty-eight of the sixty. Rather revealingly, the three had ties with the French community of Cádiz that few other merchants in Lima possessed. Sabugo, who wrote to twelve French firms, was the brother-in-law of Louis Feyt, a French merchant established in Cádiz.[75] Esteban de Urrutia, who was the agent in Lima of another eight French firms, was born in the valley of Baztán but had been educated in Bayonne in the house of the French-Basque merchant Antoine Brethous (who was closely connected to the Detchegaray brothers, a French-Basque firm in Cádiz).[76] Raimundo Marrés, who corresponded with eight French firms, had been on the verge of being expelled from Peru three years before because he was a *jenízaro* (a Spaniard of foreign parentage) of French parents, and was therefore considered by many to be a Frenchman.[77]

The crucial consequence was that, compared with Spaniards, foreigners received much less information and had fewer chances to monitor their agents' honesty and performance. As a result, foreigners were involved in far fewer transactions, and the value of those transactions was not higher than those of most Spaniards. In short, trade with Peru was for the most part dominated by Spanish merchants, because the conditions under which foreigners had to operate from the middle of the century onwards reduced their ability to trust. This problem was acknowledged by the foreigners established in Cádiz. In 1760 a survey ordered by the British Board of Trade showed that there had been no decline in the sales of British manufactures in Cádiz but that merchants were changing their methods. It was not only that by the 1760s the British wanted quicker returns than those offered by the risky and slow Spanish colonial trade. More important, the survey demonstrated that, for the British, it was better to have a debtor in Cádiz than a debtor in the Spanish colonies, the reason being that the assets of the former could be seized whereas those of the latter were in practice often untouchable. It is no wonder that the traditional figure of the Spanish front-man, the deserving object of eulogies from Jacques Savary in 1675, now began to appear untrustworthy in the eyes of foreigners established in Cádiz. In this new context it has been plausibly argued that in the 1760s the Spanish front-men were increasingly being deemed dishonest and unreliable by British and other foreign merchants.[78] Indeed, there were far greater risks associated with agency for foreigners after the mid-eighteenth century than there had been during the *galeones* era, when agents and debtors had returned to Spain once

---

[75] Sabugo to Louis Feyt, Lima, 8 May 1779, HCA 30/312/16, no. 1541.
[76] Urrutia to Brethous, Lima, 3 Apr. 1779, HCA 30/312/4, no. 648.
[77] Declaration of Antonio de Elizalde, Lima, 22 Dec. 1775, AGN, TC-GR1, caja 127, doc. 734, fo. 16.
[78] Christelow, 'Great Britain', 18–20. The British would trade directly with Spanish America only after 1796, and with Peru after 1807: Dorothy B. Goebel, 'British trade to the Spanish America, 1796–1823', AHR xliii (1938), 288–320. See also Pearce, *British trade*.

the American fairs were completed, and had made settlements with their principals and creditors. The advent of the register ships changed the pattern of trade with America in favour of Spain's indigenous merchants. However, the long distances and the problems entailed in establishing networks of communication and trade were not the only factors affecting the level of trust between merchants in the eighteenth century. Another crucial characteristic of early modern trade, which conferred great importance on trust and personal reputation, was merchants' need to keep their businesses and dealings as confidential as possible. This meant that, even when merchants lived next door to one another, there was a very thin line between trust and distrust.

PART III

TRUST AND DISTRUST

6

Confidentiality

Trade and trust were inextricably linked. Institutional arrangements, the shipowning business, variations in the pattern of trade, the quality of communication and merchants' family and *paisanos* all played crucial parts in moulding commercial networks. In different ways, and to differing extents, these factors affected the degree to which all early modern merchants were able to trust, and therefore to trade. The interaction between trade and trust can be further explored by paying attention to the most conspicuous feature of early modern trade: the need for confidentiality. Throughout the seventeenth and eighteenth centuries Spanish merchants refused to open their books to royal scrutiny because concealing their financial situation was a golden rule of trade. The social and cultural implications of this were enormous, for trade's inherent secrecy was both a necessity and, at the same time, a constant source of distrust. The sociologists Lewicki, McAllister and Bies argue that 'trust and distrust are separate but linked dimensions'. They also note that 'it is possible for parties to both trust and distrust one another, given different experiences within the various facets of complex interpersonal relationships'.[1] In the world of eighteenth-century trade, this complexity meant that merchants relied upon correspondents they trusted, but this trust was seen as fragile and, on some occasions, liable to both weakening and collapse.

Reputations

In his 1752 *Lex mercatoria rediviva*, the Englishman Wyndham Beawes gave the following advice to his merchant readers:

> A Trader should not be drawn in to employ a Factor with whose character he is unacquainted from any Motive whatsoever, even from that most prevailing one of serving for a less commission than what others commonly do. ... His first care, therefore, should be the choice of such a correspondent as he can depend on, whose Integrity will naturally lead him assiduously to sollicit and promote the Interest of his Principal unbiassed by any sinister View of his own.[2]

---

[1] R. J. Lewicki, D. J. McAllister and R. J. Bies, 'Trust and distrust: new relationships and realities', *Academy of Management Review* xxiii (1998), 439–40.
[2] Wyndham Beawes, *Lex mercatoria rediviva or the merchant's directory: being a compleat guide to all men in business*, London 1752, 33–4.

The several eighteenth-century editions of Malachy Postlethwayt's *Universal dictionary of trade and commerce* (1751, 1757, 1766, 1774) gave similar advice, as did other eighteenth-century manuals. These followed a long tradition that can be traced back to influential works such as Gerrard de Malynes's *Consuetudo, vel lex mercatoria* (1622) and Jacques Savary's *Le Parfait Negociant* (1675).[3] Of course, no eighteenth-century merchant needed Beawes, Malynes or Savary to tell him about the importance of having reliable correspondents: these authors merely stated what every merchant already knew was a crucial requirement for trade – or, to put it more dramatically, for commercial survival. Personal dependability and integrity were particularly important because merchants were extremely secretive in their dealings. Indeed, at a time when there were neither audits nor public annual balances, trade relied not only on institutional and legal support but on something as ethereal as mercantile reputations. Reputation was the backbone of trade, as it was thanks to his good reputation that a merchant had access to credit. It is no wonder that any potential threat to the reputation of its members was likely to cause panic in the mercantile community. For example, when trying to avoid an inspection of their account books in 1763, the merchants of Cádiz argued energetically that

> it might cause serious damage to many individuals and great discredit to commerce if each one's capital were known, for if it were not comparable with his reputation among the public, it might diminish his correspondents' good faith and they would cease doing business with him.[4]

By the same token, however, the degree of confidentiality meant that a merchant could be on the verge of bankruptcy without anybody knowing it, and this was a problem that the law could do little to address. The Bilbao *consulado*'s 1737 Ordinances ordered all partnerships to register their charter with a notary and to give a copy to the *consulado*. This measure was intended to provide information about starting capital, partnership duration, assets and liabilities, partners and associates, earnings and profits, thereby making trade more secure.[5] For several reasons, however, the transparency it brought to the trade was rather limited: first, most of the trade was carried out not by partnerships but by individual merchants and family firms; secondly, partners could keep trading as individual merchants; and lastly, partners could be involved in more than one partnership. In Cádiz, partnerships were surrounded by even more uncertainty. In February 1767 the members of the Cádiz *consulado* appealed to the king to oblige all merchant companies in the city (particularly the foreign houses) to register their firms' charters with

---

[3] Postlethwayt, *Universal dictionary*, 760–5; Gerrard de Malynes, *Consuetudo, vel lex mercatoria: or, the ancient law-merchant*, London 1622, 111; Savary, *Parfait Negociant*, i. 116–20.
[4] García-Baquero, *Cádiz*, i. 487.
[5] [Bilbao *consulado*], *Ordenanzas ... de 1737*, ch. x, arts iv, v.

a notary and provide a copy to the *consulado*. They recalled that there had been a similar attempt long before, in 1640, but although on that occasion the king had ordered the merchant houses of Seville to provide information about their resources, the order had been totally ignored. In 1767 the Cádiz *consulado* insisted on the importance of enforcing the measure, alleging that:

> There are many bankruptcies of houses that call themselves trading companies. But it is often the case that either there is no such trading company, or it has been created without funds ... And the creditors, confident about the opulence and external appearance of the partners, are cheated and unable to recover what it is owed to them.[6]

A royal order issued on 7 June 1767 granted the Cádiz *consulado*'s petition, but after intense diplomatic pressure it was soon revoked. In October 1775 a similar measure was adopted, and once again it was abrogated shortly afterwards.[7] It is hardly surprising, therefore, that business failures often occurred very suddenly, and could affect anyone. In 1732, after the bankruptcy of a Bilbao merchant with a debt of 16,000 *pesos*, Pedro Francisco de Irisarri, another *bilbaíno*, wrote: 'thank God I never had dealings with him'.[8] Not even the wealthiest merchants were safe from disaster, because to a large extent wealth itself was a question of reputation, and could therefore be equally deceptive. Writing from Cádiz in January 1772, the Irishman Alexis Macnamara informed the Norwich manufacturers Richard and John Gurney that '[w]e had yesterday a shocking failure here of the [French] house of Behic, Tanevot & Co, which tis said surpasses a couple of millions [of *pesos*]'.[9]

But above all, merchants feared dishonest bankrupts, those committing what the Bilbao *consulado*'s Ordinances described as failures of the 'third class'.[10] In order to avoid dealing with potentially dishonest bankrupts, the merchant had no option but to rely on often dubious sources of information such as gossip and public perceptions. Naturally, however, living close to one another in the same city made the monitoring of reputations much easier. When the company of Pedro Matías de Loygorri went bankrupt in 1758 (after just one year and thirteen days of existence), the Bilbao *consulado* stressed that Loygorri's firm 'has always been considered a house of pure

---

[6] Josiah Hardy to William Nassau de Zuylestein, 4th earl of Rochford, Cádiz, 18 Nov. 1775, SP 94/199.
[7] A printed copy of the royal order was sent to London by the British consul in Cádiz: ibid.
[8] Gonzalo Manso de Zúñiga, *Cartas de Bilbao*, San Sebastián 1949, 26.
[9] Alexis Macnamara to Gurney and Co, Cádiz, 24 Jan. 1772, Gurney papers, FHL, 2/456.
[10] First- and second-class bankrupts were not considered criminals but instead the victims of varying degrees of bad luck and mismanagement. By contrast, those of the third class were bankrupts who literally ran away from their debts, taking their account books and assets with them. According to the Ordinances they were 'public thieves': [Bilbao *consulado*], *Ordenanzas ... de 1737*, ch. xvi, arts i–iii, 126–8.

artifice', and therefore 'very few merchants of Bilbao have been affected by his bankruptcy, because those who know this [Bilbao's] trade penetrated the artifice and avoided dealing with such a house'.[11] As a result, most of those who suffered from Loygorri's third-class failure were wool merchants and flock-owners from outside Bilbao. Indeed, since they were far away and had less access to information concerning reputations, overseas correspondents were more liable to experience the expensive consequences of a business failure such as that of Loygorri.[12]

The merchant took great care in building and preserving his reputation, knowing that his actions were being closely observed by his peers. Reputation was built on previous behaviour and collective judgement. That is why the beginning of a commercial relationship with a new correspondent was always a gamble: the merchant could only assure his new correspondent that 'time and experience' would prove his competence and dependability. That first transaction, as the Spaniard established in London Juan Miguel Pérez put it to a Bilbao merchant, was considered as an *ensayo* (test) after which other, more substantial transactions might follow.[13]

Family

It is unsurprising that kinship was a very important source of trust in the secretive and uncertain world of trade. Certainly the reason why merchants associated with their relatives, and whenever possible sent them out to act as overseas agents, needs little explanation. However, it is important to stress that family members were not trustworthy *per se*. In December 1772 the Cádiz merchant Lorenzo del Arco asked his Lima correspondent Andrés Ramírez de Arellano to help a nephew whom he was about to send to Peru. 'He has been in our house for more than a year, in which I have verified his capacity and conduct', assured Arco.[14] Even so, distrust would never disappear entirely. In summer 1797 the two sons of the Bilbao merchant Simón Antonio de Goicoechea, Manuel and Miguel, were in Brest dealing with a delicate matter concerning their father's company. They neglected to do various things, such as to send a letter to Bilbao so that one of their ships could be insured, and their father became very upset: he openly accused them of living a dissolute life in Brest, and demanded a detailed report

---

[11] Bilbao *consulado's* petition to the king, Bilbao, 4 Sept. 1758, AFB, Consulado 541, fo. 164v.
[12] In an attempt to eradicate fraudulent declarations of bankruptcy, Simón Codes suggested in 1803 that only merchants with proven knowledge of commerce should be allowed to trade, and that their accounts should be examined once a year. However, his good intentions appear to have been disregarded: *Memoria*, 73–89.
[13] Juan Miguel Pérez to José Antonio del Barrio, London, 9 Feb. 1796, AFB, Corregimiento 1820/005, fo. 122.
[14] Arco to Arellano, Cádiz, 10 Dec. 1772, IRA, ARA, Epistolario.

('account by account, ship by ship') of their dealings since they left Bilbao.[15] A few days later Goicoechea wrote to them again, this time calling them 'animals' for not providing a particular piece of information in their previous letter.[16] It is possible that Goicoechea's sons were simply incompetent rather than untrustworthy, but the fact that Goicoechea and his partner Nicolás de Otero had appointed the sons to take care of a delicate matter shows that neither Goicoechea nor Otero had considered them unsuitable for the task. The difference between Goicoechea's other correspondents and his sons was that the latter were the only ones to whom Goicoechea spoke openly, even though he may have been equally suspicious of all his business colleagues. When given the chance to speak out, merchants were only too quick to reveal the extent to which distrust occupied their minds.

It was not always possible for a trader to have a relative in every place he traded with. In fact, in order to diversify risks, to have more sources of information and to monitor his correspondents, merchants tried to develop extensive networks that inevitably included many merchants who were not relatives. And yet family still played a crucial part in creating or diminishing mercantile reputations. It was not only in their public conduct that the merchant expected public honesty and competence from his correspondents. Being a trader in a world of secrecy and surface appearances in which any trivial piece of information could fuel distrust, he also judged his correspondents according to their private lives – and one thing that inspired confidence from other merchants was a model family household. The fact that very few cases of internal disagreements within the merchant families of Cádiz have been found in the notarial and judicial records (in comparison to other social groups) shows the extent to which merchants cared about keeping an immaculate image of familial peace and composure.[17] The significance of family as a source of trust was both internal and external: partners and agents were often recruited within the family, while any matter concerning a merchant's family was carefully scrutinised by other merchants.

It is no wonder that, in the eighteenth century, the frontier between business and personal or family letters was blurred. The reason why merchants often included comments on their personal lives in their letters was not only because socialising was an indispensable part of economic life, but also because merchants knew that their correspondents would be eager to know as much as possible about them. In June 1797, Goicoechea copied in his letter-book with his partner, Otero, a letter he was about to send to the Bordeaux firm Garnier and Perry. A few weeks before, Goicoechea's two sons had travelled to Bordeaux where they had met Garnier and Perry. And just before leaving for Brest the two brothers had informed their father about

---

[15] Simón Antonio de Goicoechea to Miguel and Manuel Goicoechea, Bilbao, 7 May 1797, AFB, Consulado 602, pp. 8–9.
[16] Ibid. 11 May 1797, p. 14
[17] Fernández, *Rostro*, 115–24.

the Bordeaux firm's good reputation as well as their disposition to trade with Goicoechea and Otero. So now, on 29 June, Goicoechea was writing to Bordeaux to get the correspondence underway. Using the customary phrase 'time will tell', he assured them that all their interests would be treated 'just as if we were brothers', adding that:

> It is possible that my wife doña María Josefa de Hormaeche, who has gone there [Bordeaux] for leisure, pays you a visit. I have written to her in this mail so that ... she salutes you on my behalf, and if she receives my letter she will no doubt come to you, and you will meet the mother of my sons.[18]

The importance of family in business was not an exclusive characteristic of the eighteenth century but had also been a pervasive feature in previous centuries. What was particularly significant about the second half of the eighteenth century, however, was that business practices and the role of family in providing an image of trustworthiness seem to have followed increasingly divergent paths. Aggressive marketing techniques, growing competition and merchants' increasing mobility brought a great deal of anxiety to overseas trade.

The evidence from Bilbao is patchy but revealing. It is often assumed that the hordes of English commercial travellers touring around Spain in the second half of the eighteenth century were welcomed without reservation,[19] but the truth is that Spaniards were not concerned only with the cheap prices and the good conditions that they were offered. In fact, the rapid spread of travellers provoked in the Spanish a great deal of unease, suspicion and even exasperation. In 1771 the English merchant James Roberts visited several Spanish cities with the intention of doing business, but when he arrived in Bilbao the head of the *consulado* claimed in despair that 'this man has no fixed address, something idiotic and innate to that nation [the English]. They seem vagrants'.[20] Merchants in Bilbao were used to following a social protocol that these travellers, too eager to move from one place to another, were not always ready to observe.

Although obviously the travellers in question were not vagrants, it was nevertheless considered crucial that they had a permanent address. Even those Spaniards who had moved to London after the mid-eighteenth century were a source of anxiety. In 1784 the Basque merchant Pedro de Atristain, who was long established in London, went to his home town Deusto (near Bilbao) to stay with his sisters for a few days. While there he was brought to the Bilbao *consulado*'s court by José de Echevarría y Dúo, a Bilbao merchant

---

[18] Simón Antonio Goicoechea to Garnier and Perry, Bilbao, 29 June 1797, AFB, Consulado 602, fo. 107.
[19] See Trevor Fawcett, 'Argonauts and commercial travellers: the foreign marketing of Norwich stuffs in the later eighteenth century', *Textile History* xvi (1985), 151–82.
[20] Domingo Ignacio de Mendieta to Manuel de Eléxpuru, Bilbao, 8 Mar. 1771, AFB, Consulado 543.

with whom Atristain had unfinished dealings. Echevarría tried to cast doubt on Atristain's credibility by arguing that he seemed to be travelling all the time.[21] However, Atristain said he could see nothing wrong in that. He argued that the first thing a merchant asked another merchant was whether he was married or single, and if the other man was married he would show interest in his family and place of abode. As Atristain was married to Josefa Joaquina de Retuerto, who lived in their house in London and whom Echevarría himself had met, Atristain considered that Echevarría's argument could not possibly cast any doubt on his reliability. Atristain's argument was not forgotten. Seven years later, in 1791, one of the witnesses in the Atristain case, Pedro de Orúe, would bring Atristain's words to the centre of another commercial dispute taking place in Bilbao, but on that occasion the defendant would be an unmarried merchant.

This latter case involved Juan Miguel Pérez, a London merchant from Soria who had begun his commercial career in the late 1750s as a clerk in Bilbao.[22] Around 1760 he moved to London to work for the wool merchant James Shedel, writing letters in Spanish. It was probably through Shedel that he met the leading Norwich manufacturer Jeremiah Ives, for whom he worked in the 1770s and 1780s as a commercial traveller picking up orders across Spain. In 1789 Pérez became a partner of Ives, Pérez, Echalaz and Co, but continued travelling tirelessly. And then, in late 1791, he was brought to court in Bilbao by a merchant of Madrid for a debt of 12,000 *pesos*. This time Pedro de Orúe was representing the plaintiff. He argued that Pérez's persistent mobility (he mentioned long stays in London, Bilbao, Madrid, Seville and Cádiz) meant that Pérez did not have a permanent address and therefore, according to the law, he was a *vago y vagabundo* (idler and vagabond). Pérez insisted that he travelled only for professional reasons and that his permanent residence was in London. Orúe raised serious doubts about that claim, recalling Atristain's declaration of seven years before and stressing that Pérez, unlike Atristain, was single. 'In order to prove that his residence is in London', he claimed, 'it would count for his defence if his wife were there, which would be an undisputable judicial evidence.'[23] Pérez responded, clearly infuriated, that whether or not he had a fixed address was totally irrelevant. 'It is unimportant', he claimed, 'whether [the firm] is in the fictitious country of the monkey-women, provided it is known and creditworthy', adding that, in commerce, no one asked about merchants' marital status but instead about funds. This contention bewildered Orúe. 'By asking in London about Pérez's funds what security do we have of finding something? What security of finding him who may have left for Tetuan?'[24]

---

[21] AFB, Corregimiento 1375/001, fos 39–70.
[22] AFB, Corregimiento 0547/018.
[23] AFB, Corregimiento 1375/001, fo. 190.
[24] Ibid.

Pérez saved his reputation thanks only to several Bilbao merchants who testified in his favour (he even managed to get the word *vago* crossed out in the 393 pages of the proceedings), but the anxieties brought about by his constant travelling suggest that two different mentalities coexisted in the second half of the eighteenth century: one understood the challenges posed by increasing competition, while the other, linked to certain social norms in which a permanent address and a family played crucial parts, viewed the merchant profession in a more traditional way.

But being married was not always an advantage, as Cádiz and its colonial trade revealed. Here too, trust and distrust ran parallel to the merchant's marital status. One would expect a married merchant in Cádiz to be willing to publicise his condition before travelling to America, since in the eyes of potential principals and creditors a wife and children meant a household that depended upon him, a permanent address, a place to which he was likely to return. The case of Ignacio de Torres is telling evidence in that sense: he feared that bringing his wife and daughter from Cádiz to Lima would make him look less trustworthy in the eyes of his Cádiz correspondents. Likewise, José de Moya, who was trying to recover a debt from one Pedro José de Bergara, reported to Cádiz that Bergara was 'a hard-working man, ... knows this commerce, and ... is a great lover of his family in Spain, so God gives him life to go back and pay'.[25] However, newly-married young merchants often hid their marital status from their principals and creditors, and some would even get married in secret just before leaving for America. There were two main reasons for this. First, if a married merchant whose wife was in Spain died in the colonies, it was very difficult and time-consuming to settle his accounts; and secondly, these young merchants did not want their principals to think that they would rush to sell the merchandise at any price in order to return to their wives as soon as possible.[26] In trying to avoid that second possibility, merchants travelling to America (particularly those whose married condition was known) were given both merchandise to be sold on commission and merchandise on loan to be sold on their own account. So, which was better for the merchant travelling to the colonies, to be married or to be single? In eighteenth-century Cádiz, 80 per cent of merchants got married at least once in their lifetime.[27] However, over the course of the century the pattern of marriage evolved in a manner that shows an interesting connection with the evolution of trade. Paloma Fernández states that in the first half of the century, marrying the daughter of an established merchant family was a priority for a young merchant wanting to join the colonial trade. By contrast, in the second half of the century merchants tended to marry later, after having spent some years trading. The evidence seems clear, but Fernández's explanation is rather unpersuasive. She argues,

---

[25] José de Moya to José María Enrrile, Lima, 8 May 1779, HCA 30/316/12, no. 1593.
[26] Fernández, *Rostro*, 110–14.
[27] Ibid. 127.

firstly, that in the second half of the century such merchants belonged to a generation of Cádiz-born merchants, who therefore had no need to integrate into the local community through marriage. However, that argument does not account for the majority of merchants who were born elsewhere. The second reason is that, due to the spectacular increase in imports and exports, remaining single for a longer period gave the young merchant 'freedom and independence to become rich in a few trips [to America]' before getting married.[28] This is a sweeping simplification of a far more complex process involving increasing levels of risk and competition. In fact, it was not the possibility of getting rich that encouraged merchants to postpone their marriages, but instead increasing competition and the need to stay away for several years in order both to sell their merchandise and to consolidate networks for the future.

A more plausible hypothesis, therefore, is that it was the shift from the old to the new pattern of trade that had a significant effect upon the age at which most merchants got married. Before 1740 most Cádiz merchants stayed in the colonies only for the time it took for the fairs at Portobelo and Jalapa to be completed, whereas in the second half of the century they stayed much longer. This compelled them to postpone their plans for starting a family, for few merchants were willing to get married, have children and then disappear leaving the family behind for several years. To be sure, the letters of the nine Cádiz merchants writing to their wives from Lima in 1779 shared two main themes: the desire to return to Spain on the one hand, and the difficulties of completing their dealings on the other. By 1779 most of them had been away from their wives and children for between four and eight years.[29] That Cádiz merchants married at an older age after mid-century suggests that their actions were not only driven by an economic rationale but also by an awareness of the personal costs of early marriage followed by long absences.

---

[28] Ibid. 133.
[29] Torres to María Badillo, Lima, 10 May 1779, HCA 30/312/2, no. 622; José de Moya to María Nicolasa Portusagasti, Lima, 31 Mar. 1779, HCA 30/313/3, no. 848; Domingo Millán de Acha to Gertrudis de Urruchi, Lima, 10 May 1779, HCA 30/315/7, unnumbered; Juan de Eguino to María Josefa Diton, Lima, 8 May 1779, HCA 30/314/3, no. 756; Antonio Helme to Ignacia Helme, Lima, 8 May 1779, HCA 30/313/17, no. 1069; Pedro Galesio to Juana Andresa Borca, Lima, 9 May 1779, HCA 30/314/1, no. 294; Francisco Romero to María Andrea y Arteaga, Lima, 7 May 1779, HCA 30/314/8, no. 985; Bartolomé Ramón de Muguruza to María Jesús de Urristi, Lima, 8 May 1779, HCA 30/316/14, no. 1202; Joaquín (no surname in signature) to Catalina María de Sorhaitz, Lima, 8 May 1779, HCA 30/316/15, no. 669.

Friends

In March 1785, when he was about to die, the Basque Pedro de Atristain made his last will and testament in his London house. He left several tens of thousands of *pesos* to his wife, three sisters, brother and aunt. To his partners and *paisanos*, the London merchants Alfonso de Eguino and Manuel de Garay, he bequeathed 'a ring apiece worth twenty guineas as a sign of my friendship'.[30] Historical sources usually say a lot more about family than about friends, but the fact that the concept of friendship is far more difficult to define than family is not a sufficient excuse to brush it aside. Indeed, it can be argued that a merchant's friends were as important as his own family, for his social life revolved around both.

Peter Mathias states that 'the word "friend", widely used in the eighteenth century when referring to a trusted personal acquaintance or collaborator in business, ... is resonant with the implications of personal trust and the obligations which friendship entailed'.[31] In his 1700 memoirs the Cádiz merchant Raimundo de Lantery used the term *amigo* (friend) frequently. For him a good friend would act 'without any personal interest, because there lies true friendship'.[32] Friendship entailed services to a friend such as recommending him to other friends, or even assisting him on his deathbed. Moreover, Lantery stressed that a good friend would not break off his friendship over a dispute involving money, for friends should not prove burdensome to one another. Other merchants thought likewise. Writing to Lima in 1765, Roque Aguado assured Andrés Ramírez de Arellano that 'whether we make a good or a bad business, we must keep our friendship until we die'.[33] In the correspondence, the term 'friend' was often preceded by reassuring adjectives such as dear, fine, good, old, true or intimate. Though a merchant's friends were not confined to the business world, it was nevertheless often comforting in that world to be able to deal with friends. And so, rather confusingly, the term 'friend', a marker of honesty and trustworthiness, could also be used to describe every kind of relationship from mere acquaintances to colleagues and associates, encompassing a wide spectrum of relationships which did not always correspond with Lantery's definition of friendship.[34]

Friendship worked horizontally as well as vertically. Indeed there were two models of friendship, which are not always easy to distinguish: the egalitarian and the patron/client. None the less, for the merchant, his trading network was to a large extent a network of friends. The Norwich manufac-

---

[30] Copy of Atristain's last will and testament in AFB, Corregimiento 1763/013.
[31] Mathias, 'Risk', 30.
[32] Bustos, *Comerciante saboyano*, 29.
[33] Aguado to Arellano, Cádiz, 23 Jan. 1765, IRA, ARA, Epistolario.
[34] In eighteenth-century England the term 'friend' was often used in business to mean simply a client: Hannah Barker, *The business of women: female enterprise and urban development in northern England, 1760–1830*, Oxford 2006, 81–2.

turers Stannard and Taylor referred to all their Spanish correspondents as 'friends'. To the Bilbao merchant Domingo de Oxangoiti, from whom they had had no news for a long time, they sent samples and current prices of all their articles in order to 'reclaim in this way your good friendship and correspondence'.[35] In the trade between Cádiz and Lima, merchants relied upon a group of friends to get commissions, loans, information and advice. Pedro Miguel de Arvilla, for example, informed Martín de Endara about how to avoid the payment of some taxes, adding 'tell our friends'.[36] In this usage, Arvilla was referring to fellow traders rather than superiors.

However important it might have been, the fact is that friendship could be very fragile indeed when money was involved. A Bilbao merchant who had delayed a payment for several months was reminded by Stannard and Taylor that 'with our friends, if possible, we would like to avoid quarrels and troubles'.[37] From Lima, Gregorio López de Cangas tried to convince his angry Cádiz creditor that the reason he had not cleared his debt was because 'I first tried to pay those with whom I had no friendship'.[38] Following a commercial dispute, Domingo Millán de Acha, a merchant who had been in Lima away from his wife for eight years and was desperate to return to Spain, took his best friend Juan de Alva to court. Fearing that Domingo de Urruchi, his uncle in Seville, would not approve of his decision, Acha assured him that he had been left no alternative. He had asked other merchants about the most convenient thing to do: 'They advised me that I should not lose such a large amount of money because of our friendship.'[39] These examples of quarrels between friends are not exceptions given that failure in business was as likely as success, and the chances of friends becoming foes were quite high. Lantery himself quoted in his memoirs a Castilian proverb that captures the source of this feared mutation: 'Who is your enemy? The man in your own trade.'[40]

While wary of the risk of being let down by their friends, merchants none the less expected loyalty and trust from them, as is clearly shown in the correspondence. 'Failing in my confidence and disregarding my orders, you appropriated what was mine', wrote the Lima merchant Domingo de Larrea to José de Llano, concluding that 'you have failed in our friendship'.[41] Stannard and Taylor's next letter to their Bilbao debtor was less friendly than the previous one, this time stressing that they were 'losing our patience' and

---

[35] Stannard and Taylor to Domingo de Oxangoiti, Norwich, 27 June 1767, NRO, BR 211/14, pp. 61–2.
[36] Pedro Miguel de Arvilla to Martín de Endara, Lima, 9 May 1779, HCA 30/312/11, no. 944.
[37] Stannard and Taylor to Bernardo de Guendica, Norwich, 9 Sept. 1767, BR 211/14, p. 117.
[38] Gregorio López de Cangas to Asunsolo, Lima, n.d. 1779, HCA 30/314/1, no. 278.
[39] Acha to Domingo de Urruchi, Lima, 10 May 1779, HCA 30/315/7, unnumbered.
[40] Bustos, Comerciante saboyano, 340.
[41] Larrea to José de Llano, Lima, 8 May 1779, HCA 30/315/3, no. 1822.

reminding him that he should know the importance of good faith and punctuality among merchants, for 'without them confidence is lost and correspondence ceases'.[42] Friends were desperately needed but they were hardly an absolute guarantee of trustworthiness.

If trusting a friend entailed a certain degree of risk, having to trust the friend of a friend clearly increased it. The whole Atlantic trade can be seen as a massive trading network in which not everyone knew everyone but everyone had friends who had friends. One's preparedness to use such a network depended on how much risk one was ready to take: for a chain of friends could stretch from a manufacturer in Norwich who wanted to market his articles in Peru, but knew nobody there, to a local merchant in Cuzco. Naturally, the uncertainty and distrust arising from so long a chain was too unattractive for most businessmen, which is why traders in England and France preferred to participate in Spanish colonial trade by investing in sea loans rather than sending merchandise to Spanish America on their own account. With that aim, they resorted to their Cádiz friends' ability to select reliable merchants among the Spaniards. As the Irish James Comeford wrote to the London merchant Wargent Nicholson in 1753:

> If you and your friends should think proper to conferr orders to me, on the above [a proposal for investing in a loan], I shall exert myself with the utmost care for your advantage and Don Antonio Butler *my friend and Patron* [emphasis added], will cooperate in obtaining the bonds of unexceptionable paymasters for the security of the money.[43]

One of the origins of distrust between correspondents lay in the difficulties involved in ascertaining the truth. If a debtor did not reply to several requests his dishonourable intentions were clear, but it was often the case that disputes between correspondents were not so easy to clarify. For example, if an agent made a sale at a low price or did not make it at all, and then failed to provide an immediate explanation, suspicion was likely to arise even among his best friends. The problem was that explanations relied on persuasion rather than on tangible, undisputable evidence. Few merchants were as lucky as Andrés Ramírez de Arellano, who in January 1757 left Cádiz on board the register ship *San Martín* with the French brothers Joseph and Louis Louison. Arellano and Joseph Louison were to act jointly as agents in Lima for the Cádiz merchant Lorenzo del Arco and for the French firm Magon and Co, whereas Louison's brother was appointed to Valparaiso. In Lima, Arellano and Louison resided together for seven years, until suddenly, in the summer of 1764, Louison fled to a remote village 600 miles away from Lima. Fearing that he had been cheated, Arellano accused both Louison and his brother of robbery and of being foreigners. They were both detained and

---

[42] Stannard and Taylor to Guendica, Norwich, 21 Oct. 1767, BR 211/14, p. 149.
[43] James Comeford to Wargent Nicholson, Cádiz, 12 Feb. 1753, C 111/200.

brought back to Lima, from where Louison wrote to Magon, and Arellano to Arco. Both told completely different stories. In his long and detailed letter, Louison stressed that he had left Lima with the intention only of recovering some debts. He claimed that Arellano was a traitor and a cheat who intended to appropriate their principal's money by using him and his brother as scapegoats.[44] Unfortunately, Arellano's letter to Arco is lost, but from Arco's reply it is clear that Arellano managed to be more persuasive than Louison. Indeed Arellano seized Louison's letter-book containing the correspondence between the two brothers and sent it to Cádiz. Even Magon, who had insisted on sending the two brothers to Lima along with Arellano, was now convinced of the identity of the real cheat. Acknowledging Arellano's honesty, Magon gave Arco a copy of Louison's letter. Arco translated the letter into Spanish and sent three copies to Arellano by three different mails, adding 'so that you enjoy yourself'.[45] And Arellano must have enjoyed himself greatly, for he carefully kept the three copies among his business records. On that occasion, then, truth had prevailed.

But whether because undisputable evidence of that sort was difficult to obtain or because the dispute in question was just a matter of different views, the merchant knew only too well that his ability to persuade his correspondents was the key to maintaining his reputation, and therefore, their friendship. In long distance trade, such as that between Cádiz and Lima, where the smallest detail could arouse distrust, persuasion was of paramount importance. When in 1778 Joaquín Xavier García took his partner Pedro Miguel de Arvilla to court in Lima, he was well aware that that decision could greatly undermine his chances of getting consignments from his Cádiz friends, because they were also Arvilla's friends. García asked for help from his most influential Cádiz correspondent, Simón Babil de Uriz. After explaining how bad his experience with Arvilla had been, García wrote: 'Try to obtain all the friends' favour so that they protect me and choose me for their commissions, and be assured that my correspondence and commitment to their orders will be the most exact.'[46]

The experience of Juan de Eguino

One case that encapsulates the importance of family members and friends in preserving confidentiality and personal reputation is that of the Cádiz *consulado* merchant Juan Bautista Ruiz de Eguino y López de Arregui, also known as Juan de Eguino. He was born in Mezquía, a tiny village in the Basque province of Álava, probably, on the basis of the evidence in his letters, around 1725. In his late twenties, like many other young merchants, he travelled to

---

[44] Joseph Louison to Magon, Lima, 7 Mar. 1765, IRA, ARA, Epistolario.
[45] Arco to Arellano, Cádiz, 20 Dec. 1765, ibid.
[46] García to Uriz, Lima, 14 Apr. 1779, HCA 30/314/7, no. 483.

Lima, where he stayed from 1753 to 1757 and established a close friendship with another Basque, the Lima merchant Domingo de Larrea. Just before returning to Cádiz in February 1757 he went into partnership with Larrea: Eguino would take care of their dealings in Spain, and Larrea would manage the Peru branch of the company.[47] As soon as Eguino arrived in Spain he joined the Cádiz *consulado*, and years later, having acquired a considerable fortune and a good reputation, he got married.[48] In October 1776 Eguino was living in Cádiz with his wife and two children when terrible news arrived from Lima. He became convinced that Larrea, his partner for two decades, was cheating him. Eguino's life was to change dramatically. In November 1778 he applied to the Council of Indies for a licence to stay in Peru for four years, alleging that a large quantity of clothes he had sent to Lima in 1774 were still unsold.[49] Days later he was on board the warship *Santiago* on his way to Peru, accompanied by his nephew and assistant José de la Rosa.

The ship got to Callao in late April 1779, as Eguino himself reported, 'after 158 days of navigation, having experienced its harshness and thrown ten dead people to the sea, ... with 150 ill, most of them suffering from scurvy'.[50] A man of his age was not supposed to take such risks. To his brother Benito he wrote that 'this harshness is not to be suffered more than once and being a young man, as it happened to me, but at my old age I have had to do it again with deep affliction'.[51] As soon as he arrived in Lima, Eguino wrote to Spain via Cartagena de Indias. A few days later, in early May 1779, just to make sure that his seventeen addressees would get his letters, he posted copies in *La Perla*. His relationship with those addressees, their identity, and what Eguino expected and demanded from them are key to understanding his experience of trust and distrust. Furthermore, the account of what happened in Lima between Eguino and Larrea would occupy about 80 per cent of Larrea's last will and testament, written in 1800, whilst his version of the whole affair differed substantially from that of Eguino.[52] The fact that the historian cannot determine from this evidence which version of events is true is a reminder that trust is not a question of overt truth but a matter of persuasion and perception.

Eguino went to Lima to sort out a business issue that had arisen five years earlier. On 14 September 1774 he had agreed another partnership with

---

[47] Guillermo Lohmann, 'Los comerciantes vascos en el virreinato peruano', in R. Escobedo, A. Rivera and A. Chapa (eds), *Los vascos y América: el comercio vasco con América en el siglo* XVIII, Bilbao 1989, 71–6.

[48] He probably married in the late 1760s. In 1785 Eguino would declare that he had contributed 120,000 *pesos* to his marriage with María Josefa Diton, whereas she had brought no dowry: AGN, Protocolo 968 (notary Andrés Sandoval), 22 Mar. 1785, fo. 183.

[49] AGI, Contratación 5524, N.1-R.93.

[50] Eguino to Blas Antonio Benito Jiménez, Lima, 5 May 1779, HCA 30/312/5, no. 921.

[51] Eguino to Benito de Eguino, Lima, 5 May 1779, HCA 30/316/7, no. 829.

[52] AGN, Protocolo 977 (notary Andrés Sandoval), 4 July 1800, fos 787–91.

his old friend Larrea, but this time they were joined by two new partners, Eguino's *compadre* (trusted family friend) Blas Antonio Benito Jiménez, and the Basque ship captain José Miguel de Urezberroeta. Urezberroeta had just come back from Lima with a letter of attorney from Larrea to act on Larrea's behalf. The company was agreed in Cádiz without the services of a public notary, and its duration would be the time it took to complete one single and very risky piece of business.[53] The plan was that Jiménez and Eguino would acquire a large loan in Cádiz (as it turned out they got the remarkable sum of 800,000 *pesos*) and would buy a great quantity of clothes in Cádiz and England: it would then be Larrea and Urezberroeta's duty to dispose of the goods in Peru. Needless to say this was a gamble of enormous proportions, as no merchant had shipped a cargo of that value to Peru since the time of the *galeones*. In fact, according to an anonymous observer writing in 1784, the inventories sent to Peru rarely exceeded 100,000 *pesos* of principal.[54] As it turned out, the whole venture was a complete disaster. Four years later, in 1778, most of the clothes were still unsold.

But Eguino and Jiménez were not ready to acknowledge the reality of the situation, particularly as they had heard rumours in October 1776 that Larrea and Urezberroeta, without telling them anything, had been involved in sending consignments of cocoa, wine and liquor to Chile, and had even invested in shipbuilding in Guayaquil. Eguino and Jiménez therefore suspected that their Lima partners were cheating them. Being the one who had recommended his old friend Larrea to Jiménez, Eguino took full responsibility and travelled to Lima to find out the truth, and his first meeting with Larrea confirmed his worst fears. Eguino wrote to Jiménez that '[Larrea] has denied nothing but confessed. I said to him what you may imagine, although gently and politely; and I saw him confused, not being able to reply to my charges, not even to tell me how much they owed.'[55] He asked some *amigos antiguos* (old friends) about his Lima partners' reputation, only to find out that 'everybody talks badly about Urezberroeta but they all say that Larrea is a good man, even though you and I know he does not behave as such'.[56] By contrast, Larrea said nothing about the conversation with Eguino in his letter to Jiménez. He simply assured Jiménez that the accounts he had sent to Cádiz up to then were all correct.[57]

As well as informing Jiménez, both Eguino and Larrea were very concerned about what the Lima merchant community might think of their actions. Indeed, Eguino's arrival had not gone unnoticed. For example, the *montañés*

---

[53] A copy of the company agreement in AGN, Cabildo, Cajo 1, caja 97, doc. 1486, fos 14–19.
[54] BL, MS Add. 13981, fo. 24r.
[55] Eguino to Jiménez, Lima, 5 May 1779, HCA 30/313/2, no. 921.
[56] Ibid.
[57] Larrea to Jiménez, Lima, 8 May 1779, HCA 30/313/2, no. 673.

merchant Francisco Gallegos informed his *paisano* Juan Antonio Santibáñez that '[Eguino] has not wanted to go to reside with Larrea; we presume there might be a *cuento ruidoso* [noisy affair].'[58] In fact, Eguino's refusal to reside with his partners was a way of forcing them to show their account books to him. He had told Larrea and Urezberroeta that 'if they showed me sincerely and in good faith all the accounts of all the transactions I would go to live with them'.[59] Eguino knew that it was his partners' reputation rather than his own what was being damaged by that decision. If they did not want rumours to grow then they would have to give him the account books, which they eventually did, although according to Larrea's last will and testament it was Eguino who seized all his books and papers 'despotically'.[60] Even so, despite all the resentment and disagreement, Eguino and Larrea were to share the same house for years. In December 1785 Larrea himself would declare that since Eguino's arrival, 'except for the first month', they had always co-resided.[61]

In May 1779 Eguino had two priorities in mind. First, it was essential not to draw too much outside attention to the situation. He therefore appointed a mediator to help solve the problem without having to resort to the Lima *consulado*'s court – but that did not work. Surprisingly enough, it was not Eguino who took Larrea to court but vice versa. Larrea wanted Eguino to pay him half the expenses that he and Urezberroeta had incurred since 1775 (warehouse storage, maintenance and assistants' salaries). In the forty-seven folios of the proceedings – the case took place in October 1780 – not once did Eguino accuse Larrea of mismanagement or dishonesty.[62] This court case may well have been, at least in part, a concession to public gossip. Even during the trial Larrea and Eguino resided together.

Eguino's other priority was to pay back all their creditors as soon as possible. He thought of shipping bark, copper and cocoa to Spain, but Larrea told him that obtaining those commodities could not be taken for granted because they were running short of both money and credit. They still had a large amount of unsold clothes in a warehouse, and Eguino concluded that disposing of them at a loss was the only thing that they could do in order to send cash to Spain. Despite Larrea's opposition, in late 1779 Eguino sold all the clothes to José Antonio Lavalle, Bruno Antonio Polanco and Francisco Sánchez Navarrete – a decision that he would regret for the rest of his life. In the preceding months there had been continuous rumours about the possibility of war between Spain and Britain, but nothing could

---

[58] Francisco Gallegos to Juan Antonio Santibáñez, Lima, 7 May 1779, HCA 30/316/1, no. 429.
[59] Eguino to Jiménez, Lima, 5 May 1779, HCA 30/313/2, no. 921.
[60] AGN, Protocolo 977 (notary Andrés Sandoval), 4 July 1800, fo. 789.
[61] AGN, Protocolo 1075 (notary Valentín Torres), 16 Dec. 1785, fo. 813.
[62] AGN, Cabildo, Cajo 1, caja 97, doc. 1486.

be said for certain: it was only after Eguino sold the merchandise that news of the outbreak of war arrived in Lima. There followed a severe shortage of European merchandise until 1783 – and as Larrea would remember bitterly in 1800, they lost 200,000 *pesos* in that unfortunate operation.[63]

But before all that happened, Eguino posted seventeen letters in *La Perla* (*see* table 3). The addressees can be divided into three main groups: first, his family, including his brothers Alfonso and Benito, cousin Francisco Xavier and wife María Josefa Diton; secondly, seven Basque merchants established in Cádiz; and lastly, three French firms also established in Cádiz. The three groups played important roles for Eguino, although each in a different way.

The letter for María Josefa Diton went in the envelope addressed to his intimate friend the merchant Juan Francisco de Vea Murguía. Eguino gave her precise instructions. Their situation seemed to have been rather desperate, for he wanted to know how many relatives and servants were still living with her. Eguino was particularly concerned about the education of Rufinito, their seven-year-old son, and wanted his wife to make sure that he studied as hard as possible. Furthermore, Eguino stressed that 'he should not wear any gold or silver nor even silk', and 'if it is possible he should dress down decent and humble'.[64] For anything she might need, María Josefa would have the support of Eguino's friends and family. Alfonso in London was told to write to her at least once a month, addressing his letters to Vea Murguía. To Vea Murguía, Eguino wrote: 'I have no doubt you will look after my wife and family, protecting and assisting them with anything they might need.'[65] But he did have doubts, for he asked his wife to tell him 'which of my friends visits you'.

All his other addressees were his friends, as he made clear in the forms of salutation used in his letters. His *compadre* Jiménez, the six Basque merchants and the Cádiz-born son of a Basque were all his friends as well as members of the Cádiz *consulado*. The associates of the three French firms, although for obvious reasons unrelated to the *consulado*, were also Eguino's friends. They were all to be informed about his findings in Lima through Jiménez and Zulaica. Furthermore, Eguino stressed to his friends that they could trust him if ever they required his services. Here, however, he was more effusive towards his Basque friends. To Sorozábal, for instance, he assured that 'I am an intimate friend of yours, and as such you can order me in confidence since I wish to please you.'[66] In fact, the main difference between the Basques and the French was that each group had different things to offer Eguino: his

---

[63] AGN, Protocolo 977 (notary Andrés Sandoval), 4 July 1800, fo. 789.
[64] Eguino to Diton, Lima, 5 May 1779, HCA 30/314/3, no. 756.
[65] Eguino to Vea Murguía, Lima, 5 May 1779, ibid.
[66] Eguino to Juan Pascual de Sorozábal, Lima, 5 May 1779, HCA 30/312/9, no. 209.

Table 3
Juan de Eguino's addressees, May 1779

Addressee(s)	Address	Occupation	Provenance	Relationship	HCA
Alfonso de Eguino	London	merchant	Álava (B.C.)	brother	30/315/10, no. 1431
Benito de Eguino	Cádiz	——	Álava (B.C.)	brother	30/316/7, no. 829
Francisco Xavier de Eguino	Madrid	clergyman	Álava (B.C.)	cousin	30/315/5, no. 1573
María Josefa Diton	Cádiz	——	——	wife	30/314/3, no. 756 *
count of Peñaflorida	Bergara (Guipúzcoa)	(co-founder of the Basque Society)	Guipúzcoa (B.C.)	friend	30/316/12, no. 1154
marquis of Obando	Cádiz	——	——	friend	30/312/5, no. 924
Blas Antonio Benito Jiménez	Cádiz	merchant	Granada (Andalusia)	*compadre*	30/313/2, no. 921 30/315/11, no. 66 **
Antonio Zulaica	Cádiz	merchant	Guipúzcoa (B.C.)	friend	30/316/1, no. 206 30/315/11, no. 66 **
Juan Francisco de Vea Murguía	Cádiz	merchant	Álava (B.C.)	friend	30/314/3, no. 756 *
Matías de Landaburu	Cádiz	merchant	Vizcaya (B.C.)	friend	30/313/1, no. 925
Juan Francisco de Lezeta	Cádiz	merchant	Guipúzcoa (B.C.)	friend	30/313/1, no. 920
Juan Pascual de Sorozábal	Cádiz	merchant	Navarre (B.C.)	friend	30/312/9, no. 209
Juan Martín de Aguirre	Cádiz	merchant	Navarre (B.C.)	friend	30/315/2, no. 831
Pedro José de Loyo	Cádiz	merchant	Cádiz (son of a Basque merchant)	friend	30/315/6, no. 670
Louis Lecouteaulx	Cádiz	merchant	France	friend	30/312/5, no. 922
Cayla, Solier, Cabanes, Jugla and Co.	Cádiz	merchants	France	friends	30/312/2, no. 416
Magon, Lefer and Co.	Cádiz	merchants	France	friends	30/312/4, no. 919

* Envelope addressed to Vea Murguía containing letters for both Vea Murguía and Eguino's wife.
** Envelope addressed to both Jiménez and Zulaica.

paisanos had contacts in Lima who could assist him, whereas the French were his creditors (most likely representing a consortium of French investors).[67]

For Eguino and his Basque friends, their ethnic identity was an important part of their lives. Matías de Landaburu was one of the most influential merchants in Cádiz, with correspondents in Lima, Mexico City, Buenos Aires and Guatemala. In the early 1780s he was one of the promoters of a plan to bring a Basque priest to Cádiz to assist those *paisanos* who barely understood Spanish.[68] The other five Basques were, along with Landaburu and Eguino himself, distinctive members of the Basque congregation of Cádiz.[69] Furthermore, since 1771 Eguino had been the representative in Cádiz of the *Real Sociedad Bascongada de los Amigos del País* – the Royal Society of Friends of the Basque Country, or Basque Economic Society.[70] The *Bascongada* was founded in December 1764 to encourage the education, wealth, culture and general progress of the Basque Country, and by 1789 it had 102 members in Lima. Eguino also wrote from Lima to one of its founders, the count of Peñaflorida.[71]

Eguino knew that his arrival in Lima would make clear to everyone that he had problems with Larrea and Urezberroeta. Nobody could misinterpret the situation: a merchant of his age would never have come to Lima, leaving his family in Cádiz, unless something was seriously wrong. It was a gesture of courage and sacrifice that deserved respect, but it was also a clear admission of difficulties. Once in Lima, Eguino knew that his chances of solving his problems would depend to a great extent on his own reputation. He needed to build up a good name as soon as possible, making clear to everyone that he was an honest man free of any suspicion. As the correspondence shows, it was his Basque friends who could help him to achieve that. From them Eguino got recommendations for their Lima correspondents, most of whom were also Basques.

It appears that the effect of those recommendations was positive for Eguino, at least initially. To Lezeta he wrote: 'After you recommended me

---

[67] Eguino to Solier, Cabanes, Jugla and Co., Lima, 8 May 1779, HCA 30/312/2, no. 416. The three French firms would soon be involved in the creation of the first Spanish national bank: Pedro Tedde de Lorca, *El Banco de San Carlos, 1782–1829*, Madrid 1988, 42, 46.

[68] Fernández, *Rostro*, 44.

[69] They were in fact active members of the Basque congregation; Lezeta (1777), Sorozábal (1778), Vea Murguía (1779) and Zulaica (1787) were elected *prioste* (head) of the *cofradía*: José Garmendia Arruebarrena, *Cádiz, los vascos y la Carrera de Indias*, San Sebastián 1990, 219.

[70] Eguino to Miguel de Olaso, Cádiz, 29 Oct. 1771, ATHA, FP 34/14, fo. 289. For the *Bascongada*'s membership in the colonies see Juan Vidal Abarca, 'Estudios sobre la distribución y evolución de los socios de la RSBAP en Indias (1765–1793)', in *La Real Sociedad Bascongada y América*, Madrid 1992, 142.

[71] Eguino to Xavier María de Munibe e Idiáquez, 8th count of Peñaflorida, Lima, 5 May 1779, HCA 30/316/12, no. 1154.

to your friends here, I would not be acknowledging your kindness if I did not thank you for the considerate offers they have made me on your behalf.'[72] The letters posted to Cádiz by those Lima merchants to whom Eguino had been recommended confirm their willingness to assist him. Jacinto de Segurola reported to Vea Murguía that 'to this fellow [Eguino] I shall serve according to your orders'.[73] Another of Vea Murguía's correspondents, Manuel Ignacio de Erasun, wrote that 'Eguino arrived safely, and I have provided accommodation for him near my house.'[74] Consular affiliation was no obstacle to friendship and mutual understanding. The Basque Joaquín José de Arrese, head of the Lima *consulado* between 1775 and 1777, reported to his *paisano* Lezeta that he would do 'whatever Eguino asks me, as I have already promised him'.[75] But Eguino had non-Basque supporters as well. The creole count of Sierrabella, for instance, reported to Landaburu that Eguino had given him 'your letter of recommendation, and for its observance I have offered myself to help him with what is in my reach'.[76]

The French, as creditors, had more bearing on Eguino's fortunes than his other addressees. Rather revealingly, however, they did not recommend Eguino to a merchant but to someone else – María Ventura de Guirior, the wife of the viceroy of Peru. She was an old friend of Jean Joseph Laborde, a Bayonne-born merchant established in Cádiz who had begged her to assist his French compatriots' debtor. In a letter addressed to Laborde himself, María Ventura made it clear she would help Eguino only because Cayla, Cabanes, Jugla and Co. were Laborde's friends and correspondents.[77] Although the viceroy's wife was very influential, the French merchants did not recommend Eguino to anybody else. This example adds to what has been argued about the foreigners' poor networks in Peru: rather than trade directly on their own account, the great French houses of Cádiz preferred to give a loan to a well-known, reputable and married merchant who was resident in Cádiz and had access to many contacts in Lima. But even so, success could never be taken for granted.

Eguino and his partners never managed to clear the debt entirely. Urezberroeta and Larrea would die in America, both in poverty. Eguino's wife died while he was in Peru. A broken man, he returned to Europe in 1791 following the death of his brother Alfonso. He went to London to claim his share in Alfonso's last will and testament, fearing that his nephew Francisco, son of Benito and Alfonso's partner in London, was lying about it. Eguino

---

[72] Eguino to Juan Francisco de Lezeta, Lima, 5 May 1779, HCA 30/313/1, no. 920.
[73] Segurola to Vea Murguía, Lima, 7 May 1779, HCA 30/314/3, no. 1819.
[74] Erasun to Vea Murguía, Lima, 6 May 1779, HCA 30/314/3, no. 1129.
[75] Arrese to Lezeta, Lima, 8 May 1779, HCA 30/313/1, no. 1578.
[76] Christobal Mesía y Munive, count of Sierrabella, to Landaburu, Lima, 8 May 1779, HCA 30/314/3, no. 1028.
[77] María Ventura de Guirior to Jean Joseph Laborde, Lima, 10 May 1779, HCA 30/312/2, no. 1111.

took his nephew to the Chancery Court.[78] Twelve years after having left for Lima, distrust brought him back to Europe. He was dead by 1800, his career a reminder of the vicissitudes of trade and the problems generated when trust collapsed.

---

[78] Eguino v. Eguino (1792), C 12/1401/24.

7
Risk and Competition

If the need to maintain confidentiality regarding their businesses made merchants wary of their colleagues, the same can also be said of the variety of different jurisdictions and commercial environments in which they had to operate. It is clear that the legal system played a crucial part in determining the level of trust needed between overseas merchants: the weaker the legal system (i.e. the greater the degree of contractual uncertainty) the greater the importance of trust based on social relations. Furthermore, along with the risks arising from the often dubious enforceability of contracts, in the eighteenth century, as Spain's overseas trade expanded, merchants had to cope with rising levels of competition, and as a result were inevitably compelled to take riskier decisions. This chapter explores the interaction between the legal conditions that underpinned relationships based on trust and the growing level of risk associated with increased competition. The social and cultural implications of these evolving realities added to the uncertainties of overseas trade, blurring the fine line dividing trust from distrust.

Legal frameworks

Although any eighteenth-century Spanish merchant would have subscribed to Gerrard de Malynes's assertion that '[f]aith or trust is to be kept between merchants, and that also must be done without quillets or titles of the law',[1] the fact is that the law played a pivotal role in encouraging merchants to engage in trade, or discouraging them from doing so. In the world of commerce the law was designed to guarantee the enforcement of contracts and to administer justice, so any question involving the law affected merchants' ability to trust. However, there were instances in which 'the titles of the law' were also a source of distrust for merchants. For example, by signing a written contract rather than simply accepting each other's verbal assurances, merchants were implying that, however slightly, they distrusted each other. Domingo Millán de Acha and Juan de Alva were such good friends, and trusted each other so much, that their verbal agreements were sufficient to seal their mutual contracts. In 1772 (at the time they were both in Lima), Alva introduced and recommended his friend Martín de Estenoz to Acha, assuring him he would be Estenoz's guarantor if Acha decided to sell him merchandise on

[1] Malynes, *Consuetudo*, 93.

credit. Soon after, Acha followed Alva's advice and gave Estenoz merchandise worth 16,000 *pesos* on credit. But Estenoz then took the merchandise, travelled to Arequipa, and died a year later leaving nothing for his creditor. And to add insult to injury, Alva refused to pay Acha as promised. So Acha took Alva to court, even though he knew that nothing could be proved. 'He assured me orally', wrote Acha to his wife years later, 'that he would pay in case the debtor did not. ... And since we had such a close friendship, ... I thought I would offend him if I told him that his word should go down on paper.' Acha learned a valuable lesson, acknowledging that 'it is necessary, even between father and son, to be cautious'[2].

All merchants considered the law essential in underpinning trade. The trouble was that commerce in eighteenth-century Spain was supported by a legal system that was exceedingly intricate and inappropriate – a problem noted by Juan de Hevia Bolaños in his *Curia filípica* (the Spanish procedural handbook of the seventeenth and eighteenth centuries, first published in 1617), who began the second volume, which is entirely devoted to commercial legislation, by defining the Greek term labyrinth as 'a building made up of intricate, maze-like chambers and passages so designed that a person entering one finds it difficult to find a way out', then commented that he is about to deal with a piece of legislation that should be called a 'labyrinth of trade'.[3] The term seemed very appropriate as merchants themselves often referred to their businesses as labyrinths, but it also reflects the frequent inability of the legislation to provide rapid and practical solutions to the wide range of disputes arising between merchants.

Hampered both by intricate legislation and deficient judicial facilities, the merchants of the main commercial centres of the Spanish empire relied on the *consulado* court. Merchants alleged that a mercantile court (which was elected by the members themselves) was of the utmost importance in the encouragement of business activities, for the application of its expertise meant that commercial litigations could be resolved quickly and effectively. Even though the veracity of that argument is difficult to ascertain,[4] the example of Bilbao, when placed in a wider context, shows that the good reputation of a reliable judicial framework could indeed promote business. The indigenous merchants in Bilbao considered it essential to increase the prestige of their *consulado* and to place all merchants, whether local or foreign, under the same jurisdiction. Continuing rivalry between *bilbaínos* and foreigners gave rise to the new *consulado* Ordinances in 1737, a major step towards safeguarding frameworks in which trust could operate, and it is important to stress that the *bilbaínos*' achievement had imperial implications. On the one hand they contributed to raising the educational level of all Spanish

---

[2] Acha to Gertrudis de Urruchi, Lima, 10 May 1779, HCA 30/315/7, unnumbered.
[3] Juan Hevia Bolaños, *Curia filípica, segundo tomo donde breve, y compendiosamente se trata de la mercancía y contratación de tierra y mar* (Lima 1617), Madrid 1717, ii. 2.
[4] Smith, *Spanish guild*, 112–13.

merchants (and therefore their participation in commerce) by giving them something as unusual as a commercial handbook in Spanish, and on the other the Ordinances became the procedural handbook for all *consulados* for the simple reason that it was far more useful than the updated editions of the *Curia filípica*. Every *consulado* within the Spanish empire resorted to the 1737 Ordinances.[5] It is therefore fair to say that the *bilbaínos* contributed to the expansion of colonial trade – the very trade to which they were repeatedly denied official access.

Although neither contemporary accounts nor data are available on the number of litigations reaching its court and the time it took to pass sentence, it seems that the Bilbao *consulado* was less inundated than its Cádiz and colonial counterparts. Indeed, the Lima *consulado* faced enormous difficulties in dealing with the cases reaching its court. In 1759 Juan Cranisbro, who was in Lima trying to recover a debt owed to a Cádiz merchant, wrote about the debtor that 'I have not wanted to take him to court because here litigations have no end.'[6] The case between Joaquín Xavier García and Pedro Miguel de Arvilla that started in 1778 in the Lima *consulado*'s court was, after nine sentences in favour of García and one in favour of Arvilla, still unfinished in 1792.[7] It is no wonder that in 1779 the Lima *consulado* petitioned the viceroy to allow its tribunal to deal orally with all litigations involving less than 500 *pesos*.[8] Furthermore, in Lima lack of speed was often coupled with corruption. In March 1759 Juan Cranisbro reported that some merchants in Lima were trying to send a debtor of theirs to Spain, but since the debtor (a certain Vasallo) enjoyed the patronage of important people he could walk safely in front of his dismayed creditors.[9] Twenty years later things were very similar. In March 1779 José de Vea assured one of his Cádiz correspondents that the law was more benevolent if one was the son of a minister: 'In this country', he noted in despair, 'without such circumstances litigations are everlasting.'[10]

Another important problem facing the *consulados* involved in colonial trade was the interference of other jurisdictions, which added to the trade's inherent risk. Just before the cancellation of the *galeones*, when the networks linking Cádiz and Lima were still weak, the tribunals of neither *consulado* tended to inspire much confidence in the members of the other. The *galeonistas* arriving in Lima in the 1730s petitioned the viceroy of Peru to grant them their own *consulado*, fearing that if they had any legal dispute with a local merchant the Lima *consulado*'s court would always rule in favour of

---

[5] García-Baquero, *Cádiz*, i. 400–1; Socolow, *Merchants*, 57.
[6] Cranisbro to María Valois, Lima, 1 Mar. 1759, AGN, TC-GR1, caja 119, doc. 644, fo. 41.
[7] Parrón, *De las reformas*, 59.
[8] AGN, TC-GO2, caja 5, doc. 111.
[9] Cranisbro to Lecomte, Lima, 1 Mar. 1759, AGN, TC-GR1, caja 119, doc. 644, fo. 40.
[10] Vea to Blas Antonio Jiménez, Lima, 28 Mar. 1779, HCA 30/313/2, no. 419.

its members.¹¹ Their petition was denied, but the attempt spoke loudly of the distrust that derived from being under the jurisdiction of their competitors. This occurred between the *mexicanos* and the *gaditanos* as well. In 1749 members of the Mexico City *consulado* complained that they had lost every litigation taking place in Cádiz.¹² Rather revealingly, however, this particular problem seems to have disappeared in the second half of the eighteenth century, when transatlantic relationships became more frequent and the interests of both communities became interwoven.

In addition, the interference of the military jurisdiction was a continuing source of trouble for the Lima *consulado*. This was a problem affecting only the colonies, where many members of the army engaged in trade and many colonial merchants entered the militia.¹³ Rather than transatlantic merchants, it was soldiers and lesser merchants who opted for avoiding the Lima *consulado*'s jurisdiction by resorting to their military status. In the words of the historian Leon Campbell, 'the military justices utilized a variety of tactics to insure favorable dispositions of matters brought against their soldiers'.¹⁴ This worried both the Lima- and Cádiz-based merchants for it made the recovery of debts extremely difficult. The Lima *consulado* complained repeatedly to successive viceroys, but solving this problem was not as easy as it seemed. A major concern of the viceroy was to reinforce the defence of Peru, and one way of doing so cheaply was by recruiting men for the militia. Since the militia gave no monetary reward, successive viceroys thought it essential to offer *fuero militar* or military jurisdiction to anyone joining the militia.¹⁵

Ecclesiastical jurisdiction was another source of problems in both Spanish America and Spain, for it allowed debtors to avoid (or at least delay) prosecution by taking sanctuary in churches and monasteries. Naturally, in an ultra-Catholic country such as Spain, only Catholics could take sanctuary, which suggests that non-Catholics' choice of correspondents in Spain could be affected by religious matters. In around 1664 the English merchants trading with Spain complained that:

> as many times English factors which are trusted with large estates from their friends and correspondents in England are seduced to be Papists, and others appear such out of design to defraud men of their just rights valuing themselves of Churchmen and Sanctuary when they are called to account.¹⁶

---

[11] Walker, *Spanish politics*, 188.
[12] Antúnez, *Memorias*, app. xxii, ci.
[13] Leon G. Campbell, *The military and society in colonial Peru, 1750–1810*, Philadelphia 1978, 196–200.
[14] Ibid. 197.
[15] Parrón, *De las reformas*, 63.
[16] Jean O. McLachlan, 'Documents illustrating Anglo-Spanish trade between the commercial treaty of 1667 and the commercial treaty and the asiento contract of 1713', *Cambridge Historical Journal* iv (1934), 301.

But their complaints achieved nothing in the commercial treaties of 1667 and 1713. In 1715, for example, the English merchant Daniel Lion and the Frenchman Pierre Surmone took sanctuary in two churches in Cádiz, much to the dismay of their correspondents.[17] The main problem arising from the protection offered by churches and monasteries was that bankruptcy – the only legally constituted method that put all creditors on an equal footing – could not be declared, and for creditors this was a major setback. In 1758 the scandalous third-class bankruptcy of the Bilbao merchant Pedro Matías de Loygorri involved Loygorri's seclusion in the church of San Agustín in Cintruénigo, a tiny village 130 miles away from Bilbao. And, to add insult to injury, the Bilbao *consulado* found out that while in the church Loygorri had carried on doing business through his wife.[18] In the colonies similar events seem to have occurred regularly. In 1759 Juan Cranisbro reported from Lima that the merchants Juan Verdejo and Pedro Laborda had just taken sanctuary in a local church, after having been harangued by some of their creditors. Cranisbro, who was also trying to recover debts from both, was determined to accept any repayment that they could offer, even though he admitted that what they had done was 'evil'.[19] The precise extent of this phenomenon is not easy to assess, but the very fact that in April 1764 a royal order eventually put an end to the possibility of taking sanctuary suggests that by then (precisely when both competition and risk of failure were growing) it had become a serious problem. The viceroy of Peru, Francisco Gil de Taboada (himself a churchman), was glad to stress in his 1796 *memoria de gobierno* that the decision to abolish sanctuary had extinguished 'the fire arising from [disputes over] the competence between the two jurisdictions'.[20]

It is difficult to determine the effect of the military and ecclesiastical jurisdictions on merchant networks, but there can be no doubt that their interference added to the uncertainty of trade. More conclusive as evidence of jurisdictional issues affecting both trade and networks is the case of the special jurisdiction granted to the foreign 'nations' residing in Spain. All legal cases in which a foreigner was the defendant were decided by the so-called *Juez Conservador*, who was the captain-general or governor of the Spanish province where the foreigner resided. In the foreigners' eyes the *Juez Conservador* was absolutely essential for he prevented other officials from seeing their commercial ledgers, guaranteed cheap justice, protected them against religious persecution and prevented abuses such as the seizure of goods or illegal extraction of duties. The English were granted this special jurisdiction in 1645 and the French in 1662. Furthermore, in the case of foreign countries with great diplomatic influence in Madrid (such as the French and

---

[17] AHN, Consejos, leg. 51439/exp. SN.
[18] Bilbao *consulado*'s petition to the king, 4 Sept. 1758, AFB, Consulado 541, fo. 157.
[19] Cranisbro to Antonio Butler, Lima, 1 Mar. 1759, AGN, TC-GR1, caja 119, doc. 644, fo. 46.
[20] Fuentes, *Memorias*, vi. 51–2.

the British), the decisions of the *Juez Conservador* could be greatly influenced by political pressure. In Portugal, where international trade was for the most part in the hands of British merchants established in Lisbon, Oporto and Madeira, the *Juez Conservador* was equally regarded as essential by the foreign nations.[21] *The British Merchant*, first published in 1713, explained the importance of the *Juez Conservador* in Spain:

> This perhaps will look a very strange and unnatural jurisdiction: but if we will please only to remember that Spain is a bigotted Popish Country; that the Will of the Prince is above all the Laws; and that the Inquisition prevails there, which by a secret and sudden Process can destroy any Man in a moment, and by Evidence to which he is never suffered to give an Answer; if we will but remember that our whole Nation are Hereticks in the Opinion of the Spaniards, and as such expos'd to the Fury of that People: we must needs think the Privilege of chusing our own Judge-Conservator but just sufficient for our Protection. I am almost confident no Man would ever trust the value of 100 l. [pounds sterling] of his Effects in his Factor's hands, if he did but know how much they must be exposed for want of such an Officer.[22]

When in October 1774 there were rumours that foreigners' special jurisdiction was about to be suspended, the British consul in Cádiz, Josiah Hardy, stressed that 'should it ever take place, foreigners cannot reside in this country' because they would become 'subject to the inspection of the ordinary magistrates in which case neither their persons, houses or effects would be safe'.[23] As for the Cádiz *consulado*, Hardy, like the rest of the foreign consuls, did not acknowledge its authority. In December 1775 a royal order was published obliging all commercial people to appear within a limited time before the *consulado* tribunal to declare their capital in trade. This order (which appears to have been directed chiefly towards the French) was delivered by the *consulado* to the several foreign consuls in Cádiz. Hardy replied that he 'had all regard possible for the members that Board' but he 'did not acknowledge the authority of their Tribunal'.[24] The presence of a British consul in Cádiz (and in another thirteen major Spanish ports, although not in Bilbao) was considered crucial by the British merchants resident in Spain, who argued that their consul, along with their special jurisdiction, offered them protection. However, it can also be argued that for the foreigners established in Spain, depicting the Spanish judicial system as unreliable was an effective way of attracting their own compatriots' commissions.

---

[21] Shaw, *Anglo-Portuguese alliance*, 82–94.
[22] Charles King, *The British merchant: a collection of papers relating to the trade and commerce of Great Britain and Ireland*, London 1743, 2nd edn, iii. 202–3.
[23] Hardy to Thomas Robisnon, 2nd Baron Grantham, Cádiz, 11 Oct. 1774, Grantham papers, MS Add. 24168, fo. 290.
[24] Hardy to Grantham, Cádiz, 26 Dec. 1775, ibid. 24169, fos 321–2.

In Bilbao the indigenous merchants sought to counteract that effect. The Bilbao *consulado* considered it essential to put all merchants on the same judicial footing, and with that aim in mind they banned foreign consuls and any special jurisdiction for foreigners. True, the *fueros* of Vizcaya allowed the *bilbaínos* to take decisions that not even the Spanish government was free to take, as a result of disadvantageous commercial treaties. By contrast, the situation in Cádiz, on which the efforts of foreign diplomacy were centred, differed substantially. Assisted by their special jurisdiction, the foreigners established in Cádiz attracted their compatriots' commissions and acted as brokers between foreign investors and the Spaniards involved in the colonial trade.

Sales on credit and debt-recovery

One reason why the system of consulado courts began to encounter problems in attempting to deal rapidly and efficiently with mercantile litigation in the eighteenth century was the increasing use of credit. Indeed, commercial disputes increased not only because of the expansion of trade but also due to the growing use of something as potentially controversial as credit. Despite its great importance, however, the extent to which credit was used in Bilbao's overseas trade is for the most part unknown.[25] Nevertheless, it is beyond doubt that it was increasingly used in Bilbao's trade with northern Europe. In 1754 the Spanish consul in London stressed that for the Spaniards one of the negative effects of sending wool to England was that buyers in London purchased the wool 'little by little, as they please, and on credit'.[26] He thought that Spaniards would do better if they kept the wool in Spain and forced the English to buy there at higher prices and in cash. But the consul missed an important point: if the Spaniards were willing to sell on credit it was because they trusted their debtors, their debt-collectors and the legal framework to ensure that the debt would be cleared. It was only after obtaining this relative security that they risked resorting to credit in international trade. This served to increase competition and, as competition grew, merchants were left with no option but to offer better conditions to their customers.

At the other end of the trade route, in England, the transition towards more competition and wider use of credit in the eighteenth century is better known. The changes were apparent, for example, in the English export trade in textiles (the most important as far as Spain was concerned). Until the

---

[25] The only study on commercial credit in eighteenth-century Bilbao, María Gutiérrez's work on contested bills of exchange in the 1790s, provides a rather narrow picture: *Comercio y banca: expansión y crisis del capitalismo comercial en Bilbao al final del antiguo régimen*, Bilbao 1995.
[26] Andrés Zedrón to José de Carvajal, London, 11 Apr. 1754, AGS, Estado, leg. 6923.

mid-eighteenth century most English manufacturers conducted their business on a commission basis, with one factor or agent established in London or in some other English port. But from the mid-eighteenth century onwards manufacturers increasingly began to shift to a system of direct trade with their overseas customers, selling at lower prices and on credit.[27] This daring incursion into foreign countries meant that manufacturers had to face the lender's universal problem, the recovery of debts. The letter-books of the Norwich manufacturers Stannard and Taylor show this problem clearly, as before they went bankrupt in 1769 they were primarily concerned with the difficult task of ensuring that their foreign debtors paid what they owed. For example, in 1767 they tried to recover a debt from the Bilbao merchant Bernardo de Guendica, to whom they wrote a number of increasingly angry letters, all to no avail. Then, in October, they warned him: 'you cannot complain if we ask some friend over there to help us to recover our money'.[28] That friend was the French merchant Juan Bautista de Lacoste, who was the only Bilbao merchant, apart from Guendica, with whom they had business dealings (in the summer of 1767 Stannard and Taylor offered their products to another three Bilbao merchants but received no reply). But Lacoste was not very effective because sixteen months later half of the debt was still outstanding. The Norwich manufacturers repeatedly threatened Guendica with legal action but never actually went that far.

In some cases it might have been possible for a creditor simply to travel to where the debtor lived and demand repayment in person, but often the debtor lived too far away or the creditor was too busy to travel. Therefore, as with Stannard and Taylor, in most cases merchants had to rely on a correspondent to recover their money. This form of debt-recovery, which was universal among overseas merchants, was an important source of distrust. Those correspondents in charge of reprimanding debtors always stressed their reliability and commitment, even when they were unable to recover the debt. In 1772 Joseph Merry (from the firm Peter and Gerald Merry of Seville) pointed out to the Norwich manufacturers Richard and John Gurney that 'our country chaps are become so dilatory in their payments this time past, that it is almost incredible. However, we shall redouble our endeavour towards collecting your mentioned outstanding debts.'[29] But 'redoubling endeavour' was anything but easy. Indeed, haranguing, reprimanding or threatening a debtor could have serious implications for the debt-collector himself – an important issue rarely addressed in the historiography on commercial credit. The *La Perla* correspondence shows not only that this form of debt recovery was widespread among colonial merchants but also that it had enormous social ramifications. *La Perla*'s mail demonstrates this problem in the context of Spanish colonial trade in the 1770s, and therefore many of its peculiarities (the long

---

[27] Smail, *Merchants*, 26–7.
[28] Stannard and Taylor to Guendica, Norwich, 21 Oct. 1767, NRO, BR 211/14, 149–50.
[29] Merry to Gurney and Co., Seville, 20 June 1772, Gurney papers 2/480.

distance, the conflicting legal frameworks) are not applicable to other trades. Nevertheless, *La Perla* still provides a vivid picture of a problem facing any eighteenth-century overseas merchant. In the trade between Spain and Peru the need for trust was not equally shared for the way in which the goods were marketed meant that trading from Cádiz to Lima gave rise to greater anxiety than trading in the other direction. Silver and gold represented nearly 90 per cent of the value of Peruvian exports to Spain, whereas more than 80 per cent of Spanish exports to Peru was in the form of cloth. The precious metals were either repayments or remittances. The latter could be used to purchase European merchandise or as sea loans to other merchants travelling to the colonies (usually to be paid in Lima). However, selling fabrics throughout Peru caused much more trouble. Merchants in Cádiz naturally preferred their goods to be sold for cash but by the 1760s that was rarely possible, so they wanted their debtors to be closely monitored. In January 1763 Roque Aguado ordered his Lima correspondent Andrés Ramírez de Arellano to sell on credit only to 'debtors you have within sight'.[30] Indeed, to keep an eye on these debtors, making sure that they would clear their debts, was a major task for many transatlantic merchants established in Lima. Many debtors were local merchants who knew nobody in Spain but had bought merchandise on credit from Lima merchants acting as agents for their Cádiz colleagues. But in Lima there were also debtors who had borrowed money (in the form of merchandise) in Cádiz before travelling to Peru. In 1779 the Basque Juan Francisco de Aycinena, who was unable to clear his debt, was one of those merchants. His only consolation was that those going back to Spain in the *Buen Consejo* (which had just left Callao) would tell people there about 'my life style and how much I have worked to acquit myself well in disposing of what was entrusted to me'.[31] However, his proper behaviour and hard work would only calm his creditors up to a point: they were almost sure to ask some other merchant in Lima to recover the debt.

When faced with the impossibility of recovering the money, merchants in Lima who acted as debt-collectors gave detailed explanations in their correspondence with Cádiz. For example, Juan Bautista de Sarraoa was in charge of collecting 7,800 *pesos* that a certain Eusebio Gaviña owed the Cádiz merchant Pedro Palacio. Shortly after Gaviña told Sarraoa that for the time being it was absolutely impossible for him to send any money to Palacio, Sarraoa informed Palacio that

> things are in a situation that nothing can be done, and therefore it is necessary to wait without making noise, or everything will be lost. I tell you this because, to be honest, the ineptitude of that man deserves to be treated more

---

[30] Aguado to Arellano, Cádiz, 24 Jan. 1764, IRA, ARA, Epistolario.
[31] Aycinena to Juan José de Lacoizqueta, Lima, 20 Apr. 1779, HCA 30/316/1, no. 1115.

roughly, and to make him pay by going to court. However, it is convenient to have patience.[32]

The first reason why Sarraoa was trying to avoid the Lima *consulado*'s court was because it would delay the repayment even more. The second important problem facing creditors was that if their debtors were put under too much pressure, they might declare themselves insolvent and go bankrupt. José de Moya wrote to Juan Martín de Aguirre that he was unable to collect any money from three merchants he called 'scoundrels', admitting in despair that 'if I put them in jail, I will only harm them and put an end to their trade'.[33] Likewise, Vicente Martínez Ferrer assured the French firm Causabon and Co. that he was ready to put pressure on a certain Argote in order to ensure the repayment of a considerable debt, but he also pointed out that 'much tolerance is necessary, because we are experiencing bankruptcies every day'.[34] Merchants such as Sarraoa, Moya and Ferrer feared that too much pressure on the debtors could attract other creditors and precipitate bankruptcies.

But there was a third important reason why debt-collectors might not try too hard to ensure repayment: they were afraid things would get nasty. Indeed, reprimanding debtors was an unpleasant task that not every merchant was willing to perform. The merchant in Lima usually required a *poder* or letter of attorney from the creditor in Cádiz in order to *reconvenir* (reprimand) debtors for overrunning the credit terms. A considerable proportion of the fifty-one letters that José de Moya posted in *La Perla* dealt with his attempts to recover debts in Peru, and some of those cases were particularly unpleasant. For example, after trying to get a repayment from a certain Guillermo Waujan, Moya wrote to José María Enrrile, the Cádiz creditor, that Waujan's situation was deplorable and hopeless. Moya had reprimanded and threatened Waujan, who was lying in bed at the time, but was given nothing more than a tearful show of remorse. Disgusted, Moya asked Enrrile to assign the task to some other merchant coming from Spain, 'because in this city it will not be easy to find somebody'.[35] Moya himself foresaw this problem when he asked his main Cádiz correspondent, Juan Martín de Aguirre, to lend 300 *pesos* to Miguel Blanco, a 'reliable' friend of his who was about to travel to Lima. Moya stressed that responsibility for recovering the debt should be given not to him but to Aguirre's other correspondents in Lima. In this way Moya avoided suspicions that his friendship with Blanco might be interfering in the recovery of the debt.[36] Likewise, Juan Félix de Berindoaga wrote to Francisco Martínez de Vallejo about Gregorio Xalavera's debt, stressing that it would be more appropriate to get someone else to

[32] Sarraoa to Palacio, Lima, 2 Apr. 1779, HCA 30/315/4, no. 937.
[33] Moya to Aguirre, Lima, 3 May 1779, HCA 30/315/2, no. 495.
[34] Ferrer to Causabon and Co., Lima, 7 May 1779, HCA 30/312/6, no. 110.
[35] Moya to Enrrile, Lima, 8 May 1779, HCA 30/316/12, no. 1593.
[36] Moya to Aguirre, Lima, 31 Mar. 1779, HCA 30/315/2, no. 286.

recover the debt because after twelve years in Lima he had become a good friend of Xalavera and his family.[37]

For merchants established in Cádiz who did not have several correspondents in Lima, recovering debts could therefore be very difficult. And, due to their small number of correspondents in Lima, the foreigners established in Cádiz were more likely to distrust their debt-collectors in Peru. For example, Juan Sabugo acted as agent for several French firms in Cádiz. He did his best to recover debts for them, but after several years living in Lima found the task increasingly difficult. In May 1779 he informed the French firm Galatoire Brothers and Co. that one of their debtors was now doing good business and appeared capable of clearing the debt.[38] But Sabugo did not dare try to recover the debt without a written order from the creditors: he knew the debtor well and did not want him to suspect he was the French creditors' informer. Rather than suggesting that another merchant be given responsibility for recovering the debt, Sabugo suggested to the French firm the exact words (a whole paragraph) that they should include in their letter-order (*carta orden*). When shown to the debtor, this paragraph would subtly suggest that Sabugo had previously known nothing of the debt but was somehow forced to carry out the unpleasant job of reprimanding a friend. Sabugo's other French correspondents naturally found this level of intrigue suspicious: in April 1779 the *jenízaro* Raimundo Marrés was instructed by the French firm Labat and Co. to find out whether Sabugo was lying to them. Along with their instructions the French firm sent Marrés a letter that Sabugo himself had sent them in March 1778. To the French merchants' dismay, Marrés confirmed that Sabugo had not made much effort to recover their money from several debtors.[39]

These examples are taken from the trade between Spain and Peru, but it is important to remember that the Spanish colonial trade was linked to Spain's trade with Europe, and therefore, albeit unofficially, other merchants established elsewhere in Europe also had the opportunity to participate. The main obstacle to engaging in the trade, however, was that it was very risky. In April 1772 the Norwich manufacturer Richard Gurney wrote to his Seville correspondent, Patrick Harper, saying that:

> from the distance between us [that is, between himself and his debtors in Spanish America] it may be impossible for us to administer help or give advice with propriety upon these cases, but we confide in your being well satisfied of the ability and integrity of your agents in the Indies, and therefore upon you in the first place and then upon them we must fix our dependance.[40]

---

[37] Berindoaga to Francisco Martínez de Vallejo, Lima, 3 Apr. 1779, HCA 30/314/16, no. 412.
[38] Sabugo to Galatoire Brothers and Co., Lima, 8 May 1779, HCA 30/316/9, no. 906.
[39] Marrés to Labat and Co., Lima, 6 May 1779, HCA 30/315/7, no. 1820.
[40] Gurney to Harper, Norwich, 10 Apr. 1772, NRO, BR 211/10.

But even for Gurney, who as a Quaker had great faith in human goodness, trading with Spanish America meant unbearable uncertainty. That same year he received contradictory information from his Cádiz correspondents about the state of consumer demand in Lima. One of them, an Irishman, Alexis Macnamara, assured him that 'you may take for certain, or I am prodigiously deceived, that there is more report than reality in what you seem to have heard'.[41] Based on information provided by Macnamara himself, Gurney had opted to send camblets to Lima via the Elizalde brothers the year before. Now, since he had no news from Lima, Gurney was suspicious about the Elizaldes, even despite Macnamara's assurance that 'the Elizaldes have the character of being as active, diligent, industrious and honest young fellows as there are this day perhaps in the city of Lima'.[42] Macnamara's praise for the Elizaldes was no coincidence. Up until 1764, the year he was expelled from Peru, rumour had it that the Irishman Joseph Valois had been the most important transatlantic merchant of Lima. As a foreigner he required a Spaniard to act as his front-man, which is why he employed the two young Navarrese brothers from Baztán, Antonio and Matías de Elizalde.[43] When Valois was eventually expelled from Peru the Elizaldes kept their Irish connections (they wrote in *La Perla* to several Irish merchants), but Gurney was not totally convinced of their reliability until Elizalde's reply arrived weeks later. For an 8 per cent commission they had sold Gurney's camblets on credit to eight buyers and had recovered nearly all the money.[44] However, other attempts were less successful. Another report from Macnamara, in January 1772, informed Gurney about an 'unhappy affair': two of Gurney's debtors in Buenos Aires were unwilling to repay. Macnamara depicted their conduct as 'villainous' and 'cruel' but could do nothing about it.[45] Selling on credit was clearly a sign of increasing competition, a competition in which those who could build up relationships of trust with their correspondents and debt-collectors were far more likely to take part.

Timing and decision-making

Selling on credit was an indication of increasing competition, but competition also affected merchants' ability to decide which goods should be traded and when. In fact, decision-making grew more and more risky in eighteenth-century Spain, particularly for the merchants involved in the colonial trade.

---

[41] Macnamara to Gurney, Cádiz, 19 June 1772, Gurney papers 2/479.
[42] Ibid.
[43] Deolinda M. Villa Esteves, 'Liderazgo y poder: la élite comercial limeña entre el comercio libre y la Guerra de la Independencia (el caso de Antonio de Elizalde)', in Mazzeo, *Comerciantes limeños*, 133–71.
[44] Macnamara to Gurney, Cádiz, 14 Aug. 1772, Gurney papers 2/487.
[45] Macnamara to Gurney, Cádiz, 24 Jan. 1772, ibid. 2/456.

The pinnacle of the Bourbon programme of economic reform was the publication of the *Reglamento y aranceles reales para el comercio libre de España a Indias* – the regulations and royal tariffs for the free trade from Spain to the Indies – on 12 October 1778,[46] which among other things meant the abolition of Cádiz's monopoly. A similar measure had been taken in 1765, allowing nine peninsular ports to trade directly with the islands of the Spanish Caribbean, but now those same ports, plus four more, were given permission to trade with most of Spanish America (the measure would not apply to New Spain and Venezuela until 1789). Due to their special tax system the Basque provinces were deliberately excluded. In America, twenty-seven ports were immediately open to the *comercio libre*, five of which were on the Pacific coast (from south to north Concepción, Valparaiso, Arica, Callao and Guayaquil). It is obvious that this was not commercial 'freedom' *sensu stricto* because trade remained subject to limitations at both ends. Nevertheless, it was indeed freer because it was opened to more participants, and licences to send ships were granted more quickly and without restrictions. This free yet protected commerce (Spanish products paid a lower level of duties than foreign goods) was meant to restore agriculture, industry and population in Spain and its colonies. To merchants it brought more competition and more risks associated with timing and decision-making. Indeed, the implementation of the *comercio libre* provides an exemplary case study in how increasing competition affected relationships of trust.

The economic effects of the *comercio libre* programme are still unclear. There is little doubt that between 1778 and 1796 Cádiz maintained a near-monopoly: 84 per cent of total imports from the empire came into Cádiz, and 76 per cent of exports were sent to the colonies from there.[47] In the case of trade between Spain and Peru, the participation of ports other than Cádiz and Callao was very small.[48] This is perhaps unsurprising considering the combination of robust networks built up from the mid-eighteenth century onwards and the availability of a complex infrastructure of shipping, banking, consular and warehousing facilities. Similarly, it is also clear that the share of Spanish products in total exports from Spain to Spanish America rose from 38 per cent in 1778 to 52 per cent in the period 1782–96.[49] The manufacturers of Catalonia would greatly benefit from the increase in the export of national fabrics to America. What has been a source of much controversy among economic historians, however, is the overall effect of the *comercio libre*. According to John Fisher, trade not only grew but sky-rocketed after 1783. The overall expansion of imports from Spanish America in the period

---

[46] See, for example, Antonio-Miguel Bernal (coor.), *El 'comercio libre' entre España y America Latina, 1765–1824*, Madrid 1987, and Antonio García-Baquero, *El libre comercio a examen gaditano: crítica y opinión en el Cádiz mercantil de fines del siglo XVIII*, Cádiz 1999.
[47] Fisher, *Commercial relations*, 49, 65.
[48] Ibid. 78.
[49] Ibid. 88.

1782–96 was such that annual average imports during this period were more than ten times higher than the total in the base year, 1778, while exports from Spain grew on average by 400 per cent.[50] However, Antonio García-Baquero argues rather convincingly that Fisher's estimates for 1778 are in fact highly inaccurate, and that exports from Spain did not grow but decreased 16 per cent on average, whereas imports went up not by over 1,000 per cent but just 69 per cent.[51]

According to contemporary accounts, trade between Spain and Peru did grow significantly in the 1780s. Immediately after the peace was signed in September 1783 and the *comercio libre* was finally implemented, Spanish exports to the colonies increased drastically. The dimensions of the resulting glut of European merchandise in Peru are difficult to measure with precision, particularly because it is unclear how much merchandise entered Peru by land via Buenos Aires and via Cartagena. None the less, all the contemporary accounts indicate that it was enormous. In 1786 more than 14,000,000 *pesos* in merchandise arrived via Cape Horn in a market that had previously tended to absorb only about a third as much.[52] It is hardly surprising that in 1787 the Lima *consulado* petitioned the government both to stop the trade between Spain and Peru for two years and to forbid European merchandise from entering Peru and Chile by land via Buenos Aires. But the Lima *consulado* did not succeed. The viceroy of Peru, Teodoro de Croix (1784–90), who informed the minister of the Indies, José de Gálvez, about this petition, had no doubt the merchants cared only about their own interests. 'What is more important for the state', he claimed, 'the loss of some merchants of Lima and Cádiz, or the loss of the industry of the nation?'[53] Indeed, the authorities both in Spain and in America considered *comercio libre* a very positive move. Writing in 1796, Croix's successor, Francisco Gil de Taboada, also expressed the view that the interests of merchants and the interests of the monarchy should not be confused. For him, the reason why the merchants of Lima and Cádiz were in trouble was because they had wrongly transformed 'the true free trade into an unlimited licence to bring anything they want'.[54]

Just like their Lima counterparts, the Cádiz *consulado* also recommended the cancellation of the *comercio libre*. For the historian Allan Kuethe this constitutes clear evidence that its members were only 'merchants in appearance', and that their mentality was that of 'monopolists conspiring to manipulate the royal administration as well as the markets of America and Spain in

---

[50] Ibid. 88–9.
[51] Antonio García-Baquero, 'Los resultados del libre comercio y "el punto de vista": una revisión desde la estadística', *Manuscrits* xv (1997), 303–22, repr. in his *El comercio colonial en la época del absolutismo ilustrado: problemas y debates*, Granada 2003, 187–216.
[52] 'Ydea sucinta del comercio del Perú y medios de prosperarlo … por D. José Ygnacio de Lequanda' (1794), BL, MS Egerton 771, fo. 46.
[53] Teodoro de Croix to Gálvez, Lima, 16 Aug. 1787, AGI, Lima 1546.
[54] Fuentes, *Memorias*, vi. 107.

order to eliminate any kind of competition and risk'.[55] However, it is highly questionable whether they deserve to be labelled merely 'merchants in appearance' on such grounds, for in the eighteenth century (as in any other period) there was no such a thing as a merchant who actively desired competition. As Adam Smith himself put it in 1776, 'to widen the market and to narrow the competition, is always the interest of the dealers.'[56] Certainly the members of the Cádiz *consulado* did whatever they could to reduce the uncertainty that was caused by risk and competition. True, the monopoly of Cádiz until 1778 provided an opportunity to engage in trade for merchants who otherwise, having to face more competition, would have been disinclined to do so, but the years after 1783 showed that most merchants were not afraid of the *comercio libre*.

Those historians who have studied this period agree that the glut of European merchandise was the fault of the merchants resident in Cádiz. For Guillermo Céspedes del Castillo they were the only ones to blame for 'such foolishness' since they alone were in a position to control colonial trade.[57] Likewise, Carmen Parrón states that after 1783 the merchants of Cádiz sent numerous ships to Peru 'thoughtlessly'.[58] The fact is, however, that very little is known about merchants' actual experience of the years following this date.

Printed copies of the *comercio libre* regulations arrived in Lima in late March 1779, a few weeks before the departure of *La Perla*. Predictably, merchants had plenty to say about the free trade system in their correspondence with Spain. Juan Bautista de Gárate predicted that 'commerce shall be in total disarray, bringing ruin to many'.[59] Luis Carrillo acknowledged that he was 'persuaded that free trade is useful for other kingdoms, but for our America, and particularly this city, it is the ultimate ruin'.[60] Gaspar de la Puente was equally pessimistic. 'Unless this is stopped', he wrote, 'the trade will be transformed to the detriment of the Royal Treasury, for no one will have the courage to trade with their own money, knowing the losses they are likely to suffer.'[61] But not all merchants were afraid of free trade. Manuel José de Amándarro, for example, was rather optimistic about the future in his letter to Pedro Antonio de Ibarrola. 'Do not be frightened by the *comercio libre*', he wrote, 'because before having any negative thought you must rely

---

[55] Allan J. Kuethe, 'El fin del monopolio: los Borbones y el Consulado andaluz', in E. Vila and A. J. Kuethe, (eds), *Relaciones de poder y comercio colonial: nuevas perspectivas*, Seville 1999, 38.
[56] Adam Smith, *An inquiry into the nature and causes of the wealth of nations* (London 1776), facsimile edn, London 1995, i. 409.
[57] Céspedes, 'Lima', 846.
[58] Parrón, *De las reformas*, 178.
[59] Gárate to Fermín Ramón Barrera, Lima, 9 May 1779, HCA 30/313/2, no. 50.
[60] Carrillo to Francisco Ignacio de Albizu, Lima, 3 May 1779, HCA 30/312/1, no. 686.
[61] Puente to Agustín de Amenábar, Lima, 7 May 1779, HCA 30/312/2, no. 1078.

upon my reports. You must only aspire to overcome those difficulties ... by working hard.'[62]

The outbreak of war against Britain later that year postponed the effective implementation of the comercio libre until 1783. For some, certainly, free trade was to be a catastrophe. Because of (rather than despite) the growth of imports and exports, the number of business failures in Cádiz went up sharply, as shown by the number of bankruptcies that were examined by the Council of Indies in the second half of the eighteenth century: thirty-four in the decade 1760–9, forty-three in 1770–9, sixty-four in 1780–9 and 113 in 1790–9. Presumably, cases that reached the Council of Indies were extraordinary as most failures would have been addressed at consulado level, which suggests that there were many more cases.[63] Echoing the Lima consulado's complaints (although without providing any figures), Alfonso Quiroz also stresses that in Peru 'the growth of trade in the second half of the eighteenth century increased the risk of bankruptcy'.[64] That is to say, the very long distance and the increasing complexity of the trade (via the growing use of credit and the importance of fashion) left merchants no choice but to make decisions that were increasingly risky. It is important to remember that in the second half of the eighteenth century the phenomenon of increasing risk attached to long-distance decision-making was also found in other parts of Europe, most notoriously in England.[65]

The critical period from 1783 to 1787 can be seen in great detail through the private correspondence of Juan Vicente Marticorena, a Basque merchant established in Cádiz.[66] His example clearly shows that what lay behind the glut on the colonial market was far more complex than mere foolishness. As the hundreds of Marticorena's letters held in the Archivo General de Indias show, between 1780 and 1809 he traded with the major Spanish colonial cities (Lima, Buenos Aires, Veracruz, Mexico City and Havana).[67] In the years 1782–6, however, most of his attention was focused on Lima. In July 1782, with Spain and Britain still at war, Marticorena's brother, Juan Miguel, left for Lima carrying merchandise that had been purchased in Cádiz in accordance with instructions from their cousin, Juan Bautista de Larrain, who had been residing in Lima since 1776.

Juan Miguel arrived in Lima five months later, in December 1782. That same month Juan Vicente wrote from Cádiz to report that licences had recently been granted to send three register ships to Peru. This letter arrived

---

[62] Amándarro to Ibarrola, Lima, 8 May 1779, HCA 30/313/2, no. 1072.
[63] Bernal, *Financiación*, 466.
[64] Quiroz, *Deudas*, 110.
[65] Julian Hoppit, *Risk and failure in English business, 1700–1800*, Cambridge 1987, 69–70.
[66] On the Marticorena brothers see Victoria Martínez del Cerro, *Una comunidad de comerciantes: navarros y vascos en Cádiz (segunda mitad del siglo XVIII)*, Seville 2007, 208–54.
[67] Juan Vicente Marticorena's entire correspondence can be found in AGI, Consulados 432–9.

in Lima in June 1783, roughly at the same time that Juan Miguel's first letter reached Cádiz. He noted that 'apart from the velvets, the rest promises 200 per cent profit, for nothing is to be found either in the warehouses or in the shops'.[68] A fortnight later, a second letter arrived from Juan Miguel reporting that he had sold some clothes for 26,000 *pesos* at a 100 per cent profit. 'No article is more valued than women's stockings', he added.[69] A month later, in July 1783, Juan Vicente received a letter from José de Isasi, a fellow Basque who had travelled to Lima along with Juan Miguel. The letter was dated 8 February 1783 and reported that after very good sales everything had calmed down 'all of a sudden'[70] – linen had been the best selling article but prices fell rapidly when news came that it had arrived in Buenos Aires in large quantities.

At this point the merchants in Lima must have deliberated the possibility of sending further orders or *notas* to Cádiz. Should they order more merchandise for the next year or should they just wait? Juan Miguel was determined to go ahead: on 5 April 1783 he sent a *nota* intended to reach Cádiz by mid-September,[71] and days later stated that 'the present state of war is the right moment to do business'.[72] But two months later, in early June, he received Juan Vicente's letter noting the forthcoming departure of three register ships (this was the letter posted in December 1782). At this moment Juan Miguel probably considered the possibility of writing again to cancel the *nota* that was already on its way to Spain. 'So much uncertainty always leaves us handcuffed, not knowing what to do', he confessed.[73] Furthermore, Juan Miguel was growing concerned about the possibility of peace and the effective implementation of the *comercio libre*, but eventually decided that they should keep trading: 'I deem this trade will change so much because of the abundance of register ships coming from now on, that it is necessary you proceed carefully and with much knowledge.' On 20 June 1783 he sent another large and detailed *nota* intended to reach Cádiz in early December.[74] In the letter accompanying this new *nota* Juan Miguel stressed that 'if [the merchandise] is fine, I believe it will be sold promptly'.[75]

In September 1783 (February 1784 in Cádiz) Juan Miguel reported that he had sold the merchandise that he had received in the ship *Placeres* for 75,600 *pesos* at a 50 per cent profit. But this time the sale had been made on credit – two-thirds to be paid at the departure of the next register ship

---

[68] Juan Miguel Marticorena to Juan Vicente Marticorena, Lima, 5 Jan. 1783, AGI, Consulados 432, fo. 274.
[69] J. M. Marticorena to J. V. Marticorena, Lima, 20 Jan. 1783, ibid. fo. 290.
[70] José Isasi to J. V. Marticorena, Lima, 8 Feb. 1783, ibid. fo. 319.
[71] 'Nota de géneros para Lima', Lima, 5 Apr. 1783, ibid. fo. 345.
[72] J. M. Marticorena to J. V. Marticorena, Lima, 20 Apr. 1783, ibid. fo. 357.
[73] J. M. Marticorena to J. V. Marticorena, Lima, 16 June 1783, ibid. fo. 424.
[74] 'Nota de los géneros', Lima, 20 June 1783, ibid. fos 411–12.
[75] J. M. Marticorena to J. V. Marticorena, ibid. fo. 409.

to Spain and one third a year later.[76] He did not, however, find this discouraging. For the next consignments he advised his brother to be careful and above all to follow his instructions. That same month, September 1783, peace was signed in Paris, but even without this news anxiety was already growing in Lima. In November 1783 (April 1784 in Cádiz) Juan Miguel complained that a local merchant who had agreed to buy a large quantity of merchandise was beginning to distrust him because 'he sees that everyone receives letters, and I am the only one who tells him that I have none from you'.[77] Juan Vicente's letter arrived days later via Cartagena, and Juan Miguel apologised to him for the complaint.[78]

Also in November 1783, and foreseeing the arrival of more ships, Juan Miguel wrote to his brother about a secret plan that he had discussed with some friends. The idea was to buy a 500-ton ship in Cádiz to carry their goods to Lima. Juan Vicente would buy the ship and would try (this was essential according to Juan Miguel) to keep it as secret as possible. No one should know where the ship was bound until the last minute.[79] It seems that the plan was eventually discarded, but the very possibility of it, which before the *comercio libre* did not exist, raises the question of how many other merchants had similar plans in mind. No doubt the possibility of sending ships semi-secretly would make it very difficult for merchants to assess the extent and character of competition in the years to come.

Meanwhile, in Cádiz, Juan Vicente was dealing with their suppliers. One of them was Laureano Ortiz de Paz, a woollen manufacturer of Segovia for whom Juan Vicente provided indigo and other dyes. Furthermore, Juan Vicente also gave cash to Ortiz in advance so that he could buy wool. This was very important because, as Ortiz himself pointed out, flock owners did not sell wool on credit. Ortiz also required 'samples of all the colours you want me to send you, so that I can dye and produce them [woollen fabrics] as you order, making sure they have colours of consumption'.[80] It is important to stress that Ortiz would need at least several weeks (maybe months) to buy the wool and to produce all the fabrics ordered by the Marticorena brothers. That is to say, once Ortiz received an order and the flock owners were paid, there was no way back for the Marticorenas.

While dealing with Ortiz and other purveyors, Juan Vicente received more *notas* from other friends residing in Lima and elsewhere in Spanish America. Like Juan Miguel these friends also had great faith both in Juan Vicente and their own ability to design the right *nota*. Martín de Osambela, who years later would become one of the most important merchants of Peru, was among those writing from Lima (he was another Basque whose

---

[76] J. M. Marticorena to J. V. Marticorena, Lima, 16 Sept. 1783, ibid. fo. 474.
[77] J. M. Marticorena to J. V. Marticorena, Lima, 16 Nov. 1783, ibid. fos 506–7.
[78] J. M. Marticorena to J. V. Marticorena, Lima, 5 Jan. 1784, ibid. fos 564–5.
[79] J. M. Marticorena to J. V. Marticorena, Lima, 16 Nov. 1783, ibid. fo. 509.
[80] Laureano Ortiz de Paz to J. V. Marticorena, Segovia, 22 Mar. 1783, ibid. fo. 334.

letters were amongst the *La Perla* collection).[81] In his letter, which arrived at Cádiz in September 1784, Osambela asked Juan Vicente to help his young brother Miguel Ventura to buy several goods that he had just indicated in a *nota*. 'Next year', stressed Osambela, 'there will be a lot of merchandise in this city, and, therefore, those who send something will not make any profit.'[82] However, that did not mean that Miguel Ventura should forget about sending the merchandise to Lima. 'If my brother follows my *nota*, I think he will make some profit', added Osambela rather optimistically.[83] The subjective nature of *notas* (they were based on individual perception) served to intensify competition because merchants always expected their assortment of clothes to be of better quality and more fashionable than those of their competitors.

However, in addition to a good selection of merchandise there was also another reason why merchants in Lima kept sending *notas* to Cádiz even when a forthcoming glut seemed unavoidable. It was the combined effect of fashion, regular supply and trust. For merchants in Lima were committed to supplying their network of provincial merchants, local shopkeepers and customers with fresh European merchandise as often as possible. In May 1784 (November in Cádiz) Juan Miguel complained that he had not received any merchandise in the last ship, 'letting these people become suspicious about my inaction'.[84] In fact, his colonial customers were 'already saying that I am cheating on them'. Consequently, and even though it was known in Lima that the war was over, Juan Miguel urged his brother to send merchandise regularly.[85]

Ships continued to arrive at Callao, causing an unprecedented glut of European goods. By early 1786 Juan Miguel's initial optimism had totally disappeared. The 100 per cent profit on his first sales back in January 1783 was now a thing of the past. In February 1786 (July in Cádiz), without knowing that at least ten ships were on their way to the Pacific, he wrote in despair: 'bankruptcies and delays are being uncovered in this commerce, so even if it is with smaller profits, I will ensure my sales with creditworthy individuals, which is what I have done until now; and that is why I prefer a good payment to a high price'.[86]

The example of the Marticorenas shows that it is unclear who was ultimately responsible for the glut. It was understandably difficult for merchants in Lima to asses the colonial markets precisely and to decide which merchan-

---

[81] See Teodoro Hampe Martínez, 'Don Martín de Osambela, comerciante navarro de los siglos XVIII/XIX, y su descendencia en el Perú', AEA lviii (2001), 83–110.
[82] Martin de Osambela to J. V. Marticorena, Lima, 12 Apr. 1784, AGI, Consulados 432, fo. 634.
[83] Ibid.
[84] J. M. Marticorena to J. V. Marticorena, Lima, 23 May 1784, ibid. fo. 670.
[85] Ibid.
[86] J. M. Marticorena to J. V. Marticorena, Lima, 25 Feb. 1786, ibid. fo. 1063.

dise would be more suitable for Peru. But Juan Vicente's position in Cádiz was even more problematic because he was the one who would have to make the final decision. In May 1786, when more than 14,000,000 *pesos* in European merchandise had just arrived in Peru, Juan Miguel reproached the Cádiz merchant community (including his brother) for having sent so many goods:

> The fact that merchandise is being ordered with yearning from here should not be taken at face value [over there], particularly when it is obvious and noticeable that cargoes are being shipped with as much disorder as these two years past, in which you all seem to have lost your minds.[87]

If writing a *nota* was an unpredictable art, after 1783 making decisions in Cádiz was the nearest thing to gambling that anyone could imagine. Four years of war and scarce trade with the colonies created expectations that were greatly heightened by the *comercio libre*. Juan Vicente had little idea of what other merchants would be sending to the colonies, or how many ships would depart for America and how many of those would go to Cartagena, to Buenos Aires or to Lima. Furthermore, he could only hope that Ortiz and the other manufacturers would produce his orders in time. In short, whatever decision Juan Vicente (and many others like him) took, it was bound to be a major gamble. The point was reached at which the merchant had no choice but to take huge risks if he wanted to keep trading. Naturally the possibility of failure increased accordingly, and this in turn was the cause of much acrimony and distrust between transatlantic correspondents.

The law played an important part in preserving a framework within which trust might operate, but the law on its own could not guarantee the repayment of debts. As a consequence merchants had to find other means to ensure that their debtors would reimburse the amounts owed. To a large extent, therefore, it was merchants' ability to trust in their correspondents that encouraged them to use credit and to take more risks. And yet not everything depended on trust: factors such as insufficient information or sheer incompetence could ruin a merchant, regardless of the trustworthiness of his correspondents. Trust, though necessary for trade, was not sufficient to generate success.

---

[87] J. M. Marticorena to J. V. Marticorena, Lima, 9 May 1786, ibid. fo. 1193.

Conclusion: Trade and Trust

Rather than focusing on a single community or group of merchants, this book has looked at the interaction between individuals of different national, ethnic and religious backgrounds who were involved in different commercial areas of the Atlantic. This has allowed a broader view of business collaboration than that provided by the numerous studies on early modern trading diasporas that concentrate on single merchant communities. Cooperation was an important feature of merchant communities and trading diasporas, as in the case of the Basques, but commercial relationships extended beyond the boundaries of national and ethnic groups. In order to capture the complexities and vagaries of trade, this study has focused on a feature shared by all merchants: the need to trust their colleagues.

Trust was of fundamental significance to the eighteenth-century trader. Even though most economic historians acknowledge its importance in early modern trade, the fact remains that trust is usually treated as an unimportant epiphenomenon, the implication being that trade would have existed without it. Other elements such as supply, demand, capital, infrastructure, instruments of credit and the law are seen as the main influences on the operation of trade. But it was trust that performed the role of combining all these elements, thereby constituting a prerequisite for the creation of trade.

Insofar as improvements in the legal framework helped trade to flourish, it was because those improvements increased merchants' ability to rely on other merchants. However, the mediation of the law was not absolutely necessary, for trade could also operate in a poorly developed legal framework – indeed, merchants did not necessarily concern themselves with improving the legal framework. In Bilbao it was foreigners' continuous attempts to move their trade to Santander that prompted the indigenous merchants to enhance the dependability and expertise of their mercantile court, creating and preserving public trust as a result. By contrast, the foreign merchants established in Spain, although constantly complaining about the Spanish authorities, knew only too well that their commercial success depended upon maintaining the *status quo*. If jurisdictional and legal matters were left unmodified, their compatriots would continue to rely on them rather than on the Spaniards. The *bilbaínos* improved the legal framework in order to underpin Bilbao's international trade, hoping that they themselves would benefit in the process. Unlike their colonial counterparts they had to compete with foreign merchants for the same trade. This competition became a crucial incentive to produce the Bilbao *consulado*'s Ordinances of 1737, a major contribution to Spanish commercial law. It is no coincidence that the most significant improvements in commercial law in eighteenth-century Spain occurred in a place where international commercial treaties were for the most part disregarded.

Trade was not merely an economic activity: it was also embedded in culture. At the most basic level it was the inherent confidentiality of trade that gave it a particular cultural imprint. Eighteenth-century trade was actually sustained by something as fragile as mercantile reputations, which were built not only on past economic behaviour but originated from, and were propagated by, collective judgement. Every aspect of a merchant's life – social behaviour, external appearance, habits, religious beliefs and family life – could affect his reputation and therefore his economic activities. Long distances and poor communications are usually seen as the main causes of uncertainty in early modern trade, but uncertainty also arose from the very system through which commerce was sustained.

Culture could affect trade in many different ways. In Bilbao the *huésped* institution was not meant to create links between locals and foreigners but nevertheless proved to have the decisive side-effect of forging ties between the two communities. Combined with legal and judicial improvements, the *huésped* institution explains how the *bilbaínos* managed to engage in trade with northern Europe. In 1724 Gerónimo de Uztáriz asserted that Spanish merchants would only increase their participation in international trade if some of them decided to move abroad. However, the *bilbaínos* found an alternative way to foster reciprocity and mutual understanding with foreign correspondents without having to go elsewhere. When eventually some of them moved to London in the 1750s, it was thanks to the new commercial treaty between Spain and Britain and because major transformations were occurring in the Spanish colonial trade.

Another cultural factor that helps to explain the *bilbaínos*' revival was the strong seafaring tradition of the Basques. The local supply of seamen provided not only cohesive crews but also the possibility of forging ties with ship captains whose skills and reliability were easier to ensure. Indeed, these captains played a crucial role by recruiting seamen, linking markets, monitoring correspondents, providing information and carrying mail. By performing all those crucial tasks they encouraged the merchants of Bilbao to trade.

Historians usually stress the role played by certain religious groups such as Jews, Quakers and Huguenots in creating solid commercial networks in the early modern period. The example of the Basques involved in the Spanish colonial trade has shown that the sense of common identity based on ethnic and regional origin (*paisanaje*) also contributed to the creation of relationships of trust. Religion did not distinguish Basques from other Spaniards since they were all Catholics. Furthermore, the tendency of the Basques to associate with their *paisanos* was not part of a conscious economic strategy: they got together because they had so much in common. They shared a strong ethnic identity and a peculiar language. They all left their homeland in similar circumstances, following the same pattern of emigration, and all maintained close links with their family and friends back in their home towns. They preserved their cultural identity in Cádiz and in the colonies not as part of plan to build up commercial networks but because meeting their fellow Basques was the normal thing to do. As this happened, those social and cultural networks had an impact on their economic activities, spontaneously creating trust between individuals.

The fact that in the 1770s Spanish merchants in Cádiz received more mail from Peru than any foreigners meant that the Spaniards had more information, and were therefore able to invest more trust in their correspondents. It shows that the flow of information across the Atlantic also helped to create trust by conscious intent. The Spaniards received a wide range of information not only from merchants but also from other members of colonial society. *La Perla*'s mail strongly suggests that foreigners' limited participation in trade with Peru was not due to the fact that their involvement was technically illegal but because they received relatively little information from there. As a result they preferred to give loans to Spaniards resident in Cádiz, whose dependability was easier to monitor. *La Perla*'s mail further suggests that the foreigners' direct participation in the trade with Peru was chiefly discouraged by the fact that their compatriots were not allowed to reside in the Spanish colonies.

The merchants' close links to their home towns was an emotional bond that had far-reaching cultural, economic and social ramifications. Although this study has explored the case of the Basques and other Spaniards, it must be remembered that a similar bond was shared by foreign merchants residing in Spain. In 1712, for example, the former French ambassador to Spain, Michel-Jean Amelot, celebrated the fact that many French trading houses from Nantes, St Maló, La Rochelle and Marseilles had grown powerful in Cádiz, Málaga and other principal Spanish ports. Rather revealingly, he also stressed that 'very rarely do they cut all links with the part of their family in France'.[1] Many foreigners even returned to their country after trading for several years in Spain. For the Spaniards this was intensely annoying: in June 1746 the Bilbao *consulado* complained to the Council of Castile that foreign merchants, 'after having profited handsomely due to their greater easiness in connecting and corresponding with the North, returned to their birthplaces'.[2] As that is exactly what many Basques did after spending many years in Cádiz and in America, the *bilbaínos*' complaint hardly appears justified. It does, however, provide an important insight into the mental world of the eighteenth-century merchant.

---

[1] Henry Kamen, *The war of succession in Spain, 1700–1715*, London 1969, 121.
[2] Mauleón, *Población*, 96.

CONCLUSION

The rise of merchant communities based on nationality, ethnicity and religion in certain periods and trades can be explained not only by changing economic conditions but also by the cultural imprint of trust and the conditions that helped trust to operate. Traditionally, historians explain the Spaniards' low level of participation in international trade in the seventeenth and eighteenth centuries by combining two main arguments: first that the treaties of peace and commerce favoured the activities of foreign merchants established in Spain, and secondly that the Spaniards lacked the foreigners' commercial skills. As a result, Spain's trade fell into foreign hands. There is a third possibility: that most Spanish merchants did not initially participate in international trade because there were no Spanish communities abroad. To a certain extent this third reason is a consequence of the other two, but it nevertheless deserves to be viewed as a separate factor – first because treaties of peace and commerce never prohibited merchants of different nationalities from trading with each other; and second, because the Spaniards' alleged lack of entrepreneurial spirit did not stop them from trading with northern Europe in the sixteenth century, just when there were many Spanish merchants established in Flanders and elsewhere.

The Bourbon reforms and the growing production of American silver are usually seen as the only reasons why Spanish colonial trade expanded in the second half of the eighteenth century, but the merchants themselves made an equally important contribution. Improvements in the system of transatlantic communications from the middle of the century onwards not only helped to increase imports and exports but also gave merchants the opportunity to transform the colonial trade itself. The building up of transatlantic networks contributed to the evolving complexity of exchanges between the metropole and its American colonies. After all, mere flow-charts of commodities give no indication of the full complexity of trade, nor, more important, do they say anything about trust. By forging a mutual understanding the merchants on both sides of the Atlantic bridged the gap between European manufacturers and Spanish-American consumers.

The growing importance and independence of the Spanish merchants of Cádiz in the second half of the eighteenth century is something that leading Spanish historians have observed, but the scope of their explanations is limited. This study has taken a step further by showing that three factors prompted the Spaniards to participate more actively in colonial trade after the mid-eighteenth century. First, the rise of a new pattern of trade conducted by register ships led to greater competition and a need to rely on transatlantic correspondents as never before. Second, the expulsion of foreigners from the colonies after the middle of the century, just when the pattern of trade was making it imperative to have information and trustworthy correspondents, left foreign merchants without compatriots to act as agents in the colonies. And lastly, the closer relationship between Spaniards on opposite sides of the Atlantic gave the merchants of Cádiz the opportunity to borrow money from the South Americans, thereby reducing their dependence on foreign capital. Though already a Spanish monopoly by law, the colonial trade only began to be a *de facto* monopoly after the mid-eighteenth century, when the register ships prompted the Spaniards to create a pattern of trade in which personal trust played a more important role.

The relationship between trade and trust was one of interaction. The building up of trust contributed to the expansion and shaping of trade, while the manner in which trade evolved also determined the level of trust required. But this interaction also had its limitations. Intensified trade, improvements in communication and the 1778 free trade regulations brought more competition to the Spanish colonial trade. Analysis of this has shown that the relationship between trust and trade was complex and could be, at times, full of contradictions and paradoxes. Merchants sold on credit to those whom they considered dependable, but too close a relationship with their debtors was not always advisable for it could end up making the recovery of the debt very difficult. It was more desirable for merchants to forge close ties with their debt-collectors. Furthermore, with the effective implementation of the free trade regulations after 1783, merchants were compelled to take riskier decisions because of the difficulties encountered in trying to assess the extent and character of the competition. Dealing with trustworthy correspondents was a necessary but not sufficient condition for removing the uncertainty of trade.

The origins of this book lie in an awareness of the importance of the concept of trust for the merchants themselves. Their writings are full of remarks about other merchants' reputations, reliability, trustworthiness, solvency and so forth. As well as demonstrating this fact, this study has delved deeper into the complexities of trust. Trust was and is dependent upon relationships that undergo continuous negotiation and renegotiation. Moreover, the importance of trust was confined neither to Spain nor to the eighteenth century. Indeed, sociologists, anthropologists, economists and political scientists are engaged in discussions about trust in modern societies, even though most historians do not seem to show much interest in the historical implications of these discussions. Trust is a crucial requirement for any social or economic exchange, regardless of place and period, and is therefore a worthy subject of historical inquiry.

Over the course of the nineteenth century, railways, regular steamer services and telegraph lines were to improve communications and reduce merchant anxieties about distant markets and agents. Companies grew significantly, giving rise to a new philosophy of management based on systems and efficiency, and making trade more impersonal. And yet there remained an irreducible element of risk: trust and reputation, both disconcertingly fragile, still underpinned the civility of trade, as indeed they do today.

Bibliography

Unpublished primary sources

Bilbao, Archivo Foral de Bizkaia (AFB)
Consulado 536–9, 541, 543, 549, 602
Corregimiento 0101/008, 0218/005, 0260/008, 0547/018, 0962/042, 1375/001, 1763/013, 1820/005, 2177/031, 2927/022, 4000/006

Lima, Archivo General de la Nación (AGN)
Cabildo caja 97
Protocolos 968, 977, 1075
TC-GO2 cajas 5, 6
TC-GR1 cajas 119, 127
TC-GR2 cajas 124–7

Lima, Instituto Riva-Agüero (IRA)
Epistolario Ramírez de Arellano

London, British Library
MSS Add. 13976, 13981, 13988, 24168–9, 46550
MS Egerton 771

London, Friends House Library (FHL)
Gurney papers

London, Guildhall Library (LGL)
MSS 11021/3, 19017/1–3

London, The National Archives (TNA)
C 12/668/1, 12/1401/24, 111/200
HCA 30/230–1, 30/250, 30/275–6, 30/311–16, 30/742, 32/74, 32/116, 32/124, 32/134, 32/137–8, 32/188, 32/200, 32/208, 32/227, 32/266, 32/282, 32/288, 32/334, 32/377, 32/412–15, 32/443, 32/469, 32/834, 32/1123–4
SP 34/36, 78/224, 89/69, 94/199, 94/213

Madrid, Archivo Histórico Nacional (AHN)
Consejos legs 30, 2656, 12593, 28585, 51439

Norwich, Norfolk Record Office (NRO)
BR 211/10, 211/14

Seville, Archivo General de Indias (AGI)
Arribadas 457
Audiencia de Lima 890, 1521–5, 1546, 1548
Audiencia de México 2492
Consulados 432–9
Contratación 1748, 5524
Correos 102A

Simancas, Archivo General de Simancas (AGS)
Estado leg. 6923

Vitoria-Gasteiz, Archivo del Territorio Histórico de Álava (ATHA)
FP 34/14

Published primary sources

Adams, J., *Diary and autobiography of John Adams*, ed. L. H. Butterfield, Cambridge, MA 1961
Anderson, A., *An historical and chronological deduction of the origin of commerce from the earliest accounts to the present time*, London 1764
Anon., *A brief narration of the present estate of the Bilbao trade, with some particulars by agreement, humbly tendred by the marchants trading thither*, London 1640
Anon., *Colección de los tratados de paz, alianza, comercio etc. ajustados por la corona de España con las potencias extrangeras desde el reynado del señor don Felipe Quinto hasta el presente*, Madrid 1796–1801
Anon., *Fueros, franquezas, libertades, buenos usos y costumbres del muy noble y muy leal señorío de Vizcaya*, Bilbao 1704
Anon., *Proyecto para galeones y flotas del Perú y Nueva-España, y para navíos de registro y avisos que navegaren en ambos reynos*, Madrid 1720
Anon., *Relación de las fiestas que celebró en esta muy noble villa de Bilbao, de el señorío de Vizcaya la ... muy leal nación inglesa en la gloriosa ocasión de averse coronado en Inglaterra el muy cathólico Jacobo Estuardo*, Bilbao 1685
Antúnez y Acevedo, R., *Memorias históricas sobre la legislación y gobierno del comercio de los españoles con sus colonias en las Indias occidentales*, Madrid 1797
Baquíjano y Carrillo, J., 'Disertación histórica y política sobre el comercio del Perú', *Mercurio Peruano* (Lima 1791), facsimile edn 1964, i. 209–89
Beawes, W., *Lex mercatoria rediviva: or, the merchant's directory: being a compleat guide to all men in business*, London 1752
[Bilbao consulado], *Ordenanzas de la Casa de la Contratación de la muy noble y leal villa de Bilbao*, Bilbao 1669
—— *Ordenanzas de la ilustre Universidad y Casa de Contratación de la m.n. y m.l. villa de Bilbao, (insertos sus reales privilegios) aprobadas y confirmadas por el rey nuestro señor Don Felipe Quinto (que dios guarde) año de 1737*, Madrid 1769
Bourgoing, J. F., *Tableau de l'Espagne moderne*, Paris 1797
Bustos Rodríguez, M. (ed.), *Un comerciante saboyano en el Cádiz de Carlos II: las memorias de Raimundo de Lantery, 1673–1700*, Cádiz 1983
Cadalso, J., *Cartas marruecas* (Madrid 1793), Barcelona 1994

Campillo y Cossío, J., *Nuevo sistema de gobierno económico para América* [1743] (Madrid 1789), Oviedo 1993

Cary, J., *Discourse on trade and other matters relative to it* [1690s], London 1745

Codes, S., *Memoria sobre qué providencias convendrían tomarse para precaver las quiebras o bancarrotas fraudulentas*, Madrid 1803

Covarrubias Orozco, S., *Tesoro de la lengua castellana o española*, Madrid 1611

Fuentes, M. A. (ed.), *Memorias de los virreyes que han gobernado el Perú durante el tiempo del coloniaje español*, Lima 1859

Gándara, M. A. de la, *Apuntes sobre el bien y el mal de España* [1759] (Madrid 1811), Madrid 1988

Goyeneche, J., *Executoria de la nobleza, antigüedad y blasones del Valle de Baztán*, Madrid 1685

Hevia Bolaños, J., *Curia filípica, segundo tomo donde breve, y compendiosamente se trata de la mercancía y contratación de tierra y mar* (Lima 1617), Madrid 1717

Juan, J. and A. Ulloa, *Discourse and political reflections on the kingdoms of Peru*, [1748] (London 1823), ed. and trans. J. J. TePaske and B. A. Clement, Norman, OK 1978

King, C., *The British merchant: a collection of papers relating to the trade and commerce of Great Britain and Ireland*, 2nd edn, London 1743

Labarbinais, L. G., *Nouveau Voyage au tour du monde: enrichi due plusieurs plans, vues et perspectives des principales villes & ports du Perou, Chily, Bresil et de la Chine*, Paris 1728

Larramendi, M., *Corografía de la muy noble y muy leal provincia de Guipúzcoa*, [1756] (Barcelona 1882), Buenos Aires 1950

Lee, S., *A collection of the names of the merchants living in and about the City of London*, London 1677, repr. 1863

Malynes, G. de, *Consuetudo, vel lex mercatoria: or, the ancient law-merchant*, London 1622

Moreno Cebrián, A. (ed.), *Relación y documentos de gobierno del virrey del Perú, José A. Manso de Velasco, conde de Superunda, 1745–1761*, Madrid 1983

Mugaburu, J. and F. Mugaburu, *Chronicle of colonial Peru: the diary of Josephe and Francisco Mugaburu, 1640–1697*, ed. and trans. R. R. Miller, Norman, OK 1975

Palomba, I., *El secretario de banco español y francés, en que se contiene el modo de escrivir en estas dos lenguas las cartas de comercio, en todo género de negocios y tráfico*, Paris 1768

Porras Barrenechea, R., *Cartas del Peru, 1524–1543*, Lima 1959

Postlethwayt, M., *The universal dictionary of trade and commerce, translated from the French of the celebrated monsieur Savary*, London 1751

Savary, J., *Le Parfait Negociant, ou instruction générale pour ce qui regarde le commerce des marchandises de France & des pays étrangers*, Paris 1675

Smith, A., *An inquiry into the nature and causes of the wealth of nations* (London 1776), facsimile edn, London 1995

[Stannard, P.], *The letters of Philip Stannard, Norwich textile manufacturer, 1751–1763*, ed. U. Priestley, Norwich 1994

Ulloa, A., *Modo de facilitar los correos de España con el reyno del Perú* [1765], Seville 2001

Ulloa, B., *Restablecimiento de las fábricas, tráfico y comercio marítimo de España*.

Segunda parte: que trata del comercio y tráfico marítimo que tiene España con las naciones y en la América: causas de su decadencia, Madrid 1740

Uztáriz, G. de, *The theory and practice of commerce and maritime affairs* (Madrid 1724), trans. John Kippax, London 1751

Secondary sources

Alcázar, C., *Historia del correo en América (notas y documentos para su estudio)*, Madrid 1920

Alcorta Ortiz de Zárate, E., 'Negocios familiares y circuitos laneros en Bilbao en la segunda mitad del siglo XVIII', in A. González Enciso (ed.), *El negocio lanero en España, 1650–1830*, Pamplona 2001, 175–200

Arazola Corvera, M. J., *Hombres, barcos y comercio de la ruta Cádiz-Buenos Aires, 1737–1757*, Seville 1998.

Armitage, D., 'Three concepts of Atlantic history', in Armitage and Braddick, *British Atlantic world*, 11–27

—— and M. J. Braddick (eds), *The British Atlantic world, 1500–1800*, New York 2002

Artiñano y Galdácano, G., *Historia del comercio con las Indias durante el dominio de los Austrias*, Barcelona 1917

Bailyn, B., *The New England merchants in the seventeenth century*, New York 1964

—— *Atlantic history: concepts and contours*, Cambridge, MA 2005

Barker, H., *The business of women: female enterprise and urban development in northern England, 1760–1830*, Oxford 2006

Basas Fernández, M., *El consulado de Burgos en el siglo XVI*, Madrid 1963

Baskes, J., *Indians, merchants and markets: a reinterpretation of the Repartimiento and Spanish-Indian economic relations in colonial Oaxaca, 1750–1821*, Stanford 2001

—— 'Risky ventures: reconsidering Mexico's colonial trade system', *Colonial Latin American Review* xiv (2005), 27–54

Basurto Larrañaga, R., *Comercio y burguesía mercantil de Bilbao en la segunda mitad del siglo XVIII*, Bilbao 1983

Bernal, A. M., *La financiación de la Carrera de Indias: dinero y crédito en el comercio colonial español con América*, Seville 1992

—— (coor.), *El 'comercio libre' entre España y América Latina, 1765–1824*, Madrid 1987

Bilbao, L. M., 'Crisis y reconstrucción de la economía vascongada en el siglo XVII', *Saioak* i (1977), 157–80

Booker, J. R., *Veracruz merchants, 1770–1829: a merchant elite in late Bourbon and early independent Mexico*, Boulder 1993

Borchart de Moreno, C., 'Los miembros del consulado de la ciudad de México en la época de Carlos III', *Jbla* xiv (1977), 134–60

—— *Los mercaderes y el capitalismo en la ciudad de México, 1759–1778*, Mexico 1984

Bose, W. B. L., 'El proyecto sobre 'correos maritímos' a las Indias, de 1713', *Anuario de Historia Argentina* ii (1940), 428–37

Bosher, J. F., *The Canada merchants, 1713–1763*, Oxford 1987

—— 'Huguenot merchants and the Protestant International in the seventeenth century', *WMQ* lii (1995), 77–102
Bouyer, M., 'L'Aire de recrutement des gens de mer, par le commerce nantais au XVIIIe siècle', in G. Saupin (coor.), *Le Pouvoir urbain dans l'Europe atlantique du XVIe au XVIIIe siècle*, Nantes 2000, 165–78
Boxer, C. R., 'Brazilian gold and British traders in the first half of the eighteenth century', *HAHR* xlix (1969), 754–72
—— *The Portuguese seaborne empire, 1415–1825*, London 1969.
Brading, D. E., *Miners and merchants in Bourbon Mexico, 1763–1810*, Cambridge 1971
Brown, R. F., *Juan Fermín de Aycinena: central American colonial entrepreneur, 1729–1796*, Norman, OK 1997
Brown, V. L., 'The South Sea Company and contraband trade', *AHR* xxxi (1926), 662–78
Bustos Rodríguez, M., *Los comerciantes de la Carrera de Indias en el Cádiz del siglo XVIII, 1713–1775*, Cádiz 1995.
—— *Cádiz en el sistema Atlántico: la ciudad, sus comerciantes y la actividad mercantil, 1650–1830*, Madrid 2005
Cahill, D., 'Repartos ilícitos y familias principales en el sur andino, 1780–1824', *RI* xlviii (1988), 449–73
Campbell, L. G., 'A colonial establishment: creole domination of the Audiencia of Lima during the late eighteenth century', *HAHR* lii (1972), 1–25
—— *The military and society in colonial Peru, 1750–1810*, Philadelphia 1978
Canny, N., 'Atlantic history and global history', in R. Pieper and P. Schmidt (eds), *Latin America and the Atlantic world, 1500–1850: essays in honor of Horst Pietschmann*, Cologne 2003, 25–34
Carlos, A. M. and S. Nicholas, 'Agency problems in the early chartered companies: the case of the Hudson's Bay Company', *JEcH* l (1990), 853–75
Caro Baroja, J., *La hora navarra del XVIII (personas, familias, negocios e ideas)*, Pamplona 1969
Carrasco González, M. G., *Los instrumentos del comercio colonial en el Cádiz del siglo XVII, 1650–1700*, Madrid 1996.
—— *Comerciantes y casas de comercio en Cádiz, 1650–1700*, Cádiz 1997
Carrera Pujal, J., *Historia de la economía española*, Barcelona 1943–7
Carrière, C., 'Renouveau espagnol et pret à la grosse aventure (notes sur la place de Cadix dans la seconde moitié du XVIII siècle)', *Revue d'histoire moderne et contemporaine* xvii (1970), 221–52
Céspedes del Castillo, G., 'Lima y Buenos Aires: repercusiones económicas y políticas de la creación del Virreinato del Plata', *AEA* iii (1946), 669–874
Chamboredon, R., 'Une Societé de commerce languedocienne à Cadix: Simon et Arnail Fornier et Cie. (Novembre 1768–Mars 1786)', in García-Baquero, *La burguesía de negocios*, ii. 35–55
Chaunu, P., *Séville et l'Amérique aux XVIe et XVIIe siècles*, Paris 1977
Christelow, A., 'Great Britain and the trades from Cadiz and Lisbon to Spanish America and Brazil, 1759–1783', *HAHR* xxvii (1947), 2–29
Cohen, A., 'Cultural strategies in the organization of trading diasporas', in C. Meillassoux (ed.), *The development of indigenous trade and markets in West Africa*, London 1971, 266–84
Cohen, R., *Global diasporas: an introduction*, Seattle 1997

Collado Villalta, P., 'Los consulados extranjeros en el Cádiz de Carlos III', in García-Baquero, *Burguesía de negocios*, i. 245–57

Converso, F. E., 'Españoles y americanos, agentes de un mercado regional', *AEA* xlvii (1990), 279–311

Corfield, P. J., *Time and the shape of history*, New Haven 2007

Crespo Solana, A., *El comercio marítimo entre Amsterdam y Cádiz, 1713–1778*, Madrid 2000

—— *Entre Cádiz y los Países Bajos: una comunidad mercantil en la ciudad de la Ilustración*, Cádiz 2001.

Curtin, P. D., *Cross-cultural trade in world history*, Cambridge 1984

—— *The rise and fall of the plantation complex: essays in Atlantic history*, Cambridge 1990

Dalla Corte, G., 'Recomendaciones y empeños en la sociedad colonial y postcolonial: garantías jurídicas, poder y red social', in M. Bertrand (coor.), *Configuraciones y redes de poder: un análisis de las relaciones sociales en América Latina*, Caracas 2002, 133–65

Davis, R., *The rise of the English shipping industry in the seventeenth and eighteenth centuries*, London 1962

Delgado Ribas, J. M., *Dinámicas imperiales (1650–1796): España, América y Europa en el cambio institucional del sistema colonial español*, Barcelona 2007

De Vries, J., *European urbanization, 1500–1800*, Cambridge, MA 1984

Doerflinger, T. M., *A vigorous spirit of enterprise: merchants and economic development in revolutionary Philadelphia*, Chapel Hill 1986

Domínguez Ortiz, A., *Sociedad y estado en el siglo XVIII español*, Barcelona 1976

Elliott, J. H., 'Atlantic history: a circumnavigation', in Armitage and Braddick, *British Atlantic world*, 233–49

—— *Empires of the Atlantic world: Britain and Spain in America, 1492–1830*, New Haven 2006

Eltis, D., 'Atlantic history in global perspective', *Itinerario* xxiii/2 (1999), 141–61

—— *The rise of African slavery in the Americas*, Cambridge 2000

Enciso Recio, L. M., *Prensa económica del XVIII: el correo mercantil de España y sus Indias*, Valladolid 1958

—— (coor.), *La burguesía española en la edad moderna*, Valladolid 1996

Fawcett, T., 'Argonauts and commercial travellers: the foreign marketing of Norwich stuffs in the later eighteenth century', *Textile History* xvi (1985), 151–82

Fernández de Pinedo, E., *Crecimiento económico y transformaciones sociales del País Vasco, 1100–1850*, Madrid 1974

Fernández Pérez, P., 'Bienestar y pobreza: el impacto del sistema de herencia castellano en Cádiz, el emporio del orbe, 1700–1810', *Revista de Historia Económica* xv (1997), 243–68

—— *El rostro familiar de la metrópoli: redes de parentesco y lazos mercantiles en Cádiz, 1700–1812*, Madrid 1997

Fisher, J. R., *Government and society in colonial Peru: the intendant system, 1784–1814*, London 1970

—— *Commercial relations between Spain and Spanish America in the era of free trade, 1778–1796*, Liverpool 1985

—— 'El impacto del comercio libre en el Perú, 1778–1796', *RI* xlviii (1988), 401–20

Fontaine, L., 'Antonio and Shylock: credit and trust in France, *c.* 1680–*c.* 1780', *EcHR* 2nd ser. liv (2001), 39–57
Fukuyama, F., *Trust: the social virtues and the creation of prosperity*, London 1995
Gambetta, D. (ed.), *Trust: making and breaking cooperative relations*, Oxford 1988
Games, A., 'Atlantic history: definitions, challenges, and opportunities', *AHR* cxi (2006), 741–57
Garate Ojanguren, M., *La Real Compañía Guipuzcoana de Caracas*, San Sebastián 1990
Garay Belategui, J. and R. López Pérez, 'Los extranjeros en el Señorío de Vizcaya y en la villa de Bilbao a finales del antiguo régimen: entre la aceptación y el rechazo', *Estudios humanísticos: Historia* v (2006), 185–210
Garay Unibaso, F., *Correos marítimos españoles*, Bilbao 1987
García Fuentes, L., *Los peruleros y el comercio de Sevilla con las Indias, 1580–1630*, Seville 1997
García Sanz, A., *Desarrollo y crisis del antiguo régimen en Castilla la Vieja: economía y sociedad en tierras de Segovia, 1500–1814*, Madrid 1977
García-Baquero, A., *Cadíz y el Atlántico, 1717–1778: el comercio colonial español bajo el monopolio gaditano*, Seville 1976
—— 'Permanencia y renovación en la matrícula mercantil gaditana del siglo XVIII: el componente español, 1749–1773', in García-Baquero, *Comercio y burguesía*, 69–101
—— 'Los resultados del libre comercio y "el punto de vista": una revisión desde la estadística', *Manuscrits* xv (1997), 303–22
—— *El libre comercio a examen gaditano: crítica y opinión en el Cádiz mercantil de fines del siglo XVIII*, Cádiz 1999
—— *El comercio colonial en la época del absolutismo ilustrado: problemas y debates*, Granada 2003
—— (ed.), *La burguesía de negocios en la Andalucía de la Ilustración*, Cádiz 1991
—— (ed.), *Comercio y burguesía mercantil en el Cádiz de la Carrera de Indias*, Cádiz 1991
Garmendia Arruebarrena, J., 'La Compañía de Caracas y familias donostiarras (1784–1798)', *Boletín de Estudios Históricos sobre San Sebastián* xxi (1987), 517–40
—— *Cádiz, los vascos y la Carrera de Indias*, San Sebastián 1990
—— *Tomás Ruiz de Apodaca, un comerciante alavés con Indias, 1709–67*, Vitoria 1990
Gauci, P., *Emporium of the world: the merchants of London, 1660–1800*, London 2007
Geertz, C., *The interpretation of cultures*, New York 1973
Glaisyer, N., *The culture of commerce in England, 1660–1720*, London 2006
Goebel, D. B., 'British trade to the Spanish America, 1796–1823', *AHR* xliii (1938), 288–320
Gölte, J., *Repartos y rebeliones: Túpac Amaru y las contradicciones de la economía colonial*, Lima 1980
Gómez Pérez, C., 'Los extranjeros en la América colonial: su expulsión de Cartagena de Indias en 1750', *AEA* xxxvii (1980), 279–311
Grafe, R., *Entre el mundo ibérico y el Atlántico: comercio y especialización regional, 1550–1650*, Bilbao 2005

Grassby, R., *Kinship and capitalism: marriage, family and business in the English-speaking world, 1580–1740*, Cambridge 2001
Greif, A., 'Reputation and coalitions in medieval trade: evidence on the Maghribi traders', *JEcH* xlix (1989), 857–82
—— *Institutions and the path to the modern economy: lessons from medieval trade*, Cambridge 2006
Guiard Larrauri, T., *Historia del Consulado y Casa de Contratación de Bilbao y del comercio de la villa*, Bilbao 1913–14
Gutiérrez Muñoz, M. G., *Comercio y banca: expansión y crisis del capitalismo comercial en Bilbao al final del antiguo régimen*, Bilbao 1995
Haggerty, S., *The British-Atlantic trading community, 1760–1810: men, women, and the distribution of goods*, Leiden 2006
Hamnett, B. R., 'Mercantile rivalry and peninsular division: the *consulados* of New Spain and the impact of the Bourbon reforms, 1789–1824', *Ibero-Amerikanisches Archiv* ii (1976), 273–305
Hampe Martínez, T., 'Don Martín de Osambela, comerciante navarro de los siglos XVIII/XIX, y su descendencia en el Perú', *AEA* lviii (2001), 83–110
Hancock, D., *Citizens of the world: London merchants and the integration of the British Atlantic community, 1735–1785*, Cambridge 1995
—— '"A world of business to do": William Freeman and the foundations of England's commercial empire, 1645–1707', *WMQ* lvii (2000), 3–34
—— '"A revolution in the trade": wine distribution and the development of the infrastructure of the Atlantic market economy, 1703–1807', in McCusker and Morgan, *Early modern Atlantic economy*, 105–53
Haring, C. H., *Trade and navigation between Spain and the Indies in the time of the Hapsburgs*, Cambridge, MA 1918
Hausberger, B. and A. Ibarra (eds), *Comercio y poder en América colonial: los consulados de comerciantes, siglos XVII–XVIII*, Madrid 2003
Haydon, C., *Anti-Catholicism in eighteenth-century England, c. 1714–1780: a political and social study*, Manchester 1993
Heredia Herrera, A., 'Apuntes para la historia del Consulado de Cargadores a Indias en Sevilla y en Cádiz', *AEA* xxvii (1970), 219–79
—— 'Asiento con el consulado de Cádiz en 1720 para el despacho de avisos', in *La burguesía mercantil gaditana (1650–1868)*, Cádiz 1976, 163–72
Herzog, T., *Defining nations: immigrants and citizens in early modern Spain and Spanish America*, New Haven 2003
Hoppit, J., *Risk and failure in English business, 1700–1800*, Cambridge 1987
Ibañez, I. and J. Llombart, 'La formación de pilotos en la Escuela de Naútica de Bilbao, siglos XVIII y XIX', *Itsas Memoria* iii (2000), 747–72
Imízcoz, J. M., 'Patronos y mediadores: redes familiares en la monarquía y patronazgo en la aldea: la hegemonía de las élites baztanesas en el siglo XVIII', in J. M. Imízcoz (dir.), *Redes familiares y patronazgo: aproximación al entramado social del País Vasco y Navarra en el antiguo régimen, siglos XV–XIX*, Bilbao 2001, 225–61
Janzen, O. U. (ed.), *Merchant organization and maritime trade in the north Atlantic, 1660–1815*, St John's 1998
Kamen, H., 'The destruction of the Spanish fleet at Vigo in 1702', *Bulletin of the Institute of Historical Research* xxxix (1966), 165–73
—— *The War of Succession in Spain, 1700–1715*, London 1969

Kicza, J. E., *Colonial entrepreneurs: families and business in Bourbon Mexico City*, Albuquerque 1983

Kooijmans, L., 'Risk and reputation: on the mentality of merchants in the early modern period', in C. Lesger and L. Noordegraaf (eds), *Entrepreneurs and entrepreneurship in early modern times: merchants and industrialists within the orbit of the Dutch staple market*, The Hague 1995, 25–34

Kuethe, A. J., 'El fin del monopolio: los Borbones y el consulado andaluz', in Vila Vilar and Kuethe, *Relaciones de poder*, 35–66

La Force, J. C., *The development of the Spanish textile industry, 1750–1800*, Berkeley 1965

Laborda Martín, J. J., 'El arranque de un largo protagonismo: la recuperación comercial de Vizcaya a comienzos del siglo XVIII', *Saioak* ii (1978), 136–81

Lamikiz, X., 'Bizkaitar eta gipuzkoar nekazariak 1718ko matxinadan', *Uztaro* xxxiii (2000), 21–41

—— 'Un "cuento ruidoso": confidencialidad, reputación y confianza en el comercio del siglo XVIII', *Obradoiro de Historia Moderna* xvi (2007), 113–42

—— 'Patrones de comercio y flujo de información comercial entre España y América durante el siglo xviii', *Revista de Historia Económica – Journal of Iberian and Latin American Economic History* xxv (2007), 231–58

—— 'Basque ship captains as mariners and traders in the eighteenth century', *IJMH* xx/2 (2008), 81–109

—— 'Movilidad transatlántica: navarros en el comercio directo entre España y el Perú, 1739–1796', in Rafael Torres Sánchez (ed.), *Volver a la 'hora navarra': la contribución navarra al construcción de la monarquía española en el siglo XVIII*, Pamplona 2010, 343–86

Landa, J. T., *Trust, ethnicity and identity: beyond the new institutional economics of ethnic trading networks, contract law and gift-exchange*, Ann Arbor 1994

Lario de Oñate, M. C., *La colonia mercantil británica e irlandesa en Cádiz a finales del siglo XVIII*, Cádiz 2000

Lelo Belloto, M., *Correio maritimo hispano-americano: a carreia de Buenos Aires, 1767–1779*, Sao Paulo 1972

Lewicki, R. J., D. J. McAllister and R. J. Bies, 'Trust and distrust: new relationships and realities', *Academy of Management Review* xxiii (1998), 438–58

Lockhart, J. M., *Spanish Peru, 1532–1560: a colonial society*, Madison 1968

Lohmann Villena, G., 'Los comerciantes vascos en el virreinato peruano', in R. Escobedo, A. Rivera and A. Chapa (eds), *Los vascos y América: el comercio vasco con América en el siglo XVIII*, Bilbao 1989, 54–106

Loosley, A. C., 'The Puerto Bello fairs', *HAHR* xiii (1933), 314–35

Lovejoy, P. E. and D. Richardson, 'Trust, pawnship and Atlantic history: the institutional foundations of the Old Calabar slave trade', *AHR* civ (1999), 333–55

Luhmann, N., 'Familiarity, confidence, trust: problems and alternatives', in Gambetta, *Trust*, 94–107

Luque Alcaide, E., 'Coyuntura social y cofradía: cofradías de Aránzazu de Lima y México', in P. Martínez López-Cano and others (coor.), *Cofradías, capellanías y obras pías en la América colonial*, México 1998, 91–118.

Lydon, J. G., 'Fish for gold: the Massachusetts fish trade with Iberia, 1700–1773', *New England Quarterly* liv (1981), 539–82

McCusker, J. J., *European bills of entry and marine lists: early commercial publications and the origins of the business press*, Cambridge, MA 1985

—— and C. Gravesteijn, *The beginnings of commercial and financial journalism: the commodity price currents, exchange rate currents, and money currents of early modern Europe*, Amsterdam 1991

—— and K. Morgan (eds), *The early modern Atlantic economy*, Cambridge 2001

McLachlan, J. O., 'Documents illustrating Anglo-Spanish trade between the commercial treaty of 1667 and the commercial treaty and the asiento contract of 1713', *Cambridge Historical Journal* iv (1934), 299–311

—— *Trade and peace with old Spain, 1667–1750: a study of the influence of commerce on Anglo-Spanish diplomacy in the first half of the eighteenth century*, Cambridge 1940

Malamud Rikles, C., 'El comercio directo de Europa con América en el siglo XVIII', *Quinto Centenario* i (1981), 25–52

—— *Cádiz y Saint Maló en el comercio colonial peruano (1698–1725)*, Cádiz 1986

Mannion, J., 'Waterford and the south of England: spatial patterns in shipping commerce, 1766–1777', *IJMH* vi/2 (1994), 115–53

Manso de Zúñiga, G., *Cartas de Bilbao*, San Sebastián 1949

Marks, P. H., 'Confronting a mercantile elite: Bourbon reforms and the merchants of Lima, 1765–96', *The Americas* lx (2004), 519–58

—— *Deconstructing legitimacy: viceroys, merchants and the military in late colonial Peru*, University Park, PA 2007

Martínez del Cerro, V. E., *Una comunidad de comerciantes: navarros y vascos en Cádiz (segunda mitad del siglo XVIII)*, Seville 2007

Martínez Gijón, J., 'La comenda en el derecho español, II: La comenda mercantil', *Anuario de Historia del Derecho Español* xxxvi (1966), 379–456.

Martínez Shaw, C., *Cataluña en la Carrera de Indias, 1680–1756*, Barcelona 1981

—— and J. M. Oliva Melgar (eds), *El sistema atlántico español (siglos XVII–XIX)*, Madrid 2005

Mathers, C. J., 'Family partnership and international trade in early modern Europe: merchants from Burgos in England and France, 1470–1570', *Business History Review* lxii (1988), 367–97

Mathias, P., 'Risk, credit and kinship in early modern enterprise', in McCusker and Morgan, *Early modern Atlantic economy*, 15–35

Mauleón Isla, M., *La población de Bilbao en el siglo XVIII*, Valladolid 1961

Mauro, F., 'Merchant communities, 1350–1750', in Tracy, *Rise of merchant empires*, 255–86

Maxwell, K. R., *Conflicts and conspiracies: Brazil and Portugal, 1750–1808*, Cambridge 1973

Mazzeo, C. A., *El comercio libre en el Perú: las estrategias de un comerciante peruano, José Antonio de Lavalle y Cortés, 1777–1815*, Lima 1994

—— (ed.), *Los comerciantes limeños a finales del siglo XVIII: capacidad y cohesión de una élite, 1750–1825*, Lima 2000

Molas Ribalta, P., *La burguesía mercantil en la España del antiguo régimen*, Madrid 1985

Morales Alvarez, J. M., *Los extranjeros con carta de naturaleza en las Indias durante la segunda mitad del siglo XVIII*, Caracas 1980

Morgan, K., 'Business networks in the British export trade to northern America, 1750–1800', in McCusker and Morgan, *Early modern Atlantic economy*, 36–62

Muldrew, C., *The economy of obligation: the culture of credit and social relations in early modern England*, Basingstoke 1998

North, D. C., 'Institutions, transaction costs, and the rise of merchant empires', in Tracy, *Political economy of merchant empires*, 22–40

O'Dogherty, A., 'La matrícula de mar en el reinado de Carlos III', AEA ix (1952), 347–70

O'Phelan Godoy, S., *Rebellions and revolts in eighteenth-century Peru and Upper Peru*, Cologne 1985

Odriozola Oyarbide, L., *Construcción naval en el País Vasco, siglos XVI–XIX: evolución y análisis comparativo*, San Sebastián 2002

Otte, E., 'Los mercaderes transatlánticos bajo Carlos V', AEA xlvii (1990), 95–121

Ozanam, D., 'La Colonie française de Cadix au XVIIIe siècles d'aprés un document inédit (1777)', *Mélanges de la Casa de Velazquez* iv (1968), 259–347

Padgen, A., 'The distraction of trust and its economic consequences in the case of eighteenth-century Naples', in Gambetta, *Trust*, 127–41

Parrón Salas, C., *De las reformas borbónicas a la república: el consulado y el comercio marítimo de Lima, 1778–1821*, Murcia 1995

—— 'Perú y la transición del comercio político al comercio libre, 1740–1778', AEA liv (1997), 447–75

—— 'El nacionalismo emergente y el comercio: la expulsión de extranjeros de América (Perú), 1750–1778', in *Actas del XI congreso de la AHILA*, Liverpool 1998, i. 200–18

Pearce, A., *British trade with Spanish America, 1763 to 1808*, Liverpool 2007

Pérez Cantó, M. P., *Lima en el siglo XVIII: estudio socioeconómico*, Madrid 1985

Pérez Herrero, P., 'Actitudes del consulado de México ante las reformas comerciales borbónicas, 1718–1765', RI xliii (1983), 97–182

—— *Plata y libranzas: la articulación comercial del México borbónico*, México 1988

Pérez-Mallaina, P. E. and B. Torres Ramírez, *La Armada del Mar del Sur*, Seville 1987

Phillips, C. R., 'Spanish merchants and the wool trade in the sixteenth century', *Sixteenth-Century Journal* xiv (1983), 259–82

—— and W. D. Phillips, *Spain's golden fleece: wool production and the wool trade from the middle ages to the nineteenth century*, Baltimore 1997

Pinto Rodríguez, J., 'Los Cinco Gremios Mayores de Madrid y el comercio colonial en el siglo XVIII', RI cxcii (1991), 292–326

Pradells Nadal, J., *Diplomacia y comercio: la expansión consular española en el siglo XVIII*, Alicante 1992

Price, J. M. and P. G. E. Clemens, 'A revolution of scale in overseas trade: British firms in the Chesapeake trade, 1675–1775', JEcH xlvii (1987), 1–43

Priotti, J. P., *Génesis de un crecimiento: Bilbao y sus mercaderes, h. 1520–h. 1620*, Bilbao 2004

Quiroz, A. W., *Deudas olvidadas: instrumentos de crédito en la economía colonial peruana, 1750–1820*, Lima 1993

—— 'Reassessing the role of credit in late colonial Peru: censos, escrituras, and imposiciones', HAHR lxxiv (1994), 193–230

Ramada Curto, D. and A. Molho (eds), *Commercial networks in the early modern world*, Florence 2002

Ravina Martín, M., 'Participación extranjera en el comercio indiano: el seguro marítimo a fines del siglo XVII', *RI* xliii (1983), 481–513

Ridings, E. W., 'Foreign predominance among overseas traders in nineteenth-century Latin America', *Latin American Research Review* xx/2 (1985), 3–27

Rivera Medina, A. M., 'Paisaje naval, construcción y agentes sociales en Vizcaya: desde el medioevo a la modernidad', *Itsas Memoria* ii (1998), 49–92

Rodríguez Vicente, M. E., *El tribunal del consulado de Lima en la primera mitad del siglo XVII*, Madrid 1960

Ruiz Rivera, J. B., 'Patiño y la reforma del consulado de Cádiz en 1729', *Temas Americanistas* v (1985), 16–21

—— *El consulado de Cádiz: matrícula de comerciantes, 1730–1823*, Cádiz 1988

Samuelsson, K., *Religion and economic action*, trans. G. French, London 1961

Sánchez Belén, J. A., 'Bilbao y el comercio de importación anglo-holandés durante la Guerra de Reuniones de 1684', in M. Rodríguez Cancho (coor.), *Historia y perspectivas de investigación: estudios en memoria del profesor Angel Rodríguez Sánchez*, Badajoz 2002, 269–78

Shaw, L. M. E., *The Anglo-Portuguese alliance and the English merchants in Portugal, 1654–1810*, Aldershot 1998

Smail, J., *Merchants, markets and manufacture: the English wool textile industry in the eighteenth century*, Basingstoke 1999

Smith, R. S., *The Spanish guild merchant: a history of the consulado, 1250–1700*, Durham 1940

Socolow, S. M., *The merchants of Buenos Aires, 1778–1810: family and commerce*, Cambridge 1978

Sola Corbacho, J. C., 'El papel de la organización familiar en la dinámica del sector mercantil madrileño a finales del siglo XVIII', *Historia Social* xxxii (1998), 3–22

Stein, S. J. and B. H. Stein, *Silver, trade and war: Spain and America in the making of early modern Europe*, Baltimore 2000

—— and B. H. Stein, *Apogee of empire: Spain and New Spain in the age of Charles III, 1759–1789*, Baltimore 2003

Studnicki-Gizbert, D., 'From agents to *consulado*: commercial networks in colonial Mexico, 1520–1590 and beyond', *AEA* lvii (2000), 41–68

—— 'Interdependence and the collective pursuit of profits: Portuguese commercial networks in the early modern Atlantic', in Ramada Curto and Molho, *Commercial networks*, 90–120

—— *A nation upon the ocean sea: Portugal's Atlantic diaspora and the crisis of the Spanish empire, 1492–1640*, Oxford 2007

Suárez, M., *Desafíos trasatlánticos: mercaderes, banqueros y el estado en el Perú virreinal, 1600–1700*, Lima 2001

Subrahmanyam, S. (ed.), *Merchant networks in the early modern world*, Aldershot 1996

Tedde de Lorca, P., *El Banco de San Carlos, 1782–1829*, Madrid 1988

Torales Pacheco, M. C. (coord.), *La compañía de comercio de Francisco Ignacio de Yraeta, 1767–1797*, Mexico 1982

Tord Nicolini, J. and C. Lazo García, *Hacienda, comercio, fiscalidad, y luchas sociales (Perú colonial)*, Lima 1981

Torija Herrera, C., *El libre comercio vasco con América*, Vitoria 1985

Tracy, J. D. (ed.), *The rise of merchant empires; long-distance trade in the early modern world, 1350–1750*, Cambridge 1990
Trask, R. L., *The history of Basque*, London 1997
Trivellato, F., 'Jews of Leghorn, Italians of Lisbon, and Hindus of Goa: merchant networks and cross-cultural trade in the early modern period', in Ramada Curto and Molho, *Commercial networks*, 59–89
—— 'Merchant letters across geographical and social boundaries', in F. Bethencourt and F. Egmond (eds), *Correspondence and cultural exchange in Europe, 1400–1700*, Cambridge 2007, 80–103
Turiso Sebastián, T., *Comerciantes españoles en la Lima borbónica: anatomía de una élite de poder, 1701–1761*, Valladolid 2002
Uriarte Ayo, R., *Estructura, desarrollo y crisis de la siderurgia tradicional vizcaína, 1700–1840*, Bilbao 1988
—— 'Anglo-Spanish trade through the port of Bilbao during the second half of the eighteenth century: some preliminary findings', IJMH iv/2 (1992), 193–217
Van Royen, P. C., 'Manning the merchant marine: the Dutch maritime labour market about 1700', IJMH i/1 (1989), 1–28
Vázquez Lijó, J. M., *La matrícula de mar en la España del siglo XVIII: registro, inspección y evolución de las clases de marinería y maestranza*, Madrid 2007
Vicente, M. V., *Clothing the Spanish empire: families and the calico trade in the early modern Atlantic world*, Basingstoke 2006
Vickers, D. and V. Walsh, *Young men and the sea: Yankee seafarers in the age of sail*, New Haven 2005
Vidal, C., 'The reluctance of French historians to address Atlantic history', *Southern Quarterly* xliii/4 (2006), 153–89
Vidal Abarca, J., 'Estudios sobre la distribución y evolución de los socios de la RSBAP en Indias, 1765–1793', in *La Real Sociedad Bascongada y América*, Madrid 1992, 105–48
Vila Vilar, E., 'La feria de Portobelo: apariencia y realidad del comercio con Indias', AEA xxxix (1982), 275–340
—— and A. J. Kuethe (eds), *Relaciones de poder y comercio colonial: nuevas perspectivas*, Seville 1999
Vilar, P., *Catalunya dins l'Espanya moderna: recerques sobre els fonaments econòmics de les estructures nacional*, Barcelona 1968
Villa Esteves, D. M., 'Liderazgo y poder: la élite comercial limeña entre el comercio libre y la Guerra de la Independencia (el caso de Antonio de Elizalde)', in Mazzeo, *Comerciantes limeños*, 133–71
Villalobos, S., *El comercio y la crisis colonial*, 2nd edn, Santiago de Chile 1990
Ville, S. P., *English shipowning during the Industrial Revolution: Michael Henley and Son, London shipowners, 1770–1830*, Manchester 1987
——, 'The growth of specialization in English shipowning, 1750–1850', EcHR xlvi (1993), 702–22
Walker, G. J., *Spanish politics and imperial trade, 1700–1789*, London 1979
Ward, C., *Imperial Panama: commerce and conflict in Isthmian America, 1550–1800*, Albuquerque 1993
Weber, M., *The Protestant ethic and the spirit of capitalism*, London 1930
Zabala Uriarte, A., 'Notas sobre el cabotaje vasco en el siglo XVIII', *Ernaroa* i (1985) 107–27.

—— *Mundo urbano y actividad mercantil: Bilbao, 1700–1810*, Bilbao 1994
—— 'The consolidation of Bilbao as a trade centre in the second half of the seventeenth century', in Janzen, *Merchant organization*, 155–73
Zahedieh, N., 'Credit, risk and reputation in the seventeenth-century colonial trade', in Janzen, *Merchant organization*, 53–74.
—— 'Making mercantilism work: London merchants and Atlantic trade in the seventeenth century', *Transactions of the Royal Historical Society* ix (1999), 143–58
Zylberberg, M., *Une si Douce Domination: les milieux d'affaires français et l'Espagne vers 1780–1808*, Paris 1993

Unpublished theses

Bartolomei, A., 'La Bourse et la vie: destin collectif et trajectories individuelles des marchands français de Cadix, de l'instauration du *comercio libre* à la disparition de l'empire espagnol (1778–1824)', PhD, Marseille 2007
Dilg, G. R., 'The collapse of the Portobelo fairs: a study in Spanish commercial reform, 1720–1740', PhD, Indiana 1975
Fernández-Guerra, R., 'El fletamento en el litoral cantábrico durante el siglo XVIII', PhD, Deusto 1992
Guice, C. N., 'The *consulado* of New Spain, 1594–1795', PhD, Berkeley 1952

Index

Note: Page numbers in italics refer to tables; those in **bold** type refer to maps. The following abbreviations are used in the index: *corr.* for *corregidor*; *mer.* for *merchant*; *s.c.* for *ship captain*.

Acha, Domingo Millán de (*mer.*), 151, 162–3
Achútegui, Gregorio de (*mer.*), 54, 55
Adams, John, 30, 31, 45
Adana, Isidro de, 129
agents: local commission, 4, 61–2; *peruleros*, 118–19, 130; ship captains as, 57–62. *See also* correspondents
Aguado, Roque (*mer.*), 150, 170
Aguerrebere, Juan Miguel de (*mer.*), 113, 115, 131–2
Aguirre, Juan Martín de (*mer.*), 100, 136, 158, 171
Aix-la-Chapelle, Treaty (1748), 46
Aizcorbe, Fermín de, 55
Ajeo, José de, 53
Ajeo, Juan Bautista de (*s.c.*), 53, 55, 56, 60, 67, 68
Alarcón, Melchor de, 107
alcabala de tarifa (tax on *repartimientos*), 110
alcabala real (commercial tax), 110
Aldecoa, Nicolás de (*s.c.*), 59–60
Alicante: import trade, 32
Allende Salazar, Diego (*mer.*), 38–9
almojarifazgo duties, 108
Alva, Juan de (*mer.*), 151, 162–3
Álvarez Osorio y Redín, Miguel, 5
Amándarro, Juan Antonio de (*mer.*), 128–9
Amándarro, Manuel José de (*mer.*), 105, 107, 114–15, 128, 176–7
Amat, Manuel de (viceroy of Peru), 86–7, 99
Amelot, Michel-Jean, 184
Amenábar, Agustín de (*mer.*), 130
Amenábar, Silvestre de (*mer.*), 113, 115, 128–9
Amenábar, Xavier Ignacio de (*mer.*), 113, 128

America, British: British trade with, 49; Spanish trade with, 32; and tobacco trade, 33, 37; and triangular trade, 34
America, Spanish: ban on foreign trade with, 8, 14, 133–8; and *consulados*, 16. *See also* colonial trade; Lima; Mexico City; Peru
American War of Independence (1779–83), 21, 156–7, 177–81
Amsterdam: and Spanish wool trade, 31, 39; trade with Bilbao, 33–4, 39
Anderson, Adam, 5–6, 7
Antuñiano (*s.c.*), 68
Antwerp: and Spanish factors, 5
Arambalza (*s.c.*), 68
Arambalza, María de, 67
Arazola, María Jesús, 18
arbitristas, 5
Arco, Lorenzo del (*mer.*), 100, 144, 152–3
Areche, José Antonio de (*visitador*), 104, 110–11
Armada del Mar del Sur, 77, 80
Armentia, Alonso de, 105
Armitage, David, 20
army, of Peru, 165
Arrambide, Pedro de (*s.c.*), 122
Arrese, Joaquín José de (*mer.*), 129, 160
Arriaga, Juan Antonio de (*pilot*), 63
Arriaga, Julián (minister of the Indies), 87 n. 51
Arriquíbar, José de (*mer.*), 38–9
Artamóniz, Juan Bautista de (*s.c.*), 53, 55, 58–9, 60–1, 67
Artaza, Valentín de (*s.c.*), 54
Arvilla, Pedro Miguel de (*mer.*), 151, 153, 164
Asunsolo, Lorenzo de (*mer.*), 114, 136
Atlantic history, 3–4, 17–21; and British trade, 34; and communications, 95–115; and silver trade, 18–19, 77;

201

and slave trade 4, 20 n.74, 80; and trading networks, 116–38; triangular trade, 34. *See also* Peru
Atristain, Pedro de (*mer.*), 48, 55, 146–7, 150
Austrian Succession, War of (1740–8), 21, 45
Avaría, Esteban José de, 86
avisos (mail packet-boats), 97–8, 105
Aycinena, Juan Francisco de (*mer.*), 170

Bailyn, Bernard 34
Balde, Juan (*mer.*), 39
Balde, Pedro (*mer.*), 39
bankruptcies, 142–4, 171, 177; and church protection, 166
Baquíjano, José de, 85, 108
Barcelona, import trade, 32
Barco, Domingo del (*mer.*), 44
Barco, Nicólas de (*s.c.*), 61
Barreda, Francisco de la (*mer.*), 118
Barrera, Fermín Ramón de (*mer.*), 130, 131–2
Basarrate, Manuel de (*mer.*), 47
Baskes, Jeremy, 110
Basque Country (*Euskal Herria*): and Cádiz merchants, 117, 121–5, 157–60; coastline, **64;** *fueros*, 29–30, 38, 46, 69–70, 168; iron industry, 32, 36; and Peruvian merchants, 119–20, 124, 159, 182–4; ship captains and seamen, 51–2, 62–5, 183; and tax exemptions, 30–1, 36–7, 42, 174
Basque language (*euskera*), 29, 32, 66–7, 124, 183
Baztán (valley of Navarre), 125–6, 130–1
Beawes, Wyndham, 141
Behic, Juan (*mer.*), 93
Bergara, Pedro José de (*mer.*), 148
Bergareche, Manuel de (*mer.*), 48
Berindoaga, Juan Félix de (*mer.*), 171–2
Bernal, Antonio-Miguel, 132, 134
Berría, Juan de (*mer.*), 81, 82
Bilbao: Archivo Foral de Bizkaia, 22; and commercial credit, 168; *consulado* 16, 22, 27–9, 33, 35, 40–4, 46–7, 54, 66, 146, 166, 168, court, 163–4, 182, ordinances, 41–3, 45, 55, 58 n. 33, 62–3, 142–4, 163–4, 182–3; and contraband trade, 33; foreign merchants, 18, 27–9, 33–40, 42–3, 182, 184; import trade, 31–2; and north Atlantic trade, 17–19, 21, 27–8, 32–4; population, 30; school for pilots, 68–9; and shipbrokers, 58 n. 33; Spanish merchants, 17–18, 27–50, 53, 144–7, 168–9; trade with northern Europe, 18, 31–2, 33–4, 36–40, 44–5, 47–50, 51, 70, 168, 183; and wool trade, 27, 31, 36, 38–9, 61–2, 70, 168
bill of lading, 52, 58, 101, 128
bills of exchange, 41, 43, 59, 60, 90
Bosher, John F., 8
Bourbon dynasty: and reforms, 14–17, 73, 174, 185
Bourgoing, Jean François de, 17
Bousignac, Juan (*mer.*), 55, 59, 60–1, 63
Brading, David, 119
Brazil: ban on foreign trade with, 9, 14; and Portuguese trade, 6–7, 13
Brethous, Antoine (*mer.*), 137
Brethous, Leon (*mer.*), 135–6
Britain: and Atlantic trade, 19–20, 34, 78–80; capture of Spanish merchant ships, 21; and commercial credit, 168–9; and empire of commerce, 14
The British Merchant, 167
Bruges: and Spanish factors, 5
Buenos Aires: and communications, 99; and *consulado*, 16; and trading communities, 11
Burgos: and *consulado*, 16, 18
burguesía, Spanish merchants as, 14
Burnet, John, 81
Bustos, Manuel, 126–7, 134–5
Butler, Jacinto (*mer.*), 91
Butrón, Agustín de (*s.c.*), 55

Cadalso, José, 124
Cadious, Lazaro (*mer.*), 135
Cádiz: and British merchants, 45, 137; *Cofradía del Santísimo Cristo*, 125; and colonial trade monopoly, 6, 8, 17, 49, 80, 87, 117, 133, 174, 176, 186; *consulado* 16, 44, 49–50, 80, 82, 87–8, 97, 116, creole members, 118, 119, and foreign merchants, 135, 167, and free trade, 175–6, 181, *libro de matrícula* 117, 119, ordinances 117, 127, and single traders 126–7, 142, and trading partnerships, 142–3, 153–7; and foreign merchants, 7, 19, 27, 79, 106–7, 116, 133–8; and imperial mail, 97; import trade, 32, 174; and Peruvian trade, 17, 73, 82–3, 103, 116–17, 127, 129; population, 73;

and Spanish merchants, 17, 49–50, 116, 148, 185–6
Campbell, Leon G., 165
Campillo y Cossío, José del (minister of state), 1–2, 14, 95–6
Cantolla, María Andrea de la, 114
Cape Horn trade route, 81–7, 88–9, 91, 93–4, 120, 175
capitalism, and religion, 7–8
Caracas, *consulado*, 16
Cardón, Juan Antonio de (*shipowner*), 52
Carrera de Buenos Aires, 99
Carrera de Cartagena, 98
Carrera de Indias, see colonial trade, Spanish
Carrera Pujal, Jaime, 27
Carrière, Charles, 89
Carrillo, Luis (*mer.*), 176
Cartagena: and communications, 98–9; and *consulado*, 16
cartas vivas (living letters), 105–6
Cary, John, 1
Casa de la Contratación, 74, 85, 103
cascarilla, Peruvian, 83
Castile, trade, *see* Bilbao
Castro, Juan de, 5
Catholicism: and sanctuary, 165–6; and trade, 7–8, 35, 48
Causabon and Co., 171
Cayla, Solier, Cabanes, Jugla and Co., 158, 160
Céspedes del Castillo, Guillermo, 176
Chanique, Francisco (*mer.*), 80
Charles III, king of Spain: and economic reforms, 14
charter party (*carta de fletamento*), 52–3
Chaunu, Pierre, 118–19
Cinco Gremios Mayores company, 103, 126
citizenship: and trade, 35, 39–40
cocoa, Peruvian, 83
Codes, Simón, 1, 10, 144 n.12
coercion: and *repartimiento*, 109–10
cofradías (religious brotherhoods), 125, 159 n. 69
Colbert, Jean-Baptiste, 14 n. 49
colonial trade, British, 32, 33
colonial trade, Portuguese, 8, 88 n. 53
colonial trade, Spanish: and Bilbao, 33, 50; and commodity prices, 91–4, 96, 108; and communication, 95–115, 116; and consignment trade, 89, 100; and *consulados*, 16; growth, 86–7, 108–15, 174–5, 177, 185;

liberalisation, 87; and mail, 95–100; and market information, 108–15; and married merchants, 148–9; monopoly, 5–6, 8, 14, 17–18, 49, 80, 87, 96, 117, 133, 174, 186; retail, 94; trading routes, **76**, 81–8. *See also* networks, trade; Peru
Comeford, James (*mer.*), 152
comenda (notarised contract), 58
comercio libre (free trade), 87, 174–81, 186
commissários volantes, Portuguese, 8
communications: and colonial trade, 75, 94, 95–115, 116; and information, 13, 67–8, 185; and living letters, 105–6. *See also* mail, transatlantic
companies, merchant, 42–3
competition, 111–12, 114–15, 134, 146; and credit, 168, 173; and decision-making, 173–81, 186; and postponement of marriage, 149; and risk, 162–81, 186
Condorcanqui, José Gabriel (Túpac Amaru), 111
confidentiality, 10, 128, 138, 141–61, 183; and refusal of royal scrutiny, 134, 141, 142; and reputation, 44, 141–4, 183
consignment trade, 89, 100
consulados (merchant gilds), 15–16, 18; courts, 40–1, 43–4, 156, 163–4, 168; and foreign merchants, 34; governing body, 15–16; *matrícula* (membership), 15, 117. *See also* Bilbao; Cádiz; Lima
consumer: and fashion, 94, 108–9, 113–15, 179–80; and market information, 108–15, 173
contraband trade, 19, 33, 78–81, 82–3, 87 n. 48, 88, 135
contracts, enforceability, 13, 23, 162
Corcuera, Miguel Francisco de (*mer.*), 132
Corcuera, Vicente de (*mer.*), 132
Corfield, Penelope, 22
corregimiento: in Peru, 109–12
correos marítimos (maritime mail), 98–100, 107
correspondents, 14; and British trade, 19–20; and debt recovery, 169–73, 181; and foreign traders, 6, 8, 40–1; and Spanish trade, 2–3, 141, colonial, 89–94, 96–100, 109–15, 128–9, 185, European 36, 38, 40, 44–5, 48–50, 165, and family, 144–5, and friendship, 150–3; trustworthiness, 1–3, 44–5, 94, 104, 141–4, 184, 185

203

corruption: and Lima *consulado*, 164
Cortés, Hernán, 74
Cranisbro, Juan (*mer.*), 22, 93–4, 164, 166
credit, 81, 88, 168–73; British use, 168–9; and competition, 168, 173; increasing use, 49, 110; and letters of recommendation, 107; and *repartimiento*, 110; and reputation, 142; sea loans, 89–90, 132–3, 152, 170; and trust, 9–10, 89, 93, 127, 130, 142, 168–9, 186. See also bills of exchange
crews, 62–70; as carriers of information, 106; dangers of long-distance trade, 85–6; geographical origins, 63–7, 69–70, 183
criollos (creoles): geographical origins, 118–20; as members of Cádiz *consulado*, 118, 130
Croix, Teodoro de (viceroy of Peru), 175
Cuadra, Francisco de la (*s.c.*), 52
culture: and economics, 11–13, 183; and trust, 1, 185
Curtin, Philip D., 4

Dalla Corte, Gabriela, 107
Davis, Ralph, 57, 63
De Vries, Jan, 30 n. 10
debt: case study, 153–61; and claiming of sanctuary, 165–6; recovery, 164–6, 169–72, 181. See also bankruptcies
decision-making: and risk, 173–81, 186
derecho de palmeo: duty, 108
Des Essartz, Luis (*mer.*), 59–60
Diton, María Josefa (wife of Juan de Eguino), 157, *158*, 160
Domínguez, Antonio, 18

Earle, Robert, 39
Echálaz, José de (*mer.*), 47–8
Echea, José de, 132–3
Echevarría, Luis de, 122–3, 124
Echevarría, Luis José de, 122–3
Echevarría y Dúo, José de (*mer.*), 146–7
economics: new institutional approach, 11–12; and trust, 1
education: of merchants, 123, 163–4; of ship captains, 62
Eguino, Alfonso de (*mer.*), 48, 50, 150, 157, *158*, 160
Eguino, Benito de, 157, *158*, 160
Eguino, Francisco Xavier de (priest), *158*, 160–1

Eguino, Juan de (*mer.*), 50, 136, 153–61
Eléxpuru, Manuel de, 43–4
Elizalde, Antonio de (*mer.*), 111, 113, 129, 130, 136, 173
Elizalde, José Matías de (*mer.*), 113, 130, 136, 173
Elliott, J. H., 3–4, 19
Elola, Ignacio de (*mer.*), 129
Emery, John (*mer.*), 59
emigration: from northern Spain, 121–6, 184
encomenderos (agents), 8, 85, 127–8, 132, 136
Endara, Martín de (*mer.*), 151
Enrrile, José María (*mer.*), 171
Ensenada, Zenón de Somodevilla y Bengoechea, 1st marqués de la, 14, 44, 82
Erasun, Manuel Ignacio de (*mer.*), 160
Errecarte, Juan Tomás de, 49
Errecarte, Pedro de (*mer.*), 39, 47, 49–50, 57
Escarza, Pedro (*s.c.*), 62 n. 50
escritura de riesgo (sea loan), 89–90
Esténoz, Martín de (*mer.*), 162–3
ethnicity: and merchant communities, 5, 10–11, 121–6, 159, 182–5; and ships' crews, 63–7, 183; and trustworthiness, 3, 20, 119, 126–31
Ezcurrechea, Miguel Antonio de (*mer.*), 122
Ezpeleta, Juan de (*mer.*), 131

factors, *see* correspondents
factory system, 4–5, 13
family trading networks, 10–11, 15, 20; in Bilbao, 38–9, 142; in colonial trade, 121–6; and ship captains, 62–3; and trust, 144–9
fashion: and consumer demand, 94, 108–9, 113–15, 179–80
Fernández, Paloma, 133–4, 148–9
Fernández, Pedro Celestino (*mer.*), 85
Feyt, Louis (*mer.*), 137
Fisher, John, 174–5
fleets, 18, 73; fleet/fair system, 74–80, 83, 88, 94, 126; and long-distance communication 95; weakness, 46
flotas: and colonial trade, 75, 81, 83, 86, 90–1, 96, 127; and mail, 97
Fourrat, Jaime (*mer.*), 123
Franco-Spanish War (1644), 33–4
free trade, 87, 174–81, 186

INDEX

friends: case study, 153–61; and finance, 151–2; and trust, 150–3, 162–3
Fuente, Juan Antonio de la (*mer.*), 136
fuero militar (military jurisdiction), 133, 165

Galatoire Brothers and Co., 172
galeones: and colonial fleets, 74–81, 79, 83, 84, 88, 96, 127, 164; and mail, 97; and *peruleros* 118
Gallegos, Francisco (*mer.*), 156
Gálvez, José de (minister of the Indies), 87, 175
Gálvez, Pedro Dionisio de (*mer.*), 104
Games, Alison, 4
Gana, Juan Antonio de (*mer.*), 55
Gándara, Miguel Antonio de la, 95
Gárate, Juan Bautista de (*mer.*), 111, 114, 123, 125, 131–2, 176
Garay, Manuel de (*mer.*), 48, 150
Garay y Leániz, Juan de (*mer.*), 122
García, Joaquín Xavier (*mer.*), 115, 153, 164
García, Juan (*mer.*), 47
García-Baquero, Antonio, 175
Garnier and Perry company, 145–6
Gato, Manuel (*encomendero*), 128
Gaviña, Eusebio (*mer.*), 170–1
Geertz, Clifford, 12 n. 43
Gibbs, Antony (*mer.*), 69
Gil de Taboada, Francisco (viceroy of Peru), 166, 175
gilds, merchant, *see consulados* (merchant gilds)
Glaisyer, Natasha, 9
Goicoechea, Simón Antonio de (*mer.*), 144–6
Goicoechea and Otero (Bilbao firm), 53, 56, 145–6
Goitia, Juan de (*s.c.*), 57
gold, Peruvian, 77, 83, 86, 89, 170
Golte, Jürgen, 111
good faith, 10, 43, 104
gossip, and information, 143, 156
Goyeneche, Juan de, 125–6
Guatemala: and *consulado*, 16
Guendica, Bernardo de (*mer.*), 151–2, 169
Guirior, María Ventura de (wife of viceroy of Peru), 160
Guisasola, José de (*mer.*), 82
Gurney, John, 143, 169, 172–3
Gurney, Richard, 143, 169, 172–3
Gutiérrez Cosío, Isidro (*mer.*), 78

Hancock, David, 20
Hanseatic League, 4
Hardy, Josiah (British consul in Cádiz), 167
Harper, Patrick (*mer.*), 172
Havana: and *consulado*, 16; and imperial mail, 98
Hernández Dávila, Pedro (*mer.*), 93
Hevia Bolaños, Juan de, *Curia filípica*, 163
hidalgos, 30
Hore, Vicente (*corr.*), 112
huésped (host) system, 35–6, 39–40, 51, 183
Huizi, Xavier de (*mer.*), 104

Ibañez de Zabala, Juan Ignacio (*mer.*), 52
Ibarrola, Pedro de (*mer.*), 114–15, 176
identity: Basque, 30, 183–4; common (*paisanaje*), 11, 183–4
Iguelz, Asensio (*s.c.*), 52
information: asymmetric, 9; and communications, 13, 67–8, 95–115, 185; and consumer demand, 94, 108–15, 173; and foreign merchants, 137; and gossip, 143, 156; on prices, 91–4, 96; and trust, 95, 104–5, 131, 145, 181, 184
inheritance: and family capital, 122; and landholdings, 121, 122
interdependence 12
Iriarte, Santiago de (*mer.*), 130
Iribarren, Pedro de (*mer.*), 122–3
Irigoyen, Juan Bautista de (*mer.*), 114
Irisarri, Pedro Francisco de (*mer.*), 143
Irisarri, Santiago de (*mer.*), 122
Isasi, José de (*mer.*), 78
Ives, Jeremiah (*mer.*), 147

Jalapa, fair, 127, 132–3, 149
Jenkins' Ear, War of (1739–40), 21, 79n., 81–2
Jews: and trade, 7
Jiménez, Blas Antonio Benito (*mer.*), 104, 155, 157, *158*
Juan, Jorge, 82–3
Juan de Villabaso and Co., 59
Juez Conservador, 166–7
Jussué, Bartolomé de (*mer.*), 38–9
Jussué, Miguel Antonio de (*mer.*), 39, 61, 62 n. 48
Kicza, John E., 11
Kuethe, Allan J., 174–6

205

La Coruña: and long-distance communication, 98–9
La Gazeta de Madrid, 105
La Perla (*San Francisco Xavier*): capture, 21, 101; mail, 21, 94, 100–7, 110, 111, addressees, *102*, *103*, 117–18, 126, 136–7, 154, 157–60, *158*, 184, and *corregidores*, 112, and debt recovery, 169–71, and evidence of trust, 116, 128–31, and foreign merchants 135–7, and free trade 176–7, and merchants, 116–21, 132, and *notas*, 112–15, and trading networks, 123–4, 131
Labarbinais, Le Gentil (mariner), 86
Labat and Co., 172
Laborda, Pedro (mer.), 166
Laborde, Jean Joseph, 160
Lacoa, Juan Bautista de (mer.), 122, 124
Lacoste, Juan Bautista de (mer.), 169
Landaburu, Matías de (mer.), 101, 112, 131, 136, *158*, 159–60
Landecho, Juan Martín de, 41
languages, proficiency in, 62, 123
Lantery, Raimundo de (mer.), 80, 150, 151
Larrabeiti, Adrián (s.c.), 56
Larrain, Juan Bautista de (mer.), 177
Larramendi, Manuel de (priest), 65
Larrea, Domingo de (mer.), 136, 151, 154–7, 160
Lasquívar, Domingo de (mer.), 130
Lauro, José de, 37
Lavalle, José Antonio de (mer.), 106, 114, 132, 136, 156
Lavena, Joaquín (mer.), 100
law: and Bilbao *consulado* ordinances, 41–3, 45, 55, 182–3; and contract enforcement, 13; ecclesiastical jurisdiction, 165–6; legal frameworks, 162–8, 181, 182; military jurisdiction, 133, 165; special jurisdiction, 166–8
Lecanda, Manuel de, 39
Lecouteaulx, Louis (mer.), *158*
Lecture and Gastambide company, 136
Legasa, Martín de (mer.), 130
letters of recommendation, 107
Lewicki, R. J., D. J. McAllister and R. J. Bies, 141
Lezeta, Juan Francisco de (mer.), *158*, 159–60
Lima, 17, 73, 80, 116–17, 170; Archivo General de la Nación, 22; *Cofradía de Nuestra Señora de Aránzazu*, 125; *Cofradía del Santo Cristo de Burgos*, 125; *consulado*, 16, 22, 75–8, 81–2, 104, 116, 128, court 156, 164–5, 171, and foreign merchants, 135, 175, and free trade, 175–7, geographical origins of members, 118–20, 126, 130–1, and military jurisdiction, 165; and debt recovery, 169–72; and fashion, 108–9, 113–15, 179–80; and marine insurance, 85; population, 73
Lion, Daniel (mer.), 166
Lisbon: and colonial trade, 8; English merchants in, 6–7, 13; Portuguese merchants in, 6–7
literacy: and merchants, 123
Llano, José de (mer.), 151
Llanos, Bernardo de (mer.). 66
London: Spanish merchants in, 45–50, 146–7, 150, 183; and Spanish wool trade, 31, 38, 61–2, 168
Lopes Acuña, Juan (mer.), 119
Lopes, Bernardo (mer.), 104, 119
López de Cangas, Gregorio (mer.), 151
Losada, Alfonso de (mer.), 104
Louison, Joseph (mer.), 152–3
Louison, Louis (mer.), 152–3
Loygorri, Pedro Matías de (mer.), 43–4, 143–4, 166
Loyo, Andrés de (mer.), 88, 122–3, 126
Loyo, Pedro José de (mer.), *158*
Luhmann, Niklas, 9
Lyttleton, William, 88 n. 53

Macanaz, Melchor Rafael de, 96 n. 3
McCusker, John J., 92
Macnamara, Alexis (mer.), 143, 173
Madariaga, José Antonio de (mer.), 130
Madrid: merchants, 121
Magon, Lefer and Co., 152–3, *158*
mail, transatlantic, 95–100: and *avisos*, 97–8; *correos marítimos*, 98–100, 107; *reservada* letters, 106; under-cover envelopes, 101, 103, 106. *See also La Perla*
Malynes, Gerrard de, 142, 162
marine insurance, 41, 43, 44, 61–2; register ships, 84–5
market information, *see* information
Marks, Patricia H., 116, 118, 120
Marrés, Raimundo (mer.), 136–7, 172
marriage: and Spanish merchants, 148–9
Marticorena, Juan Miguel (mer.), 177–81
Marticorena, Juan Vicente (mer.), 22, 177–81

INDEX

Martínez Ferrer, Vicente (*mer.*), 171
Martínez Shaw, Carlos and José María Oliva Melgar, 19 n. 67
Martínez de Vallejo, Francisco (*mer.*), 171–2
Mathias, Peter, 150
matrícula de mar, 69
matxinada riot, 33
Mauro, Frédéric, 4
Meager, Martin, 44
Mendoza, Lorenzo de, 105
mercantilism: and Bourbon reforms, 14, 73
merchant communities: and nationality, 3–5, 10–11, 47–8, 122–6, 182–5
merchants, British, 134, 137, 146–7
merchants, Chilean, 93
merchants, Dutch, 27, 33–5, 36, 38–40, 41–2
merchants, English: in Bilbao, 27, 33–5, 37–40, 41–2; in Cádiz, 45; and Catholicism, 165; in Portugal, 6, 167; in Santander, 36–8, 41–2
merchants, Flemish, 33–4, 134
merchants, foreign: in Bilbao, 18, 27–9, 33–40, 42–3, 182; and Cádiz, 7, 19, 27, 79, 106–7, 116, 133–8, 167; and colonial trade, 78–80, 127–8, 133–8, 184, 185; and correspondence 136–7; and lack of information, 137; profits, 134; in Seville, 19, 27
merchants, French, 7, 17, 184; in Bilbao, 33, 34, 40, 42; in Cádiz, 82, 118, 132, 134–5, 137, 167, 172; in Santander, 42; in Spanish colonial trade, 78–9, 86, 92, 126, 136–7, 157–60
merchants, German, 40
merchants, Irish, 35, 40, 91, 134, 143, 173
merchants, Italian, 134
merchants, Peruvian, 82–5, 110–14; and army, 165; and *encomendero* system, 127–8, 132, 136; and fleet/fair system, 75–8, 126, 127; geographical origins, 118–20, 121–3, 130–1; as members of Cádiz *consulado*, 117–18, 119; and register ships, 93–4; and trust, 127–31
merchants, Portuguese, 6–7
merchants, Spanish, 1–8; and attitudes to trade, 1–2; and colonial trade, 73–94, 116–17; duration of trading career, 117; and friendships, 150–3, 162–3; geographical origins, 117–20, 121; in London, 45–50, 146–7, 150, 183; and mercantile bourgeoisie, 14–15, 17, 18; mobility, 146–8; and 'nephew syndrome', 122–5; records, 21–2, 51; as shipowners, 53–7, 62–3; as single traders, 126–7, 142; and trading networks, 116–21, 126–33, 185. *See also* Bilbao; Cádiz
Merry, Joseph (*mer.*), 169
Methuen Treaty (1703) 6, 13
Mexico City: *Cofradía de Nuestra Señora de Aránzazu*, 125; *Cofradía del Santo Cristo de Burgos*, 125; and commodity prices, 91–2; and communications, 98, 105–6; *consulado*, 16, 75, 165; and fashion, 109; and trading networks, 11, 91, 132–3
Mexico (New Spain): and *repartimiento*, 110; trade with, 74–5, 81, 83, 90–2
Michel, Luis (*mer.*), 39
Micheo, Juan Francisco de (*mer.*), 129
militia, Peru, 165
Miretti, Giovanni (*mer.*), 104
Morphy, Diego (*mer.*), 91
Mortel, Juan Benito (*mer.*), 39
Mortel, Servacio de (*mer.*), 39
Moya, José de (*mer.*), 148, 171
Mugaburu, Josephe and Francisco, *Diario de Lima*, 97
Muldrew, Craig, 9
Munárriz, Pedro de (*mer.*), 90–1, 94
Murrieta, Antonio de (*s.c.*), 68
Múzquiz, Juan Angel de (*s.c.*), 65

nationalism: and trade, 8
nationality: and merchant communities, 3–5, 10–11, 47–8, 122–6, 182–5; and ships' crews, 63–7, 183; and trustworthiness, 3, 20, 119, 126–31
navío de permiso, 80
navíos de registro/registros sueltos, see register ships
navy, Spanish: recruitment for, 69–70
network analysis approach, 12–13
networks, trade, 14–15, 116–38, 185; British, 19–20, 38–9; and *consulados*, 16; and family, 10–11, 15, 20, 39, 121–6, 142, 144–9; French, 160; and friends, 150–3; and geographical origins of merchants, 118–21, 122–3, 130–1; long-distance, 73–5, 90; and reciprocity, 81, 96, 126–33, 183; and

ship captains, 51, 57–60, 68, 86; and trust, 9–14, 15, 19, 119, 126–33
New Christians (cristãos novos): in Portugal, 7
New Spain (Mexico): and *repartimiento*, 110; trade with, 74–5, 81, 83, 90–2; and trading networks, 132–3
newspapers, 96, 105
Nombre de Dios, Panama: fairs, 75, 78–80, 79
nota de efectos aparentes (inventory of articles in demand), 94, 112–15, 178–81
Nougaro, Francisco Antonio de (mer.), 54

Obregón, Francisco de (mer.), 113–14
Olarte, Manuel de (mer.), 39
Olave, Juan Clemente de (mer.), 82
O'Phelan, Scarlett, 111
O'Reilly, Charles, 104
Ormaza, Pedro de (s.c.), 68
Orobiogoitia, Juan Bautista de (mer.), 131
Ortiz, Francisco (mer.), 135–6
Ortiz de Paz, Laureano (mer.), 179, 181
Orúe, Gaspar de, 113–14
Orúe, Pedro de, 147
Osambela, Martín de (mer.), 179–80
Otaegui, Miguel Ignacio de (mer.), 123
Otero, Nicolás de (mer.), 145
Oxangoiti, Domingo de (mer.), 151
Ozanam, Didier, 118
Ozta, Juan Casimiro de (corr.), 112

packet-boats, 97–8, 105
Padgen, Anthony, 95
paisanaje (common identity), 11, 183–4
Palacio, José de (mer.), 39
Palacio, Pedro de (mer.), 170
Panama: and colonial trade, 74–5; and communications, 98–9
Parrón, Carmen, 110, 116, 118, 176
partnerships: Spanish merchants, 47–8, 126–7, 142–3, 153–60
passports, 56
Patiño, José (minister of state), 14, 127
Peñaflorida, Xavier María de Munibe e Idiáquez, 8th count of, 158, 159 n. 71
perception: and trustworthiness, 3, 13, 143, 154
Pérez, Juan Miguel (mer.), 47, 144, 147–8
Pérez del Muente, José (s.c.), 101
Peru: and Atlantic history, 20–1, 73–4; and Cape Horn route, 81–7, 88–9, 91, 93–4, 120, 175; and *corregimiento*, 109–12; and *Correos marítimos*, 98–100; and credit, 89–90; exports, 83, 174–5; and foreign merchants, 78–80, 127–8; imports from Spain, 83–4; and Indian revolts, 110–11; and long-distance communications, 95–115, 116; and marine insurance, 85; and Portobelo fairs, 75–81, 79, 83, 85, 88, 127; and Royal Philippine Company, 126; and trade with Cádiz, 17, 73–94; and transatlantic mail, 95–100. See also gold; silver
peruleros (agents), 118–19, 130
Philip V, king of of Spain, 46
pilots: Bilbao school for, 68–9
Piñero Vellorino, Juan (mer.), 105–6
Pizarro, Francisco, 74
Plencia, town of origin of ship captains, 62–3, 66
Polanco, Bruno Antonio (mer.), 156
Pombal, Sebastiao José de Carvalho e Melo, marquès de, 8
Porcel, Filipo, 104
Porto: and colonial trade, 8; English merchants in, 6
Portobelo, Panama: fairs, 75–81, 79, 83, 85, 88, 127, 149
Portugal: and colonial trade, 8, 88 n. 53; and decline in trade, 6–7; economic reforms, 8; and English merchants, 6, 167; and New Christians, 7
Postlethwayt, Malachy, 3, 142
préstamo a la gruesa aventura (sea loan), 89–90, 112
prestanombres (front men), 6
Price, Jacob M. and Paul G. E. Clemens, 20 n. 70
prices: information on, 91–4, 96, 108
principal-agent problem, 9–10, 51
promissory notes, 41
Protestantism: and trade, 7–8
Proyecto para galeones y flotas, 80
Puente, Gaspar de la (mer.), 176

Quintana, José de la (minister of the Indies), 81–2
Quintanilla, Fr Manuel de, 104
Quiroz, Alfonso W., 89–90, 116, 177
Rada, Pedro (councillor of the Indies), 136
Ramírez de Arellano, Andrés (mer.), 22, 144, 150, 152–3, 170

Ramírez de Arellano, Domingo (*mer.*), 22
Ramos, José de (*mer.*), 104, 136
Real Proyecto (1720), 80, 108
reciprocity, 81, 96, 126–33, 183
recommendation, letters of, 107
register ships: and Cape Horn route, 81–7, 88–9, 91, 93–4, 120; and cargoes, 108–15; and communications, 95, 97–8, 100, 104, 106, 116, 127; and Spanish merchants, 138, 185
Reglamento y aranceles reales para el comercio libre (1778), 174
reliability: and foreign merchants, 137–8; of ship captains, 53, 56, 183
religion: and participation in trade, 7–8, 35; and trading communities, 10–11, 182, 183, 185
repartimiento de mercancías (forced distribution and sale of goods), 109–11
reputation: and confidentiality, 44, 141–4, 183; and trust, 9–10, 101, 104, 129–30, 145, 153
Rexford, Thomas (*mer.*), 60
Richards, George (*mer.*), 38–9
Richards, James (*mer.*), 38–9
Richards, John (Juan Ricardo; *mer.*), 38–9, 61–2
Ridings, Eugene W., 120
Río, Francisco Antonio del (*mer.*). 47
Rio de Janeiro: annual fair, 88 n. 53
risk, 162–81; aversion, 87–8; and competition, 168, 173, 186; and credit, 168–73, 181, 186; and decision-making, 173–81, 186; diversification, 74, 145; and enforceability of contracts, 13, 23, 162; and trust, 13, 36, 110
Roberts, James (*mer.*) 146
Rooke, John (*mer.*) 61
ropas (textiles and clothing): Spanish exports, 83–4, 89, 94, 155, 170, 174, 177–8
Rosa, José de la, 154
Rospiglioso, Petrus Julius, 104
Royal Guipuzcoan Company of Caracas, 63–5
Royal Philippine Company, 126
Ruiz, José Blas (*shopkeeper*), 58

Sabugo, Juan (*mer.*), 136–7, 172
San Isidro, Isidro Abarca y Gutiérrez, 4th count, 106, 118, 136
San Llorente, Julián de (*s.c.*), 52

Sánchez Navarrete, Francisco (*mer.*), 156
sanctuary: in Catholic churches, 165–6
Santander: and foreign merchants, 36–8, 41–2, 182; and Spanish wool trade, 31, 36–7, 41–2, 70
Santiago, José de (*mer.*), 117–18
Santibáñez, Juan Antonio (*mer.*), 156
Sarachaga, Joaquín and Juan Matías de (*mer.*), 44
Sarachaga, Juan Bautista (*s.c.*), 68
Sarasa, Gregorio de (*mer.*), 113, 115
Sarralde, Miguel de (*mer.*), 132
Sarraoa, Juan Bautista de (*mer.*), 123, 170–1
Sarría, Juan Bautista de (*s.c.*), 53, 56, 60, 67, 68
Sarría, Juan Manuel de (*mer.*), 117–18, 130
Savary, Jacques, 5, 137, 142
scurvy: and long-distance trade, 85–6
sea loans, 89–90, 112, 132–3, 152, 170
Segurola, Jacinto de (*mer.*), 160
self-interest, rational, 11–12
Seven Years' War (1761–63), 21
Seville: Archivo General de Indias, 22; *Casa de la Contratación*, 74, 85, 103; and colonial trade, 103; *consulado*, 16, 75, 97; foreign merchants, 19, 27
Shedel, James (*mer.*), 147
shipbroker (*corredor de navíos*), 58
shipownership: joint, 53–6, 59, 60; Spanish, 132
ships: chartering, 52–3, 55–6
ships captains, 51–70; and chartering vessels, 52–3, 55–6; and colonial trade, 86–7; and crews, 62–70; education, 62; geographical origins, 62–3, 67–8, 183; and language proficiency, 62; and northern European trade, 51, 70; and *notas*, 112; as overseas agents, 57–62; reliability, 53, 56, 183; as shipowners, 52–7, 59, 60; social status, 60–1; and trust, 60–2, 63, 67–8, 70, 183; and wives, 67
ships' husbands (managing owners), 53, 56, 67
Sierrabella, Christobal Mesía y Munive, count, 160
silver, Peruvian, 18–19, 77, 83, 86, 89, 170, 185
slave trade: and Atlantic history, 4, 20 n. 74; and British merchants, 80
Smith, Adam, 176

smuggling, see contraband trade
Sobrevilla, Juan de (mer.), 93
Socolow, Susan M., 11
Sorozábal, Juan Pascual de (mer.), 157, 158
Sos, José Joaquín de (mer.), 129
South Sea Company, 82; and slave trade, 80, 81
Spain: and activity of foreign traders, 6–7, 19, 27–9, 33–40, 79, 106–7, 116, 133–8; attitudes to trade, 1–2; colonial trade monopoly, 5–6, 8, 14, 17, 49, 80, 87, 96, 117, 133, 174, 186; and *conversos*, 7; and economic reforms, 8; textile industry, 83–4, 174, 177–9; trade with northern Europe, 4–5, 18, 31–4, 36–40, 44–5, 47–50, 70, 183, 185; wool trade, 27, 31, 36, 38–9, 41, 61–2, 70, 168, 179
Spanish language, 124
Spanish Succession, War of, 32–3, 37
Stannard, Philip, 49
Stannard and Taylor (manufacturers), 151–2, 169
Stein, Stanley J. and Barbara H. Stein, 5, 93 n. 75
Studnicki-Gizbert, Daviken, 12, 75, 95
Suárez, Margarita, 119
Superunda, José Antonio Manso de Velasco, 1st count (viceroy of Peru), 108
Surmone, Pierre (mer.), 166
Suxeda, Juan de (mariner), 66–7

Tagle Bracho, Juan Antonio (mer.), 78
Tajonar, Joaquín de (mer.), 131
Tartas, Josias (mer.), 39
tax exemptions: and Bilbao, 30–1, 36–7; and Santander, 36–7, 42
taxation: and colonial demand, 108–10; and colonial fleets, 74–81; and composition of cargoes, 108; unified, 117, 134
textiles: British, 49, 146, 168–9; and fashion, 94, 108–9, 113–15, 179–80; and Peruvian trade, 108–9, 113, 170, 174, 177–9; Spanish, 83–4, 174
timing: and risk, 173–81
tobacco trade, 19, 37; contraband, 33
Tord Nicolini, Javier and Carlos Lazo García, 110
Torres y Mato, Ignacio de (mer.), 129–30, 148

trade: and Bourbon reforms, 14–17, 73, 174, 185; joint-stock companies, 126; retail, 94; Spanish attitudes to, 1–2. *See also* networks, trading
trade diasporas, 4, 8, 11
Trivellato, Francesca, 12–13, 104
trust, 182–6; collapse (case study), 153–61; and competition, 174; and contract enforcement, 13; and credit, 9–10, 89, 93, 127, 130, 142, 168–9, 186; and crews, 62–70, 183; and family networks, 144–9; and friends, 150–3, 162–3; and *huésped* (host) system, 35–6, 39–40, 51, 183; and information, 95, 104–5, 131, 145, 181, 184; institutional, 40–5; and legal frameworks, 162–8, 182; and long-distance trade, 93; and risk, 13, 36, 110; and ships captains, 60–2, 63, 67–8, 70; and trading networks, 9–14, 15, 19, 119, 126–33, 182–4. *See also* confidentiality
trustworthiness: of correspondents, 1–3, 44–5, 94, 104, 141–4, 184, 185; and gild membership, 16; perception, 3, 13, 143, 154
Túpac Amaru (José Gabriel Condorcanqui), 111
Turiso, Jesús, 120

Ullívarri, Alonso de (mer.), 105–6
Ulloa, Antonio de, 82–3, 98–9
Ulloa, Bernardo de, 96
Umaran, Cosme de (s.c.), 61–2
uncertainty, 142, 152, 162, 166, 173, 176, 178, 183–6. *See also* risk
única contribución (tax), 117, 134
Urezberroeta, José Miguel de (s.c.), 155–6, 160
Uríbarri, Joaquín de (mer.), 50
Úriz, Simón Babil de (mer.), 104, 115, 129, 153
Urruchi, Domingo de (mer.), 151
Urrutia, Esteban de (mer.), 103–4, 131, 136–7
Uruburu, José Manuel de (s.c.), 53
Utrecht, Treaty (1713), 46
Uztáriz, Gerónimo de, 2–3, 13–14, 96, 125, 183
Uztáriz, Juan Agustín (mer.), 131

Vaccarezza, Antonio (mer.), 104, 120
Valencia, import trade, 32

Valois, Joseph (*mer.*), 173
Van Lintelo, Cornelio (*mer.*), 39
Vanveen, Pedro, 39
Varas, Francisco de (president of House of Trade), 82
Vázquez Lijó, José Manuel, 70 n. 84
Vea, José de (*mer.*), 164
Vea Murguía, Juan Francisco de (*mer.*), 101, 136, 157, 158, 160
Veracruz: and *consulado*, 16; and father–son trading networks, 122 n. 23; trade with, 50, 91
Verdejo, Juan (*mer.*), 166
Verduc, Vincent and Co., 135
Vernon, Adm. Edward, 81
Vila, Enriqueta, 78 n.15, 119
Vilar, Pierre, 55, 67
Villa, Francisco de la (*mer.*), 57
Villar, José del (*mer.*), 93
Ville, Simon P., 55–6
Viollet, Luis (*mer.*), 60, 67, 68
Vizcay, Francisco (*mer.*), 91–2
Vizcaya (province): *fueros*, 29–33, 38, 46, 69–70, 168; iron and shipbuilding industries, 32, 36; and naval recruitment, 69; population, 65; ships captains and seamen, 51, 63–5, 68; and Spanish monarchy, 30

Walker, Geoffrey J., 127
Waujan, Guillermo (*mer.*), 171
Weber, Max, 7
wool trade: and Bilbao, 27, 31, 36, 38–9, 41, 61–2, 70, 168
world systems theory, 20

Xalavera, Gregorio (*corr.*), 112, 171–2
Xarabeitia, Pedro Ignacio de (*mer.*), 47, 49–50

Zabala, Nicolás de (*mer.*), 54
Zabaleta, Juan de (*s.c.*), 100–1
Zahedieh, Nuala, 10
Zaldumbide, José de (*s.c.*), 66
Zavala, Antonio de (*s.c.*), 53
Zedrón, Andrés (Spanish consul in London), 47, 168
Zelayeta, Martín de (*mer.*), 78
Zulaica, Antonio (*mer.*), 157, 158
Zumaran, Sebastián de (*mer.*), 107, 114
Zylberberg, Michael, 7

www.ingramcontent.com/pod-product-compliance
Lightning Source LLC
Chambersburg PA
CBHW070803230426
43665CB00017B/2475